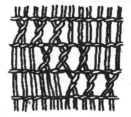

MISSISSIPPIAN VILLAGE TEXTILES
AT WICKLIFFE

MISSISSIPPIAN VILLAGE

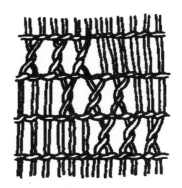

TEXTILES AT WICKLIFFE

PENELOPE BALLARD DROOKER

The University of Alabama Press
Tuscaloosa and London

Copyright © 1992 by
The University of Alabama Press
Tuscaloosa, Alabama 35487–0380
All rights reserved
Manufactured in the United States of America
designed by Paula C. Dennis

∞

The paper on which this book is printed meets the minimum
requirements of American National Standard for Information
Science-Permanence of Paper for Printed Library Materials,
ANSI Z39.48-1984.

Library of Congress Cataloging-in-Publication Data

Drooker, Penelope B.
    Mississippian village textiles at Wickliffe / Penelope Ballard
Drooker
        p.   cm.
    Includes bibliographical references and index.
    ISBN 0-8173-0592-0
    1. Wickliffe Mounds (Ky.)   2. Mississippian culture—Kentucky—
Textile industry and fabrics.   3. Mississippian culture—Kentucky—
Pottery.   4. Mississippian culture—Kentucky—Social life and
customs.   I. Title.
E99.M6815D76   1992
976.9'96—dc20   92-4722

British Library Cataloguing-in-Publication Data available

To Mike

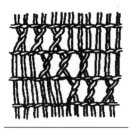

CONTENTS

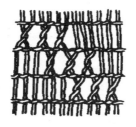

TABLES AND FIGURES

TABLES

FIGURES

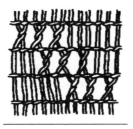

PREFACE

As a long-time weaver myself, when I first began to become familiar with the archaeology and ethnography of southeastern North America, I tried to find out as much as I could about the textiles that were made and used in this region. Although people have been living in this area for well over ten millennia, direct evidence was discouragingly sparse. Unlike the dry deserts of the Southwest, the humid forests of the Southeast were not particularly conducive to the preservation of actual textile artifacts, although some fabric fragments and artifacts did survive in bogs, dry caves, and burials. In spite of the fact that a few spectacular finds such as the textiles looted from elite mortuary contexts at Spiro, Oklahoma, did attract the attention of archaeologists, for the most part the archaeological reconstruction of southeastern prehistory necessarily has focused upon the "hard evidence" of ceramic, stone, metal, and other less perishable artifacts, together with increasingly sophisticated procedures to elicit the maximum amount of information from subsistence, settlement, and burial patterns.

Because Precolumbian southeastern textiles are relatively rare and often fragmentary, they have been almost entirely ignored as a potential source of cultural information. As a result, until recently we have known little, not only of the fabrics themselves, but also of their place within the socio-economic systems of the Southeast. Not surprisingly, archaeologists, textile historians, and nonspecialists alike are for the most part ignorant of the nature and importance of yarns and textiles made and used within this region.

Ian Brown is the person who suggested to me that a study of textile impressions on Mississippian pottery might prove fruitful. In his research on prehistoric salt-making, he had become very familiar with the large "salt-pan" vessels which often had fabric-impressed outer surfaces. I soon found that a plethora of textile-impressed sherds has been excavated during the past century, but although they have been employed widely as ceramic markers typical of the Early to Middle Mississippian, very little use has been made of them as sources of information about the Mississippian textiles industry. By analyzing in detail the fabrics impressed on pottery at a particular settlement, I hoped to be able to deduce not only some of the functions for which they originally were made but also the technology of their production and their importance in the economy and social structure of the community.

Wickliffe Mounds (15Ba4), Kentucky, proved to be a lucky site choice for me. It is a well-researched location with an ongoing program of archaeological investigation, and the working conditions for visiting researchers are excellent. Not only was there an abundance of fabric-impressed sherds to analyze, but the impressions generally were sharp and clear, and there was an amazingly wide range of yarn sizes, textile structures, and fabric types represented. The information that I have been able to glean from them is indicative of rich possibilities for future research along similar lines at other Mississippian sites. Someday soon I hope that textiles will take their deserved place as a significant component of southeastern and Mississippian culture.

This project never could have been initiated or even contemplated without the generous assistance of many individuals. Both Ian Brown and Kit Wesler, director of the Wickliffe Mounds Research Center, have been supportive and helpful in numerous ways throughout the entire time I have wrestled with the Wickliffe textile data and comparative information from other sites. During my visits to examine collections at Wickliffe, the Harvard University Peabody Museum, the University of Michigan Museum of Anthropology, the Center for Archaeological Investigations at Southern Illinois University at Carbondale, the Frank H. McClung Museum of the University of Knoxville, the Robert S. Peabody Foundation, the Ohio Historical Society, and the Program for Cultural Resource Assessment at the University of Kentucky, Kelly Lawson, Michael Geselowitz and Kathy Skelly, John Speth and David Kennedy, Francis Smiley and Brian Butler, Jefferson Chapman, Betty Steiner and Gene Winter, Martha Otto, and Gwynn Henderson and David Pollack all were extremely accommodating. Marvin and Julie Smith shared access to Milner site textiles, as did Richard Polhemus to Loy site textiles, Ian Brown to Salt Creek and Bottle Creek sherds, Ruth Truett to a large collection of relevant research materials, and Jenna Tedrick Kuttruff to the Wickliffe textile fragments and to her own research on Mississippian textiles from several different sites. Ella Baker gave valuable aid in experimental replication studies. Michael Drooker's skilled computer support was essential to the successful completion of the project. Others who answered inquiries and followed through with additional helpful information included but were by no means limited to Charles Bareis, Jeffrey Brain, James A. Brown, R. Berle Clay, Charles Cobb, Betsy Davis, Frederica Dimmick, Julie Droke, Linda Eisenhart, Richard Faust, Elizabeth Garland, James Griffin, David Hally, Michael Hoffman, Debbie Hopkins, William Johnson, B. Calvin Jones, R. Barry Lewis, Joan Miller, Jon Muller, Dolores Newton, Michael O'Brien, Christopher Peebles, Gregory Perino, Elisa Phelps, J. Daniel Rogers, Lucy Sibley, James Smith, Antoinette Wallace, Stephen Williams (to whom I owe particular thanks for furthering this project), and Virginia Schreffler Wimberly. I very much appreciate their help.

My thanks go also to Judith Knight and the staff at the University of Alabama Press, whose support and assistance during the prepublication process has been essential. In addition, the manuscript benefited immensely from expert, comprehensive, and painstaking review by Mary Elizabeth King, Jenna Tedrick Kuttruff, and a third anonymous person. Although I have clung stubbornly to my own opinion in a few matters, most of their suggestions have been incorporated into the manuscript, to its great improvement. I am extremely grateful for their help.

MISSISSIPPIAN VILLAGE TEXTILES

AT WICKLIFFE

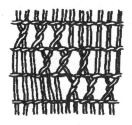

CHAPTER 1

INTRODUCTION

Seven hundred years ago on a hot, lazy summer afternoon, a woman stood working under a tree on a bluff high above the Mississippi River. Her project was one she had planned for many months, in fact for almost an entire year. She was making a mantle for herself, decorated with lacy openwork designs of tiny holes contrasted against a more opaque background. Earlier that day she had worked awhile in the village gardens. Later, when the sun approached the horizon in the sky across the water, it would be cool enough again for her to return to more active tasks. For now, though, the baby was asleep, the children were playing quietly beside her in the shade, and for a few hours she could twist the yarns around each other and watch another row of the garment slowly emerge under her skillful fingers.

In the waning days of the previous year, she and her oldest daughter had gathered plant stems, setting them to decompose in a backwater pool down in the flats of the river floodplain. When the stems had begun to come apart, they had beaten them to complete the process, separating the bleached, white fibers into long, thin hanks ready to be made into yarn. During the winter, she and the grandmother, a spinner noted for the fineness and uniformity of her yarns in spite of her now-failing sight, had spun the fiber, first twisting fibers into single strands and then plying two strands together to make the finished yarn, hundreds of meters in all. She had insisted on fine yarn, not much more than the thickness of a fingernail in diameter, because she wanted to challenge her fabric-making ability, developed over many years of producing skirts, blankets, mats, and storage bags, by creating a garment that would be the culmination of her textile art. Her aim was a fabric in which more than ten warp yarns would lie together within the width of her smallest finger. The design she planned was one traditionally worn within her clan. Her female relatives all had garments with similar motifs, but hers would be subtly different, marking it to her kinspeople as the product of her own hands.

She had only recently begun, first stringing a cord between two poles set almost as far apart as the span of her arms, then doubling the warp yarns and hanging them over the cord so that their free ends moved back and forth in the breeze. The top of the garment took shape with several close rows of twining—paired weft yarns twisting around each other and enclosing one warp yarn at a time with each twist. At either end of these twining rows, she braided the wefts together into long ties, which would secure the mantle over her left shoulder when it finally was ready to wear. Now she could start the design. Wherever she wanted a motif to show up against her sun-browned skin, she formed it by twisting the warp yarns together between each row of weft, opening up holes in the texture of the fabric. Row by row, the design would come to life under her hands. If she could find time to work like this every day over the next three passages of the moon, she could finish the mantle in time to wear it for the first time at the Corn Ceremony.

This she did, and continued to wear the garment proudly until it became shabby and torn, and it was time to plan a replacement. The fabric would not be wasted, though. She could use it, along with other available large pieces of cloth, to line the molds cut into the ground in which she formed her largest pottery vessels, the broad, rounded basins that could be used, among other things, to evaporate saline water in the salt-making process. So until it ultimately acquired so many holes that it fell apart, the mantle continued to give service, first in the production of ceramics, then as a rag. When finally it was discarded into the trash heap and gradually covered with bones, broken pottery, and other unwanted items, it slowly disintegrated until nothing of it was left to recognize.

Its maker lived out the span of her years and was buried in the village cemetery. Her funeral garments, too, deteriorated and disappeared over the years. Her village was abandoned, lying deserted for centuries. Who would ever know that she had been renowned for her fine and intricate textiles? After her village and her clan were gone, how could future generations ever piece together the techniques and designs that she and her sisters had used to make mantles, skirts, blankets, and bags, or that their men had used to knot fishing nets? Who would even remember that they had been made at all?

Today, what *do* we know of this woman, her village, her culture—and her textiles? Did she and her family have to spend most of their time in subsistence activities, scrambling to obtain enough to eat and to keep themselves warm in winter, or did they have sufficient leeway to devote time to "nonessential" arts and interactions? How might their economic situation be reflected in the village textiles industry? What sorts of textile items were produced there, and how diverse were they? Were they carefully fabricated or sloppily put together? Were they decorated or strictly utilitarian? If decorative designs were incorporated into the fabrics, what might they have signified to village inhabitants or to visitors from other settlements? Could anyone have produced the range of textiles used in the village, or must some of them have been the products of specialist craftspeople? Were they used only by the families of their creators, or were they produced for or exchanged with others? What raw materials, tools, and techniques were used to make them? How much time was devoted to their creation? How did they compare with fabrics produced and used at other southeastern settlements, including both ceremonial centers and smaller habitation sites?

These are questions whose answers are necessary for anyone seeking to build a full-dimensioned portrait of prehistoric southeastern ways of life. But how can we ever gather enough data to begin to answer them, given that probably well over 99% of the textiles produced in the Precolumbian Southeast have vanished from the archaeological record?

For the centuries during which agricultural villages flourished along major segments of the Mississippi River and its tributaries in southeastern North America—that is, for some 700 years or more, up to the time of European encroachment—we do have additional evidence. Because many textiles were pressed into pottery during the construction of large "saltpan" vessels, their images have been preserved and can be analyzed in some detail, even though most of the original fabrics have not survived. At some sites, thousands of fabric-impressed sherds have been recovered, numbers that are an order of magnitude greater than the largest number of organic fabric fragments ever recovered from any one southeastern site.

This is the evidence that was used to reconstruct the textile industry at Wickliffe Mounds, Kentucky, the location of a village active between about A.D. 1000 and 1350. The fabric impressions were studied by making modeling-clay casts from them to simulate the original yarns and textile structures. Their attributes were measured and statistically analyzed, then compared with the attributes of different types of textile artifacts in order to determine what the original functions of the Wickliffe textiles might have been. Detailed analyses of yarn construction, fabric scale, decorative designs, and edge finishes contributed to an estimation of the textiles' production complexity, a reflection of their socioeconomic value. Experimental replication allowed order-of-magnitude estimates of production times for typical fabrics, and thus an assessment of the place of textile production in the round of subsistence activities at Wickliffe. Although textile data from other sites of this time period still are relatively sparse, it did prove possible to make tentative comparisons of Wickliffe textile data to similar data from contemporaneous settlements, confirming that regional similarities and differences apparently do exist and warrant additional investigation.

Almost all previously published information on Mississippian textiles—and on southeastern textiles in general—describes them out of context, as disembodied fragments unconnected to the socioeconomic matrix within which they actually functioned. This book is an initial attempt to re-place them within the larger framework of Mississippian day-to-day subsistence, ceremonial life, and worldview.

To set the scene, Chapter 2 briefly summarizes Mississippian lifeways and textiles in contrast with those of preceding time periods, as well as describing at somewhat greater length the characteristics, production, and use of Mississippian fabric-impressed pottery. Within that framework, Chapter 3 paints a portrait of Wickliffe Village as it is known from the archaeological record, including its environment, settlement pattern, chronology, regional affiliations, and selected artifact types. In Chapter 4, the procedures followed in analyzing textile impressions are described, along with the diagnostic attributes of Mississippian textile artifacts from which the original functions of the Wickliffe impressed textiles were reconstructed. In Chapter 5, the Wickliffe fabrics are illustrated, described, and compared. Chapter 6 discusses the socioeconomic information extracted from these impressed textiles: their probable original functions, the spinning and fabric-construction technology used to produce them, the amount of labor invested in them, and the social "messages" embedded in their designs. Chapter 7 compares quantitative data on textiles from different Mississippian sites in an effort to identify regional and temporal similarities and differences. This section of the book provides site-by-site summaries of the available attribute data on textiles impressed into pottery and on fabrics preserved in their original form; compares them regionally, temporally, and by site type and recovery context; puts this information into perspective within the context of Mississippian subsistence, ceremonial life, and exchange patterns; and assesses the place of Wickliffe fabrics within the larger Mississippian textile complex. Included as appendixes are a glossary of textile terminology and a discussion of methodological details for analyzing fabric-impressed sherds.

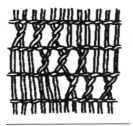

CHAPTER 2

SETTING THE SCENE

Mississippian textiles were not made and used in a vacuum. As just one of many day-to-day activities, fabric production was accomplished only after basic subsistence needs were met. Materials were obtained from particular environments and processed according to the season. If the desired materials were not available locally, they had to be obtained from elsewhere through travel or exchange. Both utilitarian items such as bags or blankets and decorated, symbolic items such as elaborate headdresses were fashioned using socially sanctioned, traditional "blueprints," to serve particular purposes within the group and in its members' contacts with outsiders.

To provide a context within which to consider Wickliffe Village and its textiles, this chapter briefly summarizes the subsistence activities, settlement patterns, and regional interactions of Mississippian peoples, as distinct from those of other regions and time periods. A short introduction to current baseline knowledge and some of the outstanding questions in Mississippian fabric studies is included as a prelude to the more detailed discussion in Chapter 7. Finally, the characteristics of Mississippian "saltpan" vessels relevant to their use in textile research are described.

MISSISSIPPIAN LIFEWAYS

"Mississippian" designates a cultural manifestation in southeastern North America spanning the approximate time period A.D. 900–1600. From the

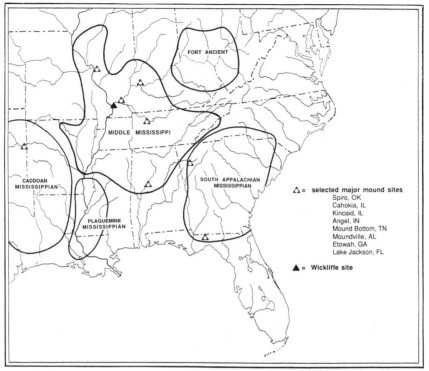

Figure 1.
Major Mississippian culture areas and archaeological sites (after Coe et al. 1986:54).

upper Midwest to Florida, Mississippian and related peoples lived in nucleated, year-round settlements, practiced maize horticulture supplemented by
hunting and gathering, made shell-tempered pottery, constructed flat-
topped mounds crowned with public buildings, and participated in a ranked
social organization. Like the climate and the physical environment, their
culture was by no means uniform over this vast area and long time period,
but similarities and continuities allow us to discuss "the Mississippian" as an
entity while keeping regional and temporal variations in mind. (For a discussion emphasizing cultural variability, see Muller and Stephens 1991.)

The larger Mississippian settlements were located along major river valleys
within the Mississippi River drainage system and to its southeast (Figure 1),
indicating an emphasis on floodplain horticulture. In general, such towns
were organized around a central, open plaza surrounded by mounds and
often were entirely or partially enclosed by palisades. The biggest of them,
Cahokia (opposite modern-day St. Louis), covered over 5 square miles
(1340 ha), had thousands or even tens of thousands of residents, and in-

cluded more than 100 mounds, the most prominent of which encompassed 16 acres (6.5 ha) and rose to 100 feet (30 m) above the surrounding area (Fowler and Hall 1978). Settlement size ranged downward from Cahokia's impressive statistics to far smaller communities, but even small towns included platform mounds that would have required planning and cooperative work by dozens, scores, or hundreds of people. Near major "cities" and large towns some sort of hierarchical settlement pattern often occurred, with large mound sites surrounded by smaller villages and outlying hamlets or "farmsteads" (Griffin 1983; Muller 1983; B. Smith 1978).

Mississippian culture incorporated far-ranging exchange systems that dealt with both raw materials and finished products. The latter included both utilitarian objects such as chert hoes and ceremonial objects such as incised shell gorgets and drinking vessels, repoussé copper plates, carved stone "effigy" pipes, negative-painted ceramics, and other artifacts that shared certain designs and symbols such as the cross-in-circle, forked eye, and bilobed arrow motifs (the "Southeastern Ceremonial Complex"). Exchange extended to related cultures located to the west and southeast of the primary Mississippian area, with types of items involved varying from region to region and site to site (Brose et al. 1985; J. Brown 1971, 1975, 1983; J. Brown et al. 1990; Cobb 1989; Curry 1950a, 1950b; Galloway 1989; Hamilton et al. 1974; Howard 1968; B. Jones 1982; Kneberg 1959; Muller 1987; Peebles 1971, 1978; Phillips and Brown 1978; Schambach 1990; Waring and Holder 1945; Willey and Phillips 1944; Williams and Brain 1983).

Many exotic and elaborate artifacts connected to exchange networks have been discovered in mortuary contexts interpreted as elite. In fact, analysis of their patterns of disposition has been instrumental in demonstrating that within many areas of the Southeast the social structure was hierarchical and at least some aspects of leadership were hereditary. Cahokia, Etowah, Moundville, and Spiro (Figure 1) are examples of large ceremonial centers where such high-ranking individuals were interred (J. Brown 1971; Fowler 1975; Larson 1971; Peebles 1971).

By approximately A.D. 1450, a great number of the major settlements in the northern Mississippian "heartland" no longer were active. In fact, Williams (1980, 1990) has designated this area—north along the Mississippi River to above Cahokia, south to below Wickliffe, east along the Ohio River to beyond Angel, and up the Tennessee and Cumberland rivers to central Tennessee—as a "vacant quarter" after that time. Where settlements did continue to exist, such as the Caborn-Welborn phase sites in southern Indiana and north-central Kentucky and the Armorel phase sites in extreme southeastern Missouri, they differed in significant ways from their predecessors (Green and Munson 1978; Price and Price 1990). Because of this discontinuity, tying residents of a given Early-Middle Mississippian settlement within this northern region to any historically known Native American group is virtually impossible.

Farther south, Mississippian cultural characteristics persisted longer, and the earliest European explorers, notably the 1539–1543 de Soto expedition, encountered a number of rich, mound-building chiefdoms (Bourne 1904; Hodge and Lewis 1907). The longest-lived, best-known such group were the Natchez of southwestern Mississippi, who were defeated and dispersed by the French in 1731 (Le Page du Pratz 1763). Elsewhere, most mound building had ceased well before that time, although the nucleated villages and subsistence pattern consisting of maize agriculture supplemented by hunting, gathering, and fishing that were characteristic of the Mississippian persisted in most parts of the Southeast until they were broken up by disease, warfare, and U.S. government policy over the centuries following European incursion.

Largely because of the prominent earth mounds associated with many of them, Mississippian archaeological sites evoked increasing interest, speculation, and investigation by curious Euro-Americans during the course of the nineteenth century. Organized, "scientific" excavation of relevant sites occurred largely in the twentieth century, accelerating during the 1930s and becoming increasingly refined and comprehensive after World War II (Stoltman 1973). During different periods of investigation, analysis and interpretation of Mississippian archaeology has centered on pottery seriation, settlement pattern analysis, subsistence studies, and investigation of exchange networks and hierarchical social organization through ceremonial objects such as engraved gorgets. Some investigations of craft specialization and production of utilitarian items have been carried out (e.g., Cobb 1989; Muller 1984; Yerkes 1989), but because of their relative rarity in the archaeological record, artifacts of fiber, wood, and other perishable materials ordinarily have received far less attention than items of stone, shell, metal, or fired clay.

MISSISSIPPIAN TEXTILES

In general, prehistoric peoples of southeastern North America have not been celebrated for their textiles. Unlike the dry Southwest, the humid Southeast is far from ideal for the preservation of organic material. Only a comparatively few fragments of fabrics and a miniscule number of complete or near-complete textile artifacts have been recovered from archaeological contexts, and almost no direct evidence of fabric production technology has been discovered. Although native-made baskets, bags, and sashes dating to early historical times may be displayed by museums, museum dioramas and illustrations for popular publications frequently depict Mississippian and earlier southeastern people wearing skin rather than fabric clothing. When textile fragments are mentioned at all in site reports, they are simply described or pictured. Almost never is any effort made to assess their social or economic importance, other than perhaps a speculative guess at their original function.

Thus, anyone who bothered to think about the subject at all might perhaps be excused for believing that pliable textiles constructed from yarn elements played little part in the daily lives of Native Americans in the Southeast. Such a belief, however, would be very far from actuality. A variety of fabric-making techniques were being utilized in the region at least as early as the eighth millennium B.C. (Chapman and Adovasio 1977), and a sophisticated textile complex was in place by at least the sixth (Andrews et al. 1988). From small items like sandals and sashes, to bags and garments, to large fishing nets and mats, enough evidence has survived to hint at the magnitude of what has been lost.

For the Mississippian, ceremonial regalia such as headdresses, tapestry mantles, and complex basketry containers have been recovered from elite mound burials at Spiro, plus lesser amounts from a few other sites like Etowah. More utilitarian fabric items have come from rock-shelters and caves at various locations, but little has been obtained from village contexts. Here, fabric impressions on pottery have the potential to extend greatly our knowledge of everyday Mississippian textiles, since sherds carrying textile impressions are hundreds to thousands of times more common on Mississippian sites than are organic fabrics.

Besides the few surviving whole items, additional evidence for textile use in the Mississippian is available from images of clothed people in various two- and three-dimensional media such as stone statues and effigy pipes, ceramic effigy pots, and engraved shell cups and gorgets. In many cases, early historical accounts also can be useful in supplementing the archaeological record.

The earliest-published comprehensive, detailed illustrations and descriptions of North American textiles were by Holmes (1884, 1888, 1896). Many of these fabrics (e.g., Figure 2a–e, g–h) are typical of the Mississippian as well as of earlier periods. Unfortunately, although Holmes's publications convey much important information, they lack any sense of the significance of regional and temporal variation. In spite of a laudable interest in fabric-

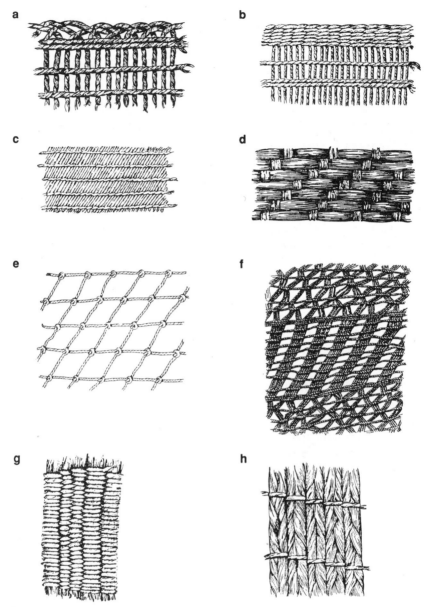

Figure 2.
Drawings by William H. Holmes of textiles impressed on pottery (Holmes 1896:40, 42–44):
a, plain twining; *b*, plain twining with grouped-weft-row bands; *c*, alternate-pair twining over
closely spaced warps; *d*, 3/1 straight twill interlacing; *e*, knotted netting; *f*, plain twining with
openwork design formed by extra weft twists; *g*, weft-faced fabric; *h*, plain twining over
braided warps.

making technology, his attempts to reconstruct production methods for twined textiles (e.g., 1884:Figures 74, 75, 92) are merely speculative, with no connection to methods known to have been used historically.

Miner (1936) was the first to summarize textile-structure variations among eastern North American culture groups from different time periods and locations and to draw attention to the importance of textile evidence in the interpretation of cultural differences and relationships among groups. In 1960 Rachlin presented a detailed tabulation of her assessment of fabric structures present in eastern North American culture groups from Archaic through modern times. From Miner's and Rachlin's data, as well as from additional archaeological evidence reported during the past 30 years, it seems that one hallmark of Mississippian fabrics compared to earlier textiles is an increased number of complex structural variations (e.g., Figure 2f). Virtually all fabric structures and decorative techniques from earlier contexts were retained, some were elaborated to greater complexity, and new ones were added. The "new" types of textile structures—new, that is, to the archaeological record—apparently were used primarily if not exclusively for visual impact, and, to date, the most complex and elaborate examples have been reported from elite mortuary contexts. This apparent trend toward elaborate display in Mississippian textiles parallels the increased social complexity deduced from Mississippian settlement configurations, architecture, artifacts, and burial practices. However, complex fabric structures also are known from eastern North American mortuary contexts of apparently simpler societies as far back as the Early Woodland period (ca. 700 B.C.–A.D. 100) (Heckenberger et al. 1990; M. E. King 1968). In seeking general trends, researchers must keep in mind the extremely limited amount of prehistoric textile evidence at their disposal.

Large-sized Mississippian textile artifacts, like those from earlier contexts, typically were rectangular and made as units, either as flat shapes (skirts, mantles, blankets) or as three-dimensional entities (bags, pouches). Little direct evidence of the techniques used to produce these large fabric items during the Mississippian has survived. Fragmentary early historical accounts plus analysis of extant artifacts points to a production process that employed free-hanging warp yarns suspended from a stick or cord, but this may not have been the only method used. Mississippian spinning technology likewise is debated in the literature. Attribute analysis of yarns and fabrics impressed on pottery can provide additional input toward resolving these questions.

Who were the textile makers in the prehistoric Southeast? No direct evidence in the form of pictures or figurines has yet been found to tell us whether women or men were the primary producers of fabrics during the Mississippian and earlier. However, not a single early historical account casts men in this role. Women frequently are mentioned or depicted as makers of garments, bags, baskets, and mats (Adair 1968:422–423; du Ru 1934:29; Le Page du Pratz 1763:2:229–231), while men have been described only as makers of nets for fishing and hunting, using cordage spun for them by women (Cleland 1982:763).

Diagnostic attributes of Mississippian textile artifact types will be discussed in Chapter 4, as a preliminary step in the interpretation of fabrics impressed on Mississippian pottery. After the detailed case history of textile production and use at the Wickliffe Mounds site (Chapters 5 and 6), the final chapter will summarize and compare all available quantitative data for impressed fabrics and textile fragments from other Mississippian sites, using this as input toward an interpretation of the importance of textiles in everyday life and ceremonial contexts during the Mississippian.

MISSISSIPPIAN "SALTPANS"

Before the advent of radiocarbon dating techniques, ceramics seriation was of prime importance in establishing temporal relationships among sites in the Southeast. One distinctive and valuable marker of the Mississippian has been its so-called "saltpan" pottery. Because many "saltpan" vessels carry fabric impressions on their exteriors, these ceramics also offer a wealth of information about the Mississippian textiles industry, information that to date has barely begun to be utilized. To take full advantage of this source of data, it is helpful to know the sizes and shapes of the "saltpan" vessels, their temporal and geographic distribution, and theories of how and why fabrics were used in their manufacture. The information summarized below is discussed at more length by Drooker (1989b); further details are available from I. Brown (1980).

"Saltpan" Vessel Attributes

Mississippian "saltpans" are large, relatively shallow vessels, usually of coarse shell-tempered pottery, thick-walled and heavy. They are sturdily utilitarian in design, in contrast to more refined Mississippian ceramics such as effigy vessels or negative-painted plates and bottles. Although these pans are common at many Mississippian settlement sites, they have been found in particular abundance at saline springs and other locations where water was boiled down to form salt. From their probable function at these saline locations comes the name by which they generally are known. Both smooth and fabric-impressed varieties occur.

Many different named varieties of Mississippian fabric-impressed pottery have been designated, including Hawkins Fabric Marked, Kimmswick Fabric Impressed, Kincaid Net-Impressed, Langston Fabric Marked, Morris Fabric Impressed, Saline Fabric Impressed, Tolu Interior Fabric Impressed, and Yates Net Impressed. Salt Creek Cane Impressed is a type defined by impressions of matting rather than cloth. Phillips proposed that all textile-impressed "saltpan" ware in the Southeast be grouped into a supertype, designated Kimmswick Fabric Impressed. His definition was based on vessel form, paste composition, and decoration: "Outsize round or flat-bottomed bowls or vats, 20–30 inches in diameter, of coarse, shell-tempered ware, bearing impressions on the exterior of fabrics of various kinds of simple twining. Matting and (rarely) leaf impressions are specified as minority features." He specifically distinguished "fabric-impressed" pottery, which bears the impression of large, whole pieces of cloth, from "fabric-marked" pottery, malleated with a fabric-wrapped hand or paddle (Phillips 1970:95–96).

Phillips's definition and the Kimmswick Fabric Impressed name are in general, though not universal, use at the present time. However, if Kimmswick Fabric Impressed is to be regarded as an overarching supertype, the definition perhaps should be extended somewhat. In terms of size, vessels up to 66 inches (1.7 m) in diameter and as small as 11 inches (28 cm) have been found (Griffin 1938:293; O'Brien, 1977:375–376; I. Brown 1980:22). Although twining does predominate as the major type of impressed fabric, other textile structures such as interlacing and knotting have been reported. Placement of fabric impressions occurs not only on exterior surfaces but also sometimes on interiors (Webb and Funkhouser 1931:379–380). And although shell-tempering, generally taken to be diagnostic of Mississippian ceramics, is most common, some clay- or grog-tempered (mixed or unmixed with shell) fabric-impressed "saltpan" ware also has been found in Mississippian contexts (Baldwin 1966:250; Clay 1984:107–108; R. Lewis 1986:46; Young 1962:62, 64).

Just as vessel size varied greatly, "saltpan" shapes also were by no means consistent (Figure 3), and a number of different shapes might occur at any given site, from shallow and flat-bottomed to almost hemispheric and bowl-like (e.g., Muller 1984:487; Orr 1951:317–318). Fabric-marking might extend all the way to the vessel lip, or it might be terminated by smoothed rims as wide as 8 centimeters (3 in) (Williams 1954:Figure 52).

At some sites, such as Kincaid, Angel, and Tolu, all in the lower Ohio River Valley, there was great variety in the textiles impressed on "saltpan" pottery (Orr 1951; Rachlin 1955a; Webb and Funkhouser 1931), while at

Figure 3.
Mississippian "saltpan" forms: *a*, "usual form of large salt vessels or vats" (after Holmes 1903:Plate 3); *b*, pan from Kimmswick, 75 centimeters (30 in) in diameter (after Holmes 1903:Plate 10); *c*, pan forms from Kincaid, 45–55 centimeters (18–22 in) in diameter (after Orr 1951:Figure 3); *d*, smoothed rims of Kimmswick Fabric Impressed pans from Crosno, Missouri (after Williams 1954:221); *e*, type of bowl-like form found at Great Salt Spring, Illinois (after Muller 1984:497). Arrows indicate position of fabric impressions.

others such as Williams, Kentucky, and Mound Bottom, Tennessee, textile structures and scale apparently were more restricted (Webb and Funkhouser 1929; Kuttruff 1987b; Kuttruff and Kuttruff, 1986). Vessels might be impressed with single pieces of cloth or with a patchwork of two, three, or more pieces, differing in structure and scale (Bushnell 1914:Plate 57; Orchard 1920:19–20).

Temporal Variation

Although on occasion "saltpan" vessels do occur in non-Mississippian contexts (I. Brown 1980:42), they are typically Mississippian. The fabric-impressed type is concentrated in the Early to Middle Mississippian, with the smooth-surfaced "saltpan" gaining prominence in the Late Mississippian (I. Brown 1980:54–58).

No general study has been made of variations in "saltpan" shapes over time, but some temporal differences were noted at particular sites. At Crosno, Williams found that Kimmswick Fabric Impressed vessels with wide, smoothed rims occurred later than vessels with fabric impressions extending up to the top of the rim (Williams 1954: 220). At Kincaid, both pan thickness and lip shape changed over time, and the pan form as a class tripled in frequency from Early to Late Kincaid at the same time as the percentage of textile-impressed versus smooth pans declined (Orr 1954:315, 320–321).

Geographic Distribution

Geographic occurrence of smooth and textile-impressed "saltpans" has been exhaustively compiled by I. Brown (1980:25–30, 42–59). Fabric-impressed "saltpan" ware has been found as far west as interior Arkansas, along the Mississippi as far north as the vicinity of St. Louis, as far south as southern Alabama and central Georgia, east along the Tennessee River to northeastern Tennessee, along the Cumberland River, and along the Ohio River and its tributaries in Illinois, Indiana, Kentucky, and Ohio as far east as the West Virginia line. Rachlin gives it a still wider distribution, from the Atlantic coast to Oklahoma (personal communication 1990). It is concentrated, however, in eastern Missouri, southern Illinois, southwestern Indiana, western Kentucky, and northwestern and eastern Tennessee.

Because of the significant size and weight typical of "saltpan" vessels, it is probable that most were produced very close to where they were used and ultimately deposited. There is no evidence that they ever functioned in inter-site trade.

"Saltpan" Production

Enough archaeological evidence has accumulated to know that "saltpans" were made in or over molds. In the case of fabric-impressed vessels, the textile would have been inserted between the clay and the mold.

Fabric impressions on a large proportion of "saltpan" sherds are deep and clear, implying that significant pressure was exerted during their application. The process of forming large, thick-walled vessels in basin-shaped molds cut into the ground has been portrayed in picturesque terms by William Haag: "They stamped them out in a pit in the ground with their feet and they didn't have delicate toes" (quoted in Williams 1971:7). Pottery artifacts inter-preted as trowels, found at many Mississippian sites, are an alternative tool for pressing the clay into place (Orr 1951:317). Several sites have yielded pit molds in association with the raw materials of pottery-making: quantities of mussel shells and unfired clay. For example, at Kincaid two clay-lined basins of approximately the same diameters as Kincaid "saltpans" were excavated in association with clay and shells; in addition, the clay-lined fire pits used as hearths at this and many other Mississippian settlements could have served as pottery molds (Cole 1951:53, 139; Orr 1951:316, 318; I. Brown 1980:32). The Great Salt Spring, a salt-production site approximately 80 kilometers (50 mi) northwest of Kincaid, yielded clay-filled storage pits, large quantities of mussel shell, and "unfired clay-lined basins that may have been mixing basins or molds (or both)." As well, there were many separate, semi-spherical, baked-clay hearths, from 50 to 100 centimeters (20–40 in) in size (Muller 1984:500, 504). At the Cole, Missouri, salt-making site, Keslin discovered a 35-inch (89 cm) diameter, basin-shaped, packed-earth depres-sion in which was found "a large fabric impressed sherd with the fabric impressed side against the basin wall," which he interpreted as a saltpan manufacturing mold (Keslin 1964:72–73).

At other sites, "saltpans" may have been formed over convex molds rather than in concave depressions. At Equality, Illinois, and Tolu, Kentucky, mounds of appropriate shape and size have been found, and a minor percent-age of Tolu "saltpan" vessels actually had both interior and exterior fabric impressions. I. Brown summarizes, illustrates, and discusses the details of this proposed process, noting that it also could account for the occasional textile impressions found inside jars, such as at Kincaid (1980:32–35).

Granted that fabric was used in the manufacture of a large proportion of "saltpan" vessels, and to some extent in other types of ceramics as well, many different theories have been advanced as to the primary function served by these textiles and by the impressions they left in the pottery. A number of researchers have advocated a decorative purpose for fabric impressions (e.g., Bushnell 1914:664; Holmes 1884:398; Linton 1944:373). However, few people if any have proposed a completely nonfunctional purpose for them. Drawing at least to some extent on ethnographic data, Holmes advocated their use "as exterior supports in holding or handling the vessel while it was still in a plastic condition," noting that cloth-wrapped exteriors also "would serve to prevent quick drying and consequent cracking of the clay along a weak line" (Holmes 1903:71). Webb and Funkhouser essentially concurred and drew attention to the worn state of many of the fabrics used, as evidence against a primarily ornamental function (1931:378–380). A modern potter who has replicated aboriginal pottery, Tammy Barnes, has suggested that because textile impressions on much "saltpan" pottery are so deep and well-formed, they must have been made while the clay was extremely wet, then the fabric left on the vessel, facilitating a slow drying process, until the clay was hardened (Joan Miller, personal communication 1990; see also Drooker 1989b:242–243).

Bushnell believed that "saltpans" at Kimmswick, Missouri, were molded in baskets. He rejected the necessity, proposed by some, of burning off basketry molds to remove them from the pottery, postulating rather that contraction of the clay as it dried would permit its easy removal from the basket (Bushnell 1914:664–665). Although some nineteenth-century writers claimed to have observed Native Americans of their day forming pots in baskets, then burning the baskets, the evidence is not reliable (I. Brown 1980:31). Most theoreticians would agree with one Professor Wyman, quoted by Holmes (1884:398): "It seems incredible that even an Indian would be so prodigal of time and labor as to make the necessary quantity of well-twisted cord or thread, and weave it into shape for the mere process of serving as a mold which must be destroyed in making a single copy."

Orr was another researcher who viewed fabrics and other materials such as leaves found impressed on Kincaid "saltpans" as "mold linings," functioning to separate the vessel from the mold—but an earthen rather than a basketry mold (1951:316). Keslin, as well, saw fabrics functioning to facilitate removal from an earthen mold (1964:50, 72, 74). Nothing would prohibit pottery makers from peeling textiles off nearly dry "saltpans" and reusing them repeatedly (Webb and Funkhouser 1931:380; Keslin 1964:50; Kuttruff and Kuttruff 1986:8). It is quite possible that fabrics were not merely helpful in separating vessels from molds but actually necessary to support the heavy, unwieldy pans in such manufacturing steps as lifting them from their molds (I. Brown 1980:32).

How much time would have been invested in each "saltpan"? Production steps include gathering raw materials, removing impurities, burning and crushing the shell temper, mixing clay and temper, aging the damp clay, forming the vessel, drying it, and firing it (Million 1975, 1976). Although elapsed time to produce a large pottery vessel can be many days, actual hands-on time for a single molded vessel would be more a matter of hours, considering the fact that drying, firing, and at least some of the preparation of materials is done in bulk (Drooker 1989b:242–243).

The nature of textiles impressed on "saltpans"—coarse or fine, open or dense, standardized or diverse, in pristine or ragtag condition—can give clues as to how they might have been used in the manufacturing process, and whether they originally were made for that purpose alone. To date, only one formal study has considered this question.

In her analysis of 510 fabric-impressed sherds from Mound Bottom, Tennessee, Kuttruff postulated that a limited variety in the textiles (i.e., standardization) would provide evidence to support the idea that they were created specifically for use in pottery manufacture, while a greater variety might imply that they were "created for other purposes or were considered as a means of decoration." In addition, to be suited for pottery-making, fabrics should have the qualities of strength, durability, and flexibility. In fact, Kuttruff found that the vast majority of textiles used at the site were of relatively simple construction. However, only a small percentage used plied yarns, considered a hallmark of strength. Although she stopped short of concluding that the fabrics were made solely to aid in manufacturing pottery, she emphasized that "these textiles were at least selected, if not created, to function in the pottery manufacturing process" (Kuttruff and Kuttruff 1986:14–15; Kuttruff 1987b).

Who would have made these vessels? The overwhelming evidence from early historical reports is that all across the Southeast, pottery-making was women's work (Swanton 1946:549–555). Evidence for the same situation in prehistoric times comes in the shape of a ceramic vessel from a Mississippian mound in southern Indiana that depicts a female potter at work (Holmes 1903:Plate 28).

"Saltpan" Use

Textile function vis-à-vis "saltpan" vessels need not necessarily have been limited to the manufacturing process: fabric impressions might have been functional in some aspect of vessel use. However, the way(s) in which "saltpans" actually were used still is a matter of some debate.

"Saltpan" sherds are found in extremely large numbers at salt-spring sites, where these vessels undoubtedly were employed in the evaporation of saline water to obtain salt. Such sites include Kimmswick, Kreilich, and Cole, Missouri (Holmes 1903; Bushnell 1907, 1914; Keslin 1964), French Lick, Tennessee (Thruston 1973), Equality and Great Salt Spring, Illinois (Sellers 1877; Muller 1984), and sites in Clarke County, Alabama (Wimberly 1960; I. Brown, personal communication 1991). However, "saltpan" sherds also occur in significant numbers at many Mississippian settlement sites, often far from saline localities. At such places, they most likely were used for cooking and/or eating. Some researchers have proposed their use as communal eating bowls, perhaps indicating significant changes in cultural patterns of food preparation and consumption between pre-Mississippian and Mississippian times (e.g., Goggins and Fairbanks, in Williams 1971:6–7; Webb 1952:93). However, it would seem that the size and weight of the larger vessels would make them extremely awkward to lift and carry when full of hot food.

Various ways that these vessels may have been used for cooking and the evidence for each type of use are summarized by Drooker (1989b:18–21). These include stewpots, bread ovens, and drying/parching surfaces (Lorant 1946:91, 93, 255; Adair 1968:407–408; Linton 1944). Textile-roughened surfaces have been proposed as factors that could increase "gripping ability and heatable surface area" (Pauketat 1987:7).

The very great range of sizes and shapes classified as "textile-impressed saltpans" (large versus small diameter, deep versus shallow shape, rounded versus flat bottom) and the range of use patterns (embedded in the ground or not, blackened by fire or not) all imply the possibility of significant differences in function or technique of use, rather than mere stylistic fads. In addition, the fact that "saltpan" forms were not invariably present at Mississippian-period settlements (e.g., the sites in northern Georgia studied by Hally [1984, 1986]) may have functional significance. However, there seem to be no quantitative studies of variation in "saltpan" form between geographic regions, between different sites, between portions of a given site, between salt-producing versus non-salt-producing sites, or between over-fire versus not-over-fire usage that might be employed to correlate form and exterior texture with function. A single bit of relevant data is Black's passing remark comparing "saltpans" at the salt-making sites of the Saline River, Gallatin County, Illinois, with those from settlement sites like Angel. At Saline River, it appeared to Black that vessels were made on the spot, used once, and abandoned: "They are, more often than not, thick, rather crude, and poorly fired in comparison with sherds of the same type found within and upon permanently occupied sites" (Black 1967:581).

A comprehensive study of fabric impressions on "saltpans," such as that carried out for Wickliffe, has the potential to contribute not only to knowledge of the Mississippian textile complex but also to knowledge of how textile-impressed ceramic vessels were made and used. Comparative studies of fabric-impressed pottery from several types of sites, including both saline and village locations, would add still further to our understanding of Mississippian lifeways.

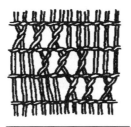

CHAPTER 3

WICKLIFFE VILLAGE

Wickliffe Mounds, the archaeological site chosen for this case study of impressed textiles, is located in western Kentucky within the northern Middle Mississippi region. The village at Wickliffe was intermediate in size and early to intermediate in time within the Mississippian tradition.

In order to obtain the maximum amount of technical and socioeconomic information from the Wickliffe fabrics, it will be important to consider the natural and social environments in which they were made and used. Below are summary descriptions of the site itself, its excavation history, its chronology, its regional affiliations, its "saltpan" pottery, and the little evidence other than impressed fabrics of its textile industry.

SITE DESCRIPTION

The Wickliffe Mounds site (15Ba4) is typical in many ways of moderate-sized Mississippian settlements. It lies approximately 5 kilometers (3 mi) south of the confluence of the Ohio and Mississippi rivers on the east bank of the Mississippi River, in the town of Wickliffe, Ballard County, Kentucky. The prehistoric village was situated on a bluff overlooking the Mississippi River to the west. At this spot, the river floodplain at present is approximately 400 meters (¼ mi) in width, and the adjacent bluffs are approximately 12 to 15 meters (40–50 ft) in height. Corn has been excavated at the site, and agriculture is presumed to have taken place in the rich bottomlands of the

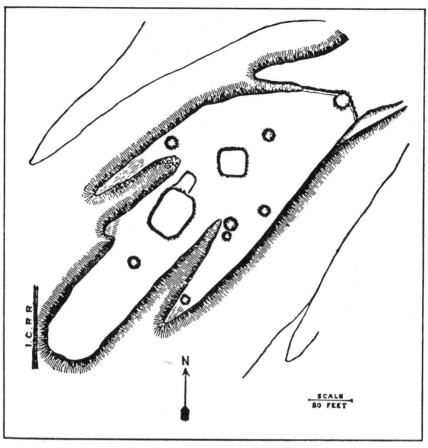

Figure 4.
The Wickliffe site in the 1880s (after Loughridge 1888:185).

floodplain. Adjacent upland forests were a potential source for many plant and animal foods to be hunted and gathered, and river and marshlands could provide fish, birds, and additional vegetable resources. Remains of deer, smaller mammals, turtles, birds, fish, mollusks, and several kinds of nuts have been excavated at the site. From the point of view of riverine transportation, defense, and available resources for food, shelter, and clothing, the settlement was very well situated (R. B. Lewis 1986:121–128; Wesler 1985:1–3).

The earliest representation of the site, a map rendered by Robert Loughridge in the 1880s (Figure 4), shows two large rectangular mounds and eight smaller round mounds, plus an indication of an embankment cutting off the neck of the relatively narrow bluff on which the village was located. The largest mounds probably surrounded an open plaza area typical of Mississippian settlement layouts. As discussed below, during the time that the flat-topped platform mounds were in active use, houses were located toward the periphery of the site. The two southwest-northeast-trending gullies may or may not have been present in Mississippian times. Since Loughridge's day, the gully contours have been altered, and the western edge of the bluff has been truncated by road building.

This was not a large community. At any one time, it probably included no more than 250 people (Wesler, personal communication 1988). Unlike other regions that encompassed larger towns such as Kincaid and Angel (Green and Munson 1978; Muller 1978), the area around Wickliffe shows a non-hierarchical settlement pattern, with villages of similar size located every 10 to 13 kilometers (6–8 mi) (Wesler, personal communication 1988; e.g., see R. B. Lewis 1986, 1987; Sussenbach and Lewis 1987). No large "paramount center" has been discovered in the nearby region of western Kentucky and southeastern Missouri (Wesler, personal communication 1989).

EXCAVATION HISTORY

After highway construction in 1930 uncovered archaeological deposits along the western edge of the bluff, the Wickliffe site was purchased by Fain W. King, who owned and operated it as a tourist attraction with his wife, Blanche, until 1946. It continued in the same function for 35 more years and then, in 1983, was donated to Murray State University. Archaeological excavations took place during the 1930s, supervised for the most part by King, an amateur, and from 1983 onward. King's records were sparse, and publications about the site were few (T. Lewis 1934; F. King 1936; B. King 1936, 1937a, 1937b, 1939) until excavations resumed in the 1980s. Artifacts in the Wickliffe Mounds collection from the 1930s excavations were sorted and cataloged only in 1984.

Figure 5 shows the site essentially as it looks today, including locations of recent excavations. The area where the Mound A excavation shelter previously stood has been backfilled. A parking lot occupies the area between the gate and the office building, the construction of which involved extensive bulldozing.

Starting in 1932, King first excavated the center of Mound A, the major platform mound. Very few cataloged artifacts from this dig have been located. In 1984 and 1985 Wesler excavated at the east side of the mound, which had been built in stages. King found two buried surfaces, at 1.5 meters (5 ft) and 3 meters (10 ft) below the top, both with postholes and the remains

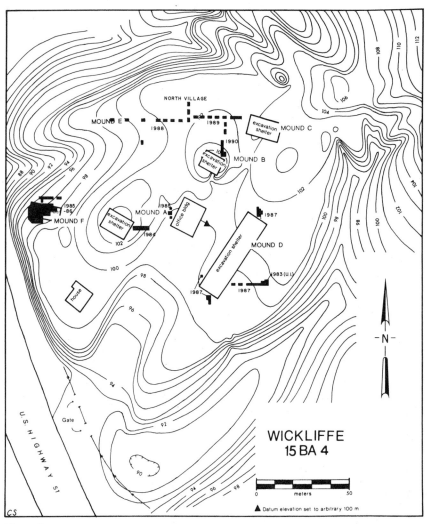

Figure 5.
The Wickliffe site in the 1980s (overlay by Kit W. Wesler on map by Charles B. Stout). Used
by permission of Wickliffe Mounds Research Center. Base map used by permission of the
Western Kentucky Project, University of Illinois at Urbana-Champaign.

of burned structures. Wesler identified a minimum of three construction
episodes within the mound core and two within the outer mound. Below the
level of King's excavations, Wesler uncovered a submound midden, including a hearth and two wall trenches (Wesler 1985, 1986; Wesler and Neusius
1987).

Much of Mound B also was excavated by King, again with sparse documentation and few cataloged artifacts. On display in the excavation shelter, at a level at least 1.5 meters (4–5 ft) below the surface of the mound, are features including postmolds, a hearth, and a possible storage pit. Unfortunately, however, the building floods during heavy rainfalls, and these features may well have been reconstructed repeatedly since they first were excavated. Excavations in 1989 and 1990 found a dense midden zone adjacent to this mound as well as possible middens on what remained of earlier summits. Wesler's preliminary analysis raises the possibility that Mound B served as the base for an elite residence (Wesler 1990c).

The Mound C excavations by King partially uncovered a cemetery, containing the remains of many adults and some older children (Wesler 1990b). According to T. Lewis (1934:27–28), at least two types of interment were present. Most common were fully extended, natural-flesh burials, but bundle burials also occurred. One woman, buried with five trowels and two rubbing stones, was thought to be a potter. Lewis pointed out the "abnormally" large number of associated effigy pots, among which was little or no repetition in form. He also noted "numerous artifacts of mica, hematite, fluorite, lead, copper, cannel coal, marine shells, bone and stone" associated with burials, as indicative of widespread exchange contacts. Only a few artifacts from Mound C were labeled or cataloged. In 1988 a complete survey of extant cemetery remains was carried out (Haskins 1990), and in 1991 the excavation was completed. Initial interpretations of Mound C stratigraphy from 1991 operations include a Middle Wickliffe village midden capped by a basket-loaded mound, followed by Late village deposits. The cemetery is within Late midden, and may be intrusive (Wesler, personal communication 1991). As this is written, final analysis of cemetery materials has just begun.

"Mound D" was indicated on the Loughridge map as two round mounds rather than a single large mound. King exhibited his excavation of this location as the "Infant Burial Mound." Remains of both infants and adults were discovered there, along with submound features including possible storage pits and postmolds from at least two rectangular houses. In general, the 63 infant burials, like those excavated elsewhere on the site, were associated with deposits at the base of the mound, whereas the adult remains, including two extended burials covered with bark, came from within the mound (B. King 1939:44–45, 50; F. King 1936; Wesler 1990b:4, 7–8, 1990c:10–11). Also coming from within this mound were an "unusual and large" fluorspar pendant (B. King 1939:81), several possible caches of stone projectile points, bone tools, disks and discoidals, and 8 of the 12 conch-shell effigies found at the site (Wesler 1990b:8, 10). Wesler suggests that the in-mound adult burials may have been of elite individuals (1990b:12).

Most of the artifacts from the early Mound D excavations were labeled by provenience and retained on-site, but two large lots of ceramics from the north end of the mound were sent to the University of Chicago and the University of Michigan by King. Excavations in 1983 and 1987 provided additional data from three locations around the periphery of the King excavations (R. B. Lewis 1986; Wesler 1989a). The unit excavated to the east of Mound D was interpreted as midden.

No field notes survived from King's excavation of Mound F, and information about artifacts and features is anecdotal at best. In 1985–1986, Wesler and Neusius excavated truncated submound features and midden still remaining to the west of the mound (Wesler and Neusius 1987).

Mound E apparently was completely leveled by King, who retrieved thousands of artifacts, carefully labeling them by provenience within a five-foot grid system. Unfortunately, the location and exact orientation of the grid itself—and thus Mound E—are unknown. In 1988 excavations were carried out near the area marked "Mound E" in Figure 5, in an effort to locate the mound. Although a portion of one of King's 1932 tests of Mound E was uncovered, the main excavation remained elusive. Instead, a residential area was discovered that has been designated the "North Village" (Wesler, personal communication 1988, 1989, 1990).

The 1985 excavations included test pits in the driveway area and just west of the office building. Remnants of a pre-1930 shallow plow zone penetrating to subsoil in the latter area were interpreted as consistent with the presence of a nonoccupied plaza in the center of the settlement (Wesler and Neusius 1987:20–32) . No archaeological evidence has yet been found of the "earthworks" that cut off the neck of the bluff in the Loughridge map.

CHRONOLOGY

Analysis of ceramics excavated in 1984–1986 from Mounds A and F resulted in a three-period chronological sequence. Based on the juxtaposition of deposits within and under Mound A, time periods were characterized as follows. Early Wickliffe deposits—the underlying midden—contained relatively less incised and punctate-decorated pottery (0.5%) and relatively more red-filmed pottery (3.1%). In Late Wickliffe deposits—the outer mound—the relationship was reversed: 1.5% versus 0.6%. Middle Wickliffe deposits of the mound core contained 1.8% and 2.9% of incised versus red-filmed pottery. Mound F ceramics from both mound fill and submound midden and features conformed to the Late Wickliffe assemblage from Mound A (Wesler 1988).

Mound B chronology is much like that of Mound A: most of the mound is

Middle Wickliffe, the base is Early, and the final cap is Late (Wesler, personal communication 1991).

Most sherds from within and around Mound D fit into the Late Wickliffe typology. However, some of the lowest levels excavated at the north end of the mound appear to represent Early Wickliffe, and ceramics from the lowest levels at the south end of the mound have been designated as Middle Wickliffe (Wesler 1988, 1989a:58–60).

Mound E ceramics may be mixed, or they may be Late/Middle stratified. They include the only examples on the site (five sherds) that may date to the late 1300s (Wesler, personal communication 1991).

Although a sample of Mound C ceramics "tends to the late profile," it was not large enough to be definitive (Wesler 1988:12). The cemetery depositional context is complex, containing both Middle and Late Wickliffe components, and is just now being studied in detail. "North Village" deposits excavated in 1988 and 1989 appear to belong primarily to Late Wickliffe, but some Early-Middle Wickliffe material also is present (Wesler, personal communication 1988, 1989, 1991).

Through 1989 radiocarbon analysis had been carried out on 16 samples from in and around Mounds A, D, and F (Wesler 1988:12–16, 22, 1989a: 54–76; 1989b, 1990a:3–4, Table 3, personal communication 1990). On the basis of these data and intersite ceramics comparisons for an estimate of the beginning of Early Wickliffe, absolute dates for the Wickliffe intrasite chronology were interpreted as follows (Wesler 1989a:75):

	uncorrected (a.d.)	calibrated (A.D.)
Late Wickliffe	1200–1300	1260–1300
Middle Wickliffe	1100–1200	1200–1260
Early Wickliffe	1000–1100	1000–1200

In a recent article (1991), Wesler summarized all ceramic and radiocarbon dating information for Middle and Late Wickliffe, concluding that Late Wickliffe extends into the early fourteenth century; Middle Wickliffe continues to be assigned to the early-middle thirteenth century.

RECAP: THE SHAPE OF WICKLIFFE

What is currently known about Wickliffe chronology implies a settlement in which living areas were shifted outward from the center as mounds were constructed on top of earlier domestic sites during the thirteenth century. Mounds A, B, D, and F are known to have been superimposed on previous house locations. The earliest-dated such location was in the area presently occupied by Mound A, the largest substructure mound on the site. Houses covered by the two "Mound D" mounds also date to Early Wickliffe, as well as to Middle Wickliffe. Village middens north of Mound B have some Middle Wickliffe but date primarily to Late Wickliffe. Living areas to the east of Mound D, under Mound F, and in the vicinity of Mound E likely date to Late Wickliffe. They are located toward the periphery of the site. The area surrounded by Mounds A, B, and D probably served as an open plaza.

Mound C, covering the "adult cemetery," was located just beyond the plaza-ringing mounds, behind Mound B. The wide variety of grave goods, including exotic materials, buried with villagers at this location would seem to argue for a somewhat egalitarian society, although there is a certain amount of evidence, in the artifacts and adult remains taken from Mound D during the 1930s excavations and in the possible middens atop Mound B, for elite residences and elite burials indicative of social stratification.

All indications are that village occupation ceased prior to European contact (Wesler 1989a:75–76, 1989b:10, 1990a:4, 1991).

REGIONAL AFFILIATIONS

The Wickliffe artifact assemblage has yet to be compared in detail with assemblages from other Mississippian settlements, although on the basis of general material culture it has in the past been grouped with the major sites of Kincaid and Angel to the east (Cole 1951:229) and the smaller Crosno, Missouri, site to the southwest (Williams 1954:121). Miner grouped the Wickliffe textile structures with those from six other locations generally in the lower Ohio Valley region: Mouth of the Wabash, Indiana; Saline River and Kincaid, Illinois; Tolu and Williams, Kentucky; and Crowder, Missouri (Miner 1936:191).

During the past decade, the "Western Kentucky Project" has been amassing data on archaeological sites in the Jackson Purchase area of the state. The settlement pattern is one of hamlets, villages, and towns rather than farmsteads, hamlets, and small villages surrounding a single "paramount center" like Cahokia, Kincaid, or Angel (R. B. Lewis 1991:290, 293). An expanded edition of the Western Kentucky Project's first report (R. B. Lewis 1986) groups Wickliffe, on the basis of site layout and 1983 excavation results, with approximately 20 Mississippian towns of roughly similar size near the Mississippi River in Kentucky and Missouri. It is compared specifically with the Adams and Sassafras Ridge sites, some 40–50 kilometers (25–30 mi) to its south, all of which exhibit "the same basic tool kits, technology, and raw material sources" (R. B. Lewis 1986:154–155). However, whereas decorated ceramics such as negative-painted wares and effigy vessels at the three sites were very similar in all respects, implying exchange, utility wares differed significantly in paste from site to site.

The material culture of the western Kentucky region is considered to be more similar to that of Kincaid and sites in the Lower Tennessee–Cumberland River drainage and western Tennessee such as Jonathan Creek, Tinsley Hill, and Obion than to that of sites in the Memphis region farther south along the Mississippi or the Cahokia area to the north (Figure 1) (R. B. Lewis 1986:2, 153–161, 1990a:56–57, 1991:291–293). Recent ceramics analysis by Sherri Hilgeman places the Angel region, to the east of Kincaid, firmly within the Lower Ohio Valley sphere (Wesler, personal communication 1991). It is of interest that the major mound-building phase at Kincaid, like that at Wickliffe, occurred during the thirteenth century (Butler 1990:270–271). Although "beaten copper ornaments" have been reported from Wickliffe (B. King 1937:87), they were not described in detail, and the importance of copper as an exotic item of exchange is unknown for the site. Artifacts designated by J. Brown as "High Value Exchange Items"—shell cups and embossed copper headdress ornaments—generally have not been found at Mississippian sites in southeastern Missouri, western Kentucky, and the Ohio River Valley, although they do occur in southwestern Illinois and the Cahokia region, as well as at major centers such as Spiro, Etowah, and Moundville (J. Brown 1983:147; J. Brown et al. 1990:261).

The western Kentucky–lower Tennessee–Cumberland region does appear to be at most only very sparsely populated after about 1450, but debate continues among archaeologists working in and around this area as to whether it was peopled into protohistoric times. The view that "the Kincaid locality and the lower Ohio region in general does fit, to some extent, the 'Vacant Quarter' scenario," and that "by ca. A.D. 1400 Mississippian population aggregates had largely dispersed and moved south" has been advocated by Butler, among others (1991:272, 1987:75). Lewis argues for "cultural continuity into the sixteenth century," hypothesizing that the scarcity of archaeological evidence for this period may be due to the decimating effects of European diseases (R. B. Lewis 1986:8, 1991:290). Wesler also has entered into the debate (1989b, 1990a, 1991), contending that, at least at Wickliffe, occupation ceased well before 1400.

TEXTILES

If an attempt were made to reconstruct the Wickliffe textile industry from surviving fabrics, the going would be rough indeed. Only one organic textile

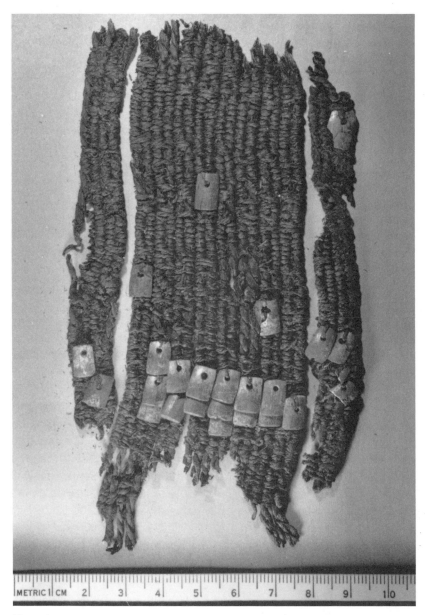

Figure 6.
Decorated weft-faced textile from Wickliffe. It consists of 1/1 and 2/2 plain interlacing, with bone beads attached to some weft elements. Photograph by Jenna Tedrick Kuttruff. Used by permission of Wickliffe Mounds Research Center.

Table 1. Summary of textile attributes for organic fabrics from Wickliffe

Attribute	Weft-faced interlaced fabric (Figure 6)	Plain-twined fabrics	
		Edge finish	Body
Warp diameter, mm	1.8–3.0	1.0	2.0
Weft diameter, mm	1.0	1.0	1.0
Number of warp plies	2	2	2
Number of weft plies	2	2	2
Warp twist category	3	3	3
Weft twist category	2	3	3
Warp elements per cm	4	7	4
Weft elements per cm	16	20–30	4
Fabric count	20	32	8
Warp density	8	7	8
Weft density	16	10	2
Total density	24	17	10
Complexity Index No. 1	7	5	4
Complexity Index No. 3	12	10	9

Note: Data from Kuttruff 1990, samples 2B and 2E. See Appendix A and Chapter 4 for definition of terms.

of any size survives from the King excavations (Figure 6). This fragment, approximately 7 × 14 centimeters (2.8 × 5.5 in) in size, has been analyzed by Jenna Kuttruff (1990:3–7). The fabric is interlaced, with a dense, weft-faced structure, approximately 4 warps and 16 wefts per centimeter (Table 1). Most of the textile consists of 1/1 interlacing, but there are narrow bands of 2/2 interlacing at intervals across the fabric. It was constructed in three pieces, with two narrow sections, each 4 warps wide, flanking a wider fragment, 16 warps wide, and is ornamented with overlapping rectangular bone "beads," each approximately 0.6 × 1.0 centimeters (0.2 × 0.4 in). These beads seem to be strung on the weft yarns, thus apparently were attached as the weaving progressed. Yarns are two-ply, of **Z**-spun singles twisted together in the **S** direction (see Appendix A: "Twist direction," and Figure 12 below), with warp diameters ranging from 1.8 to 3.0 millimeters and wefts of approximately 1.0 millimeter. Precise identification of fibers has not yet been accomplished, but they are vegetal and very likely some type of bast. The exact provenience of this fabric within the site is unknown (Wesler, personal communication 1988).

No similar textile has been reported from any other Mississippian site. The combination of 1/1 and 2/2 weft-faced interlacing, the co-occurrence of narrow and wide strips, most likely woven as a unit, and the flat, rectangular bone beads all are unusual. Kuttruff suggests that this may have formed the end of a sash, such as those depicted on many Mississippian engraved artifacts (e.g., see Phillips and Brown 1978:96–97). By means of her Textile Production Complexity Index (see Chapter 4), Kutruff rates the complexity of this fabric as slightly in excess of the average high-status textile from Spiro, a ceremonial center from which many elaborate fabrics were recovered (Kuttruff 1988, 1990:6).

In addition to the decorated fabric, only small fragments survive from one or possibly two textile artifacts that are more utilitarian (Kuttruff 1990:7–10). The major remains were tagged "Parts close woven bag. March 5, 1938" and undoubtedly refer to the lone textile described in Blanche King's book (1939:70):

> On March 5, 1938, . . . an unusual fabric container was excavated from a portion of Mound D here at the King Mounds. Due to carbonization, the type of weave and material can be determined. The bag or container was filled with charred prehistoric corn and cobs. The corn was much larger than any we had found previously; apparently the largest ears had been placed in the bag for next year's planting.

Kuttruff analyzed five of the fragments, the largest of which is 2 × 4 centimeters (0.8 × 1.6 in), in detail (Table 1). They include separate examples of both weft-faced and spaced twining (Figures 2g, 2a). Two of the weft-faced fragments (2A and 2B), one of which may be an edge finish with warp ends turned back into the fabric, consist of three-strand twining, while the others were too small for their structures to be recognizable. The largest fragment of spaced twining (2E) is plain twined over single warps, with weft rows approximately 0.5 centimeter apart. Yarns are two-ply, constructed of plant fibers, **Z**-spun and **S**-plied, with average diameters of 1 millimeter. Kuttruff interprets these remains as from a single fabric, with the first two fragments representing starting and/or terminal edges and the last-described representing the main body of the textile. Two other very small fragments may have been side edges, so this may have been a flat textile wrapping rather than a bag (Kuttruff 1990:9). During the 1991 excavation season, a few additional pieces of charred fabric or cordage were found in association with a burial, but they have yet to be analyzed (Wesler, personal communication 1991).

The poor condition, small sizes, and minute number of fabric fragments, along with the singular nature of the decorated textile, are illustrative of the problems associated with attempts to reconstruct the Mississippian textile complex from organic fabrics alone. Statistically, so few have survived that there is no way to know what the complete range of fabric types actually was.

Fortunately, although actual fabrics recovered at Wickliffe have been few, fabric-impressed sherds have been relatively abundant. Analysis of the impressed textiles and comparison of them with actual textile artifacts from Wickliffe and elsewhere in the Southeast can give a much broader and more rounded picture of fabric production and use at Wickliffe than would be possible with extant textiles alone.

"SALTPAN" POTTERY

At the Wickliffe site, there is no indication of any but a utilitarian function for "saltpan" vessels. Both smooth and fabric-impressed examples have been recovered.

Textile-impressed pottery at Wickliffe makes up on the order of 2% of the ceramics. "Saltpan" sherds are present in most locations and levels, but they decline in proportion to other ceramic types from Early to Late Wickliffe. Wesler (1990a:Table 1) gives these frequency ranges:

Early Wickliffe	2.0–4.1%
Middle Wickliffe	2.1–4.3%
Late Wickliffe	0.8–2.1%.

All Wickliffe textile-impressed ceramics, with the exception of red-filmed ware, have been classified as Kimmswick Fabric Impressed. The nondecorated coarse shell-tempered pottery classified as Mississippi Plain makes up the bulk of the ceramic assemblage at the site (Wesler 1986a:20, 1988:21, 1989a:19–20, 1990a:Table 1; Wesler and Neusius 1987:41, 59). No comprehensive analysis has yet been done of vessel shapes of either ceramic type, so no data are available to determine relative frequency of "saltpans" in textile-impressed versus plain ware.

According to Blanche King, "We have excavated three types of shallow plate, many of them measuring 14 inches in diameter at least. Two types were similar, with the exception, however, that one has fabric impressions on the outside, showing that a fabric bag was used as a mold until it was air dried" (1939:102–103). Sherds of part of a large, shallow, smooth-surfaced "saltpan" with possible smoothed-over fabric markings on its exterior are displayed supposedly in situ on a pedestal in the Mound D excavation building. They are located in a basin-shaped depression with a rounded bottom, approximately 60 centimeters (2 ft) in diameter and 5–8 centimeters (2–3 in) deep. The shape is similar to that illustrated in Figure 3c, left.

Unfortunately, relatively few large sherds from fabric-impressed vessels remain in the collection, and to date no textile-impressed saltpans have been reconstructed. However, although no complete survey has been done of "saltpan" vessel forms at Wickliffe, some general assessments can be made.

Fabric-impressed pottery used at Wickliffe was by no means uniform in shape. At least two different forms were present. The largest rim sherds seem to indicate vessels with gradually sloping sides (Figure 7b), but the frequency of occurrence of this shape is not known with any certainty. The smooth-surfaced pan in the Mound D excavation shelter is relatively shallow, but whether or not this is representative of Wickliffe "saltpans" in general is not known.

Rim forms varied considerably. One easily distinguishable type (Figures 7d, 7f) had a flat, smoothed rim up to 6 centimeters (2.4 in) wide, similar to those illustrated in Figure 3d. Some 24 examples were found, representing 13% of all rim sherds. The remainder of the rim sherds were not so easily separated in form, since variation seemed to be almost continuous among them. Shapes varied from slightly out-curving to thickened, knobby, and everted. On the simpler shapes, textile impressions generally continued right up to the edge of the lip, while on thickened rims the upper 1–2 centimeters might be smoothed.

Small sherd size, irregular rims, and uncertainty as to vessel shape made it difficult to assess textile-impressed "saltpan" diameters with any precision. At Mound Bottom, O'Brien (1977:374) found that "no precise wall angle can ever be obtained from a single sherd or even from three or four connecting rim sherds because of the great unevenness of the vessels. This lopsided effect also makes the measuring of the rim diameters tenuous at best." At Wickliffe, the same sort of problem prevailed.

A total of 194 rim sherds were examined. Inside diameter could be measured for 101 cases. Outside diameter could be measured for 93 cases, and both measurements were available for 77 cases. For these 77 cases, the mean of the average of the two estimates of diameter (Appendix B) was 79 centimeters (31 in), with minima and maxima of 25 and 107 centimeters (10 and 42 in).

This range falls well above the typical sizes reported by Blanche King. Because of measurement uncertainties, in a conservative estimate of vessel size perhaps diameters as large as 79 centimeters should be thought of as falling within an upper range rather than as representative. Fabric-impressed "saltpans" at the Adams site, about 40 kilometers (25 mi) south of Wickliffe,

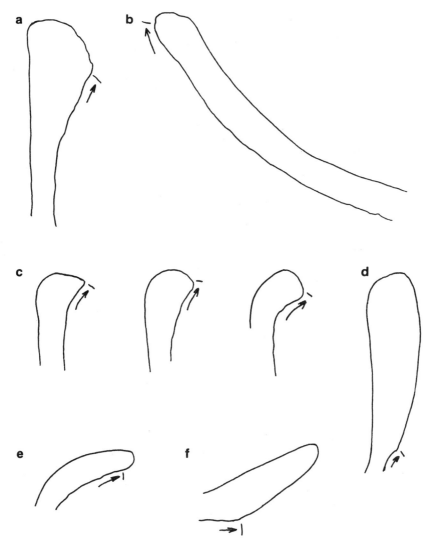

Figure 7.
Examples of rim sherd profiles from Wickliffe fabric-impressed pottery. Arrows indicate position of fabric impressions.

while difficult to measure because of inadequate sherd size, were at least 42–46 centimeters (17–18 in) in diameter (R. B. Lewis 1986:35). It does seem likely that Wickliffe "saltpans" at least matched those from Adams in size, but the true extent of their size range has yet to be determined. The average probably falls between 40 and 80 centimeters (16–31 in).

Within the Wickliffe sherds classified as Kimmswick Fabric Impressed there was considerable variation in the shell-tempered matrix. Sherds ranged from lightweight and crumbly to dense, heavy, and solid. One instance of a very sandy matrix was noted, but more may have been present. Its thickness was 6 millimeters (0.2 in), whereas most sherds were at least 1 centimeter (0.4 in) thick. Ten comparatively thin textile-impressed sherds, ranging from 3 to 5 millimeters (0.1–0.2 in) in thickness, were measured. Two, possibly three, instances of textiles impressed on Bell Plain sherds were found.

Most textile impressions were on vessel exteriors, but three examples of textile impressions on vessel interiors were discovered, two of which occurred on sherds classified as Bell Plain.

Although formal tabulation of the relative frequency of smoke-marked fabric-impressed sherds was not part of this study, it can be said that while nonmarked sherds were the norm, smoke-marking on both interior and exterior of sherds did occur. For some examples, the marking was apparent on broken edges as well, as might occur if pieces of a broken vessel fell into a hearth.

Types and attributes of the textiles impressed on pottery at Wickliffe are detailed in Chapter 5, along with the relationships of fabric structures to the form of the vessel on which they were impressed. In Chapter 6 these data are utilized to reconstruct, as far as possible, how the Wickliffe impressed textiles were made and used. However, before the results of the Wickliffe textile attribute study are reported, it will be useful to consider the methodology employed in obtaining them.

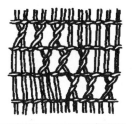

CHAPTER 4

GLEANING INFORMATION FROM FABRIC IMPRESSIONS

Methodology and Comparative Data

At first consideration, it might seem that analysis of fabric impressions on pottery can yield little more than descriptions of textile structure types. Indeed, previous researchers have cautioned strongly against jumping to unwarranted conclusions based on the restricted nature of the data available from textile impressions (M. E. King 1978:90–91). For the most part only small pieces of fabric can be studied, since most impressions are preserved on relatively small-sized sherds. The textile "images" cannot be turned over or unraveled to investigate their structures, nor can their fibers be analyzed directly. Almost always they lack even one selvage, a feature essential for determining the details of how a fabric was manufactured. They provide no records of entire textile items, like skirts or bags, only of portions of cloth.

The surviving collection of southeastern textile artifacts, however, although spanning some 8,000 years, is sparse and uneven in its coverage. Mississippian fabric items have been preserved at only a few locations, primarily in mortuary contexts. They fully represent neither the complete range of textile types nor the total numbers of textile artifacts produced. How can these artifacts best be utilized to learn more about the fragments of fabrics visible on Mississippian pottery sherds? How, in turn, can the comparatively large available sample of fabric impressions on pottery be used to enrich our knowledge of textile production and use during the Mississippian?

Only by employing these two sets of data in conjunction and by supplementing them with information from ethnographic textiles, from Mississippian art depicting clothing and other fabric items in use, and from early historical accounts of Native American textile production and use can we begin to construct a fully rounded picture of the importance of fabrics in Mississippian life. At a minimum, relevant questions include the following: How, and from what materials, were they made? How much time and skill were required for their production? How were they used? What types of artifacts were made from them? Were they primarily utilitarian? Ceremonial? Were they a major or a minor part of the economy? These are the kinds of questions that this case study of textiles impressed on pottery at Wickliffe Mounds was designed to answer.

This chapter is concerned with the methodology and comparative data used to analyze the Wickliffe impressed textiles per se, and to determine tentatively for what function or functions they originally were made. In the following two chapters this methodology is applied to an analysis of the Wickliffe impressed fabrics, after which the final portion of the book addresses some of the larger socioeconomic implications of the textile complexes at Wickliffe and at other Mississippian sites.

While the research reported here centered on an in-depth study of impressed textiles from a single Mississippian village site, every effort has been made to generalize the methodology employed so that it will be useful as a model for future similar studies. Both quantitative and qualitative analysis are used, but the former is an essential precursor to the latter. Thus, the major part of such a study consists of detailed measurement of textile attributes from fabric impressions present at a given site. Also important in assessing fabric size and function are measured attributes of the vessels on which they were impressed. These data are reduced statistically so that textile attributes can be compared among subsets of the sample, and ultimately between the sample and comparable data from other Mississippian sites. Finally, the attributes of the impressed fabrics are compared with measured attributes of complete or nearly complete Mississippian textile artifacts, with the aim of determining the function(s) for which the impressed fabrics originally were made.

The nature and significance of the measured attributes are discussed below, followed by a summary of diagnostic characteristics of Mississippian textile artifacts. Information about measurement techniques is provided in Appendix B, while definitions of textile terminology can be found in Appendix A.

Figure 8.
Examples of textile-
impressed sherds *(right)*
and casts made from
them *(left).*

TEXTILE ATTRIBUTES STUDIED

Because of the depth of most textile impressions on "saltpan" pottery, shadows make it very difficult to see details of yarn and fabric construction. For this reason, it is necessary to make a cast, or "positive mold," of each impression, thus reproducing the actual appearance of the original textile (Figure 8). Materials and methods for making such casts are discussed in Appendix B, along with the details of measurement methods and a summary listing of attributes that were measured or noted.

As far as possible, equivalent measurements were taken from both the fabric-impressed sherds and the textile artifacts with which they were compared. For each fabric, the following attributes were measured or noted: fabric structure(s) present, twining twist direction, warp and weft yarn diameters, yarn twist direction and angle, yarn ply, numbers of warp and weft elements per centimeter, structural designs, structure of any finished edges, condition of fabric, and overlapping or joining of fabrics. In addition, average yarn diameter, fabric count, fabric density, and modified Textile Production Complexity Indices were computed from the raw measurements. For rim sherds, the estimated vessel diameter and fabric orientation relative to the rim also were recorded. Following is a brief discussion of each of these variables, including both the definition and the significance of each attribute.

The fundamental identifying characteristic of any fabric is its *structure*— the way its elements are put together. All structural categories employed in this study follow Emery (1966), whose classification is divorced from any implications of manufacturing technique. Fraser's more detailed classification for weft-twined fabrics (1989) was used to supplement that of Emery as needed.

The three major structural categories represented at Wickliffe were twining, interlacing, and knotting (Figures 9 and 10, Appendix A). The overwhelming majority of textiles examined were twined, with the two primary structural subcategories being plain twining and alternate-pair twining. If warp elements are not spaced too close together, alternate-pair twining exhibits a characteristic zigzag warp pattern (Figure 9b). However, with closely spaced warps the fabric is not so distinctive (Figure 2c), and care must be taken not to mistake it for plain twining.

Also present, but rare, were three-element braided twining and twining around two warps without alternation between warp pairs. The former may be difficult to recognize. Although twining with more than two yarns is known from the southeastern archaeological record (e.g., J. Brown 1976b:327), it is difficult to identify such structures by examining only a single side of a fabric. One side of a textile twined with three wefts looks like plain twining, but the wefts on the reverse side overlap each other's positions, each passing across two warp elements (Emery 1966:Figures 315–316). If the twining yarns simply spiral around each other, both sides of the fabric will show an identical twining twist. However, if the twining yarns are braided, twining twists on either side of the fabric will appear to be in opposite directions (Figure 9c). It is the presence of weft twining elements that overlap and encompass two warp elements at a time that gives a clue to the possible presence of twining with three wefts in an impressed textile. Whether it is spiraled or braided twining cannot be determined from an impression.

Weft-faced textiles (Figures 2g, 10c) posed a special problem in identifica-

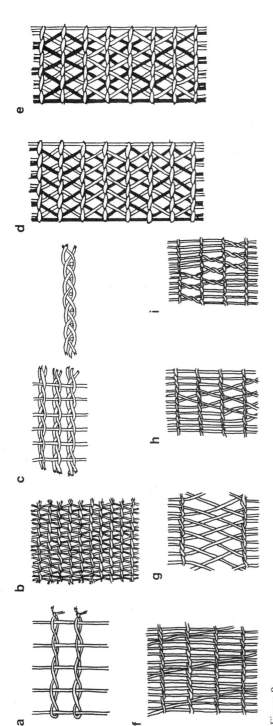

Figure 9.

Twining structures: *a*, plain twining (two weft elements twisting around one warp element at a time), with twining twist in **S** direction; *b*, alternate-pair twining (sometimes called "diagonal," "split-pair," "twilled," or "zigzag" twining); *c*, three-element braided twining, with cross-section (after J. Brown 1976b:Figure 67); *d*, two-color double-faced crossed-warp twining with warp elements of each color following parallel zigzag paths; *e*, two-color double-faced crossed-warp twining with warp elements of each color following nonparallel zigzag paths (*d* and *e* after Rogers 1980:Diagrams A1, A2); *f*, plain twining with diverted warp patterning—diagonal lines are built up from successive small diversions of different warp elements; *g*, plain twining with oblique interlacing; *h*, plain twining with transposed crossed diverted warps—each diverted warp element continues in an oblique path away from its original position; *i*, plain twining with transposed interlinked warps ("octagonal openwork" in the older literature). On one side of a fabric, structure *c* appears identical to ordinary two-element plain twining, twisted in either the **S** or the **Z** direction. On the reverse side of the fabric, however, the structure looks like two-element twining over two warp elements at a time (rather than one), twisted in the opposite direction to the first side; that is, on one side, the structure looks as if it were twined in the **S** direction, while on the other side it looks as if it were twined in the **Z** direction. Terminology follows Emery (1966). (Structures *d* and *e* from Drooker 1990c:Figure 1. Copyright 1990 The Kent State University Press; used by permission.)

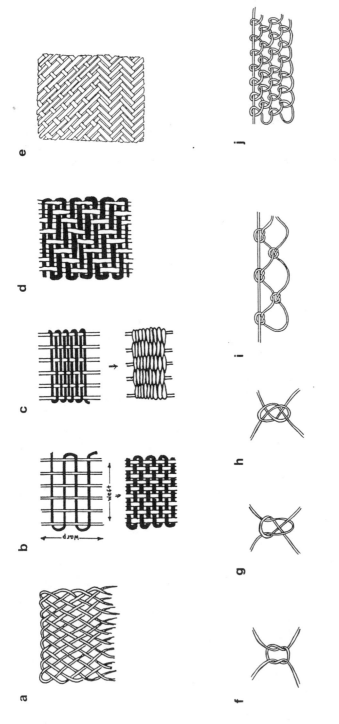

Figure 10.

Interlacing and knotting structures: *a*, plain interlacing with one set of elements (oblique interlacing); *b*, balanced plain interlacing with two sets of elements; *c*, weft-faced interlacing, structure and appearance; *d*, balanced 2/2 twill interlacing; *e*, combination of straight 3/3 twill and broken 4/1 twill (oriented as for oblique interlacing), common structures in southeastern mating and baskets; *f*, square knot; *g*, sheetbend knot; *b*, fishnet knot (*f*, *g*, and *b* are frequently used in knotted netting); *i*, knotted netting with overhand knot; *j*, looping. (Structures *a–d*, *f–i* from Drooker 1990c:Figure 2. Copyright 1990 The Kent State University Press; used by permission.)

tion, because unless some weft yarns were worn away, it usually was impossible to discern the difference between weft-faced plain twining and weft-faced plain interlacing. For this reason, a fourth category, "weft-faced," was utilized for record keeping, even though it did not correspond to a single unique fabric structure. Weft-faced alternate-pair-twined textiles were not included in this category because they could be identified by their brick-like appearance, caused by the alternating positions of their twining twists (see below, Figure 23).

Under interlacing, the two primary subcategories encountered in North American textiles are plain (1/1) and twill interlacing. Twill, in turn, occurs in a wide variety of structural variations (e.g., Figures 2d, 10d, 10e).

An attempt was made to categorize knotting by knot structure, but this was not always possible because only one face of the fabric was visible. At least three different structures, including square, overhand, and sheetbend knots (Figures 10f, 10i, 10g), were employed.

Different textile structures can have widely differing functional qualities. The functional characteristics of different combinations of yarn types and fabric structures—the factors that a craftsperson takes into account when planning how to construct a particular item—are discussed below, in the section "Functional Characteristics of Textile Types."

It should be emphasized that identification of textile structure does not automatically carry with it identification of the technique by which a fabric was made. Many structures can be produced in several different ways, for instance, with one set of elements as in oblique interlacing, or with two sets of elements as in woven interlacing. Selvage structure often gives a clue to the technique by which a fabric was produced. A particularly good example of this is interlacing with one set of elements versus interlacing with two sets, each of which can be identified by the angle at which their yarn elements meet the selvage (Figures 10a and 10b). Often more than one selvage is required to determine which set of elements is warp and which is weft, if two or more sets are present. Unfortunately, in the present study few textiles examined included a selvage, so it usually was impossible to demonstrate with certainty which direction was "warp" and which was "weft." However, from archaeological and historical textile artifacts, it seems a virtual certainty that the twining technique employed for all southeastern textiles of any significant width was weft twining rather than warp twining, so this terminology has been followed throughout the present report except in the few cases where a structure clearly is warp twining, as in some edge finishes.

Many of the twining subcategories consist of combinations of two or more structures. These include weft-faced twining with spaced twining; plain twining with alternate-pair twining; plain twining with oblique interlacing;

plain twining with transposed, crossed warps; plain twining with transposed, interlinked warps; and alternate-pair twining with twining over non-alternating paired warps (Figures 2b, 9f, 9g, 9h, 9i). Additional combinations of textile structures have been found at sites other than Wickliffe (Chapter 7). Such combinations are of interest because they can be employed to create decorative designs in contrasting textures on a fabric. Some types of fabric structures, such as twills (Figure 10d), double-faced twining (Figures 9d and 9e), and tapestry (Appendix A), can be used in combination with more than one color of yarn to produce decorative motifs; from the structure alone, it sometimes is possible to reconstruct the design shapes.

Decorated textiles are analogous in interpretive importance to any other decorated artifact, from negative-painted pottery to engraved gorgets. Their motifs and/or complexity can mark them as having been employed by a particular segment in society (elite versus nonelite, male versus female, old versus young) or by a particular "ethnic" group. Decorative motifs can send visual "messages," either directly through the symbolism employed, or indirectly through other attributes. For example, the scale of an item of apparel such as a headdress or the scale of motifs on a garment such as a mantle can indicate whether it was intended to be viewed close at hand, such as by family members or close associates, or at a distance, such as in a ceremonial context (Wobst 1977). Ethnographic research in the Southeast indicates that differences in costume served not only to distinguish group or "tribe" affiliations but also to distinguish members of different bands within the larger group, as in the case of Choctaw pouches and tattoo markings (Swanton 1946:489, 1918:66).

In recording information from each sherd, *design motifs* formed by the juxtaposition of two or more textile structures, such as horizontal bands, diagonal lines, and geometric shapes, were described and/or sketched. The total *number of structures within each fabric* was noted, to be utilized in the computation of the Textile Production Complexity Index, discussed below. The number of structures included only those within the body of a fabric; weft-faced or warp-faced twining typical of some edge finishes was treated separately.

Twining twist direction can be **S** (\), **Z** (/), or a combination of **S**- and **Z**-twisting (Figure 11). "Countered" twining—alternating rows of **S** and **Z** twining twist—has an appearance almost like knitting, if it is weft-faced, and can be used for special decorative effects. It is more common to find a consistent pattern of twining than to find random changes in twining twist direction within the same row, because the latter situation can result in a structurally unsound fabric.

A number of researchers consider twining twist direction to be closely

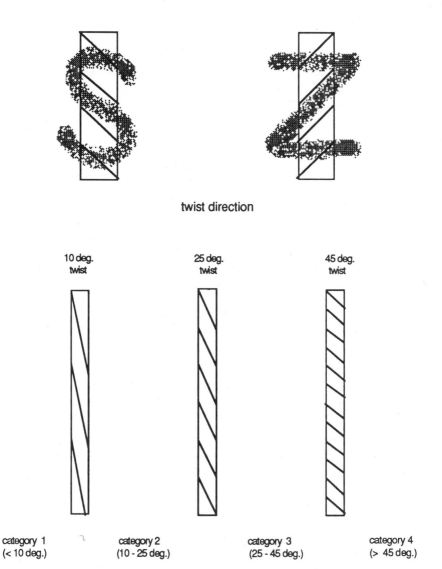

twist direction

10 deg.
twist

25 deg.
twist

45 deg.
twist

category 1
(< 10 deg.)

category 2
(10 - 25 deg.)

category 3
(25 - 45 deg.)

category 4
(> 45 deg.)

Figure 11.
Twist angle chart. The same terminology is used for yarn spin direction, yarn twist, yarn ply, and twining twist. Note that for all these applications, the twisted fibers or yarns must be viewed vertically, not horizontally, as this makes a difference in the slant direction. (Drooker 1990c:Figure 4, after Emery, 1966:11–12. Copyright 1990 The Kent State University Press; used by permission.)

correlated with culture-group identity. For example, Adovasio and Carlisle have stated that "there are virtually no ethnographic parallels for the coexistence of both twining twist directions in the same residence unit unless two different populations of weavers have been amalgamated" (1982:844). This assertion would seem to be an overstatement, since individual differences and other factors can enter into the equation, as Newton has shown in her analysis of cordage twist and twining type employed by members of two Brazilian tribes (Newton 1971:278–301, 1974). However, with large samples of fabrics it often is possible to find statistical differences between groups.

Besides being affected by individual and cultural differences, twining twist direction also can be related to technological considerations such as whether or not a weaver is working with warps attached to a frame, whether twining is done horizontally or vertically, and whether the final twist of the twining yarn is **S** or **Z**. Such questions are discussed in Chapter 6, in the section "Spinning and Fabric Production Technology."

The number of *yarn elements per centimeter*—warp, weft, or both—is a standardized measurement that can be used as one indicator of the fineness or coarseness (scale) of a fabric. Although the number most commonly employed as an indicator of fabric scale is the sum of warp and weft elements per centimeter ("fabric count"), the number of warp elements per centimeter alone ("warp count") sometimes can be a good simple indicator of scale, because in a twined textile it is influenced not only by the size of the warp yarns but also by the size of the weft yarns.

In measuring *warp elements per centimeter,* I counted warp yarns within as wide as possible a segment of fabric, then calculated the elements per centimeter (Appendix B). The number of *weft twining rows per centimeter* was measured in a similar fashion to the warp ends per centimeter, then *weft elements per centimeter* were calculated as twice this number unless there was good evidence that twining had been done with more than two elements. For interlaced textiles, the number of weft elements per centimeter is equal to the number of weft rows per centimeter. For the sake of consistency, the "number of elements per centimeter" was retained as the unit of measure for knotted netting; however, it should be realized that since such fabrics are made with a single continuous element, it is not elements that are being counted but intervals at which the yarn zigzags to form the sides of the mesh (Figure 10i). "Mesh size" is the attribute more commonly measured in netting.

The *warp yarn diameter* was measured in millimeters. Because in most of the textiles examined the yarn diameters were not consistent, either from element to element or even within the same element, the recorded diameter typically was an informal average of several measurements (Appendix B).

The *weft yarn diameter* was measured similarly to the warp diameter. However, in tightly twined textiles it sometimes was difficult to measure a single twining element. It also should be noted that the twining process can twist a yarn tightly enough to reduce its diameter to less than it would be if serving as a warp.

A measurement that was not taken, but which would have been useful to have, was the *diameter of the twining row*. Its size generally falls between the weft yarn diameter and twice the weft yarn diameter, varying with the tightness of the twining twist but tending to be closer to the former than the latter. For example, in a sample of 233 impressed textiles from another Mississippian site, weft yarn diameter averaged 1.5 millimeters, while twining row diameter averaged 2.1 millimeters (Drooker 1990b).

The *number of elements plied together* to make a yarn was recorded for both warp and weft. If this could not be determined visually, as with faint fabric impressions or with tightly twined weft yarns, it was set arbitrarily to 1. Again, with faint impressions, if at least some but not necessarily all of the warp yarns appeared to be two-ply, the higher number was used.

The *final direction of yarn twist*, **S** (\) or **Z** (/), was recorded (Figure 11). This always was visible for plied warp yarns, although not always apparent for singles. In the case of tightly twined weft, yarn twist direction, as opposed to twining direction, often was difficult to determine. If spin or twist direction within elements that had been plied together could be seen, it was recorded, but it often was not visible. A few warp yarns appeared to be three-strand braids rather than twisted elements (Figure 2h).

Final yarn twist is regularly employed by many archaeologists as an indicator of culture-group identity. Comparison of yarn twist direction percentages among different sites can be a very useful operation, particularly when only cordage is available for analysis rather than complete fabrics. However, care must be taken both in assuring an adequate sample size and in interpreting the results of such a study. Just as with twining twist direction (above), other factors can enter the equation, including personal choice or habit, fiber type (some fibers such as flax twist naturally in a particular direction, which is then exploited by spinners), spinning technology employed (e.g., thigh spinning vs. the more versatile spindle spinning), and cultural decisions (such as constructing yarns for mortuary fabrics differently than those for day-to-day garments). The combination of relevant cultural and individual factors may or may not result in a yarn twist pattern consistent enough to be decipherable in the archaeological record. As Petersen and Hamilton point out, it is the use of yarn twist and twining twist "in conjunction with other attributes" that most reliably distinguishes among groups of people known only from the archaeological record

(1984:433–434). The variables listed above are discussed at more length in Chapters 6 and 7.

As one indicator of the amount of labor involved in fabric production, the *angle of final twist in the warp yarn* was recorded. This is formally measured as the angle of deviation from the vertical axis of the yarn, with lower numbers indicating yarns that are more loosely twisted. Because of the variation among yarn twist within a given fabric fragment, this attribute was determined by category rather than by exact measurement of the angle of twist (Figure 11, bottom; Appendix B). The amount of twist in weft yarns was rarely possible to measure, since it almost always was affected to greater or lesser degree by the twining twist.

Edge structures are important diagnostic attributes, analogous to rim sherds on pottery but perhaps even more significant. They often are indicative of the function of a fabric. For instance, very sturdy and secure finishes typically are employed for the rims of bags, while more flexible finishes, like fringes, often are used for the bottoms of garments. Edge structures also are important indicators of the time invested in constructing a fabric. In fact, the more elaborate edge finishes can take almost as long to construct as the fabric itself. Edge structures can be used to infer the techniques employed in constructing a textile. For example, a flat textile constructed on free-hanging, separate warps can have three distinct types of edges—starting, side, and terminal—whereas a textile constructed on a continuous warp, fixed in a frame or attached to a backstrap loom, potentially can have near-identical selvages on all four sides. Selvages can be used to distinguish interlaced fabrics constructed from a single set of elements from fabrics woven using separate warp and weft elements (Figures 10a and 10b). Likewise, fabrics knotted from a set of separate elements ("macrame") will have different edge structures than knotted netting made from one long, continuous yarn element (e.g., Figure 10i).

Because of their relative complexity and variety, edge structures probably are good candidates for traits that can be used to distinguish between "ethnic" groups. However, a comparatively large sample would be required, far larger than the number of extant examples from organic fabrics. Textile impressions may well prove useful in enlarging this data base.

Descriptions and sketches were made of every edge structure encountered in the data set. In addition, each one was classified as a potential starting, side, or terminal edge, to aid in determining the type(s) of technology that might have been used in their construction. *Starting edges* typically are formed by folding warp yarns over a cord or stick that will hold them during construction. In flat weft-twined textiles, starting edges consist of a row of warp loops parallel to the twining rows (Figures 2a, 13b, below). A *terminal edge*, where the free-hanging warps are secured, will be located on the opposite side to a starting edge. It may consist, among other things, of fringe (knotted, twined, or otherwise secured), a hem, or warp ends bent back and enclosed in the final few rows of weft twining. *Side edges* occur where twined or interlaced wefts either reverse course and reenter the fabric for a succeeding row, or where the wefts are terminated by knotting them together or otherwise securing them. Specific edge structures that are associated with particular types of Mississippian artifacts are discussed below in the section "Diagnostic Characteristics of Mississippian Textile Artifacts."

The *condition of each textile* was noted. If any yarns were torn or missing, the fabric was designated as "worn." The nature and extent of damage to individual fabrics can be useful in interpreting how the textiles may have been used in the pottery-manufacturing process and whether they were used exclusively in pottery-making or served some other function, either previously or contemporaneously. Particular functional interpretations of wear on impressed textiles are discussed later in this chapter.

It is worth noting that missing yarns can change the apparent structure of a fabric. For instance, if one weft yarn is removed from a row of plain twining, the resultant structure is that of plain interlacing, and if one of the two twining wefts is removed from a series of rows of alternate-pair twining, the resultant structure is that of 2/2 twill interlacing (e.g., Figure 23 below, top left). If a fabric appeared to be very worn, this was taken into account when designating its structure.

If two *fabrics* were *overlaid on the same sherd*, the relationship between them was described (e.g., parallel or nonparallel warps and wefts, complete or incomplete coverage of one by the other, similar or dissimilar fabric characteristics). Overlays might be the result of impressing into the wet clay a double fabric such as a bag, a flat fabric folded back on itself, or two or more overlapping fabrics. Two separate fabrics also might be impressed on the same sherd if they were sewn together, but in that case they would not overlap.

Like the degree and frequency of damage in impressed textiles, the frequency, orientation, and completeness of coverage of overlapped fabrics can help indicate how they were used in the pottery-manufacturing process, for instance, whether or not they were used to lift vessels from molds, a function for which single large-sized fabrics would be optimum. By taking into account vessel size together with frequency and nature of overlapping, it is possible to estimate the size range of fabrics impressed on a given sample of sherds.

Yarn fiber type and amount of processing are helpful in ascertaining for what type of artifact a particular textile might have been intended. Unfortunately, unambiguous determination of yarn fiber is not feasible from impressions alone. It did prove possible in many cases to discern at least whether the fibers of a yarn had or had not been highly processed, although no formal analysis was made of this attribute.

Kuttruff, working with actual yarns in a study of Caddoan Mississippian textiles, categorized vegetable-fiber yarns by degree of shredding: little or none, coarse ("some separation of fibrous strips"), medium ("thin narrow strips"), fine, and very fine (1988a:136). In the impressions on pottery, it was possible to distinguish little or no shredding, coarse to medium shredding, and fine to very fine shredding. In the middle category, which appeared similar to experimental impressions in clay of modern machine-made "dry-spun" linen yarns, long, uniform fibers were clearly visible in the yarns. In the fine category, fibers were either very fine or not visible in the yarn, although two elements plied together might be clearly visible; these impressions appeared similar to those of modern linen yarns spun in the presence of water ("wet-spun") or to yarns of short animal hairs such as rabbit. (Linen is a bast fiber yarn made from the stem of the flax plant, directly analogous to Native American yarns made of fibers such as wild hemp and nettle stems.)

From the above "raw data," taken directly from the fabric-impressed sherd and textile cast, some additional traits were calculated.

The *mean yarn diameter* for a given fabric was determined by averaging its warp and weft yarn diameters. This number was used primarily for comparison with published data from other sites for which warp and weft diameters were not given separately.

Fabric count is a widely employed, but actually only partial, measure of textile scale (fineness vs. coarseness). It is defined as the number of elements per square centimeter and is calculated as the number of warp elements per centimeter (warp count) plus the number of weft elements per centimeter (weft count). Fabric coarseness or fineness in reality is dependent on both fabric count and yarn diameter. Fabric count can be used to give an approximate relative indication of the amount of time invested in a textile, with high-count fabrics requiring more time to construct than low-count ones in the same structure. (Absolute time requirements must take into account fabric structure, warp and weft count, and yarn size and structure.)

It should be noted that textiles made in the same structure and with the same fabric count still can have very different appearances and functional qualities, depending on whether their warp and weft yarns and warp count and weft count are the same or different. Thus, separate warp and weft counts are more useful than fabric count as descriptive attributes of textiles.

However, computed fabric counts are necessary for comparison with published data from other sites in which only fabric count has been reported.

The *density* of a fabric (i.e., the proximity of its component elements) may give some indication as to its intended use. Opaque fabrics are likely to have different functions than nonopaque fabrics. For instance, a winter robe is more likely to be dense than to be open and full of holes, whereas a decorative shawl intended for summer use might well be reticular and lacy. Likewise, a bag intended to store hulled corn would be much denser than one employed in the hulling process. In general, dense fabrics take more time to make than open fabrics, but this also is a function of textile structure and scale: fine, dense fabrics in a given fabric structure will be slowest to construct, while coarse, open fabrics will be fastest.

Many researchers consider weft density to be a primary structural factor and set up separate textile structure categories for "close" and "open" or "compact" and "spaced" twined fabrics. Unfortunately, criteria for separating these categories vary significantly among published reports. Moreover, fabrics at a given site generally tend to grade gradually between "open" (widely spaced weft rows) and completely weft-faced. For these reasons, I did not use density as a structural category but considered it as a separate attribute.

The most accurate calculation of weft density for a twined fabric is weft row diameter × number of weft rows per centimeter. Because weft row diameter was unavailable for the Wickliffe textiles, weft density was approximated as weft diameter (mm) × number of weft rows per centimeter. Warp density was computed as warp diameter × number of warp elements per centimeter, and total density as the sum of warp and weft density. (A warp density of 10 indicates a textile in which the warp yarns are just touching.) A visually dense fabric will have warp and/or weft yarns so close together that the textile is opaque. Visual density also is affected by textile scale, since coarser fabrics have fewer, larger holes per square centimeter and will appear more open than finer fabrics with the same computed density.

In order to rank construction labor input, Kuttruff developed a *Textile Production Complexity Index* (TPCI), described as "a comparative, ordinally scaled index of the amount of work need to produce pre-industrial textiles" (1988a:202). Nine factors were included in this index, encompassing scale, patterning, coloration, yarn, and fiber. The factors were fabric count (expressed as an index number, with 1 = 0.0–4.9, 2 = 5.0–9.9, 3 = 10.0–14.9, etc.), number of structural techniques, number of added surface techniques (e.g., painting, embroidering), number of different colors, number of different yarn types, average number of yarn components (elements making up a yarn), average amount of final yarn twist (per Emery's categories [1966:12]), number of different fibers used, and average amount of fiber preparation or processing (Kuttruff 1988a:263).

Because several of these factors (coloration, some of the surface techniques, type of fiber used) cannot be determined from textile impressions, a Modified Textile Production Complexity Index had to be used for the Wickliffe data. Since some attributes were available for almost all of the Wickliffe sherds, while others could be measured only for a limited number of examples, three different versions of the modified Index number were computed. The first was calculated as fabric count index number plus number of structural techniques present. This number could be computed for most of the Wickliffe textiles analyzed. The second and third were closer to Kuttruff's index in scope but could be computed for fewer textiles. Modified Index No. 2 was calculated as Index No. 1 plus the average number of elements plied together in warp yarns and weft yarns. To this number, Index No. 3 added the warp yarn twist index number. Weft yarn twist was not included because so little data were available. Likewise, amount of fiber processing was not included because it had been determined for only a small portion of the Wickliffe textiles.

These indices are useful for comparing the relative amount of labor expended on textiles from different archaeological contexts. Kuttruff, for example, used her TPCI to compare fabrics from elite versus non-elite mortuary contexts within the Caddoan Mississippian region, finding a positive correlation between high index values and high social status (1988a, 1988b). Besides their potential use as indicators of social status, they also can be used directly to indicate the relative economic value of different types of textiles within a given site or of textile assemblages from different sites, reflecting allocation of time, resources, and effort.

It may well be difficult to visualize what these attributes mean in terms of an actual fabric. To give a basis for numerical comparison, Table 2 lists the measured attributes of modern, machine-made burlap (1/1 interlacing).

"SALTPAN" ATTRIBUTES STUDIED

A number of "saltpan" attributes have direct relevance to interpreting the nature of textiles impressed upon them. These were included, along with textile data, in the information recorded from Wickliffe fabric-impressed sherds. They are formally described and discussed below, along with a few other attributes that were noted primarily for the purpose of elucidating the function of fabrics in the pottery-making process.

Table 2. Modern burlap textile attributes

Attribute	Value
Warp diameter, mm	1.2
Weft diameter, mm	1.0
Yarn diameter, mm	1.1
Number of warp plies	1.0
Number of weft plies	1.0
Warp twist category	2.0
Warp elements per cm	4.8
Weft elements per cm	4.8
Fabric count	9.6
Warp density	5.8
Weft density	4.8
Total density	10.6
Complexity Index No. 1	3.0
Complexity Index No. 2	4.0
Complexity Index No. 3	6.0

The difficulties of obtaining accurate estimates of Wickliffe "saltpan" *vessel diameters* were described in Chapter 3. To circumvent them to some degree, a three-step measurement procedure was adopted (Appendix B). Vessel diameter can be used together with frequency of occurrence of impressed fabric edges to estimate minimum widths of fabrics used in "saltpan" manufacture at a given site. For example, if edges never appear in fabric impressions from a large sample of sherds, it can be concluded that the impressed textiles were wider in their smaller dimension than the diameters of the vessels on which they were impressed. In addition, correlations of a vessel's size and the scale or structure of the fabric(s) impressed upon it could give clues as to the function of fabrics in the pottery-making process. For instance, it can be hypothesized that relatively sturdy textiles would be necessary to lift large-diameter, heavy vessels out of their molds.

Fabric orientation relative to vessel rim was measured for all rim sherds, in degrees of weft-row deviation counterclockwise from the horizontal (Appendix B). This measurement has relevance both to how fabrics were used in vessel manufacture and to whether or not their impressions served a primarily decorative purpose on "saltpan" vessels. The proposal that "saltpans" were made inside baskets or bags can be tested by seeing whether warp elements are consistently oriented perpendicular to the rim, as they are in small, flowerpot-shaped fabric-impressed molded vessels from Mexico (Nunley 1967:515). Some researchers (e.g., Bushnell 1914:664) have equated the orientation of a fabric edge or decorative motif parallel to a sherd rim as evidence of decorative intent. However, a single sherd is not evidence enough: entire vessels or a statistically significant sample of sherds must be examined in order to demonstrate the validity of this hypothesis. A decorative impression parallel to an entire rim could be made by wrapping a fabric horizontally around a vessel. Such an orientation, however, would not be consistent with certain postulated utilitarian functions such as using a textile to lift a vessel from its mold.

Exterior versus interior location of textile impressions was noted, both as a factor in determining the average size of textiles and as an indication of whether a vessel likely was formed in a concave mold or over a convex one.

Textile impressions do occur on Mississippian vessels other than "salt-pans," although very rarely (e.g., Black 1967:405; Orr 1951:318). Presence of fabric impressions on sherds of finer matrix or notably thinner walls than typical "saltpans" was recorded, for possible correlation with fabric characteristics such as scale.

FUNCTIONAL CHARACTERISTICS OF FABRIC TYPES

Tentative determinations of the original functions of Wickliffe impressed textiles were made primarily by comparing measured attributes of impressed fabrics with measured attributes of various types of Mississippian textile artifacts. However, a far wider range was found within each attribute class for the sample of impressed fabrics from Wickliffe than for the relatively small sample of extant Mississippian textile artifacts. Therefore, to supplement quantitative data taken from artifacts, I also had to consider in general terms what textile qualities would be appropriate to the function of various types of artifacts. Plain and alternate-pair twining, along with knotting and, to a lesser extent, interlacing, have been the mainstays of textile production in eastern North America for millennia (e.g., Adovasio and Andrews 1980; Andrews et al. 1988; Chapman and Adovasio 1977; Petersen and Hamilton 1984). Throughout that time, craftspeople could hardly help learning how to tailor the qualities of their fabrics to fit the jobs they were intended to perform. In and of themselves, combinations of particular textile structures, fiber types, yarn types, and edge finishes can give clues to the intended function of a fabric, since variations among them will result in textile products with a wide range of functional properties. Some of the most important are highlighted below.

Plain twining (Figure 9a), if executed tightly and in close rows, produces a firm, rather stiff fabric, with warps never quite touching and sometimes actually spaced quite far apart. Relative closeness of warps depends not only on tightness of twining twist but also on relative diameter, flexibility, and density of warp and weft yarns: a thick, firm weft yarn will separate warps significantly, while a thin, soft weft may separate them little. Perhaps contrary to intuition, tightly twisted twining separates warp yarns more than loosely twisted twining. If spacing between weft rows is increased, the resultant fabric structure will be more flexible and, if warp yarns are soft and relatively thick, may allow them to expand to touch each other between rows, adding to visual density. Unless twining rows are spaced close together, use of thick, dense weft yarns will result in prominent ridges uncomfortable to sit or lie on.

Alternate-pair twining (Figure 9b), because of the coupling together of pairs of warp yarns and the zigzag connection between yarns, can be both denser and more flexible than a comparable plain-twined textile. (See Figures 22 and 23 below for differences in density between plain-twined and alternate-pair-twined textiles constructed from very similar yarns.) Although logically it might seem to be a more complex structure, in fact its execution takes less time than plain twining because there are only half as many twining twists per fabric width, even though it may take a bit more time to pick up two yarn elements at a time rather than one.

Weft-faced and warp-faced fabrics of any structure (e.g., Figures 2g, 10c) are denser, smoother, and usually firmer than their more balanced counterparts in which both warp and weft are visible. Firmness depends on the actual amount of yarn packed into a given space: if thick, soft wefts are gently woven or loosely twined into place, they may cover the warp and still result in a relatively flexible fabric, but if dense weft yarns are beaten tightly into place, the textile will be stiff, firm, heavy, sturdy—and it will use a very large amount of yarn. The absolute and relative diameters of warp and weft yarns, along with their fiber content, also will affect density, flexibility, and weight of a weft-faced textile.

Interlaced structures (e.g., Figures 10a, 10b, 10c, 10d) differ in their functional qualities in ways analogous to relationships among twined structures. Twill structures can be relatively denser yet more pliable than 1/1 interlacing constructed from similar yarns, and they increase in density and flexibility as their component warps and wefts pass over and under greater numbers of wefts and warps (e.g., 4/4 vs. 2/2 twill). Oblique interlacing, because its component yarns are not perpendicular to the fabric edge, is stretchier and more flexible than comparable two-element interlacing (weaving). Unlike twining, warps and wefts of interlaced fabrics can shift position relative to each other, so it is difficult if not impossible to weave an extremely open interlaced fabric that will hold its structure. Dense interlaced textiles, however, can be thinner and of lighter weight than twined textiles made from similar-size yarns because they do not contain pairs of wefts twisting around each other. This also means that they can use less yarn for a given area of fabric.

Interlacing is faster to do than twining, but it is less secure. Unlike twining, if warp yarns are broken, an interlaced fabric unravels easily. Narrow oblique interlaced fabrics—braids—are not difficult to construct because the elements can easily be held in order by one hand. However, because of the tendency of pliable elements to unravel and to tangle, broad oblique interlaced textiles are difficult to construct on free-hanging warps unless they utilize relatively stiff elements. In ethnographic textiles, wide oblique-interlaced fabrics such as those used for hammocks seem to be most commonly constructed using the technique of sprang, where the yarn elements are fixed at both ends, and a set of sticks is used to keep the structure from unraveling while work is in progress (Cardale-Schrimpff 1972; Collingwood 1974; Junius Bird, personal communication 1981).

Knotted netting (e.g., Figure 10i), extremely flexible yet with yarn elements firmly fastened together, is a fabric that will hold its form even under considerable physical stress. If the appropriate knot is employed, yarns will not slip relative to each other and mesh size will remain uniform, even if a knotted fabric is tugged and jerked or used to carry heavy weights. Because it is covered with protuberances, knotted netting generally is uncomfortable to sit or lie on unless it is extremely fine.

The *planning and preparation of yarns* is another essential element in the creation of a fabric intended for a specific function. Yarn fiber type affects such textile qualities as ability to insulate and to absorb or to "wick off" moisture. The amount and type of processing that yarn fibers receive determines their softness, hardness, scratchiness, stretchiness, flexibility, and strength. Besides being softer and more flexible, loosely spun yarns made from highly processed, numerous small-diameter fibers will be able to trap more air and thus insulate more effectively than yarns tightly twisted from dense, unshredded fibers. All other things being equal, twisted yarns are stronger than untwisted yarns, as are yarns composed of comparatively longer fibers. Amount of twist is directly related to strength, as are the diameter of a yarn and the number of elements plied together to make a yarn. Tightly twisted yarns are stiffer than loosely twisted yarns, with the same relationship holding true for large-diameter versus small-diameter yarns.

Final yarn twist direction relative to twining twist direction can be important to textile characteristics and to ease of construction. If yarns are twined in the opposite direction to their twist, they can untwist, become softer and less dense, and eventually pull apart. Yarns twined in the same direction as their twist will become more tightly twisted (e.g., see C. Samuel 1982:87). However, they will not naturally hold their structure unless they are knotted or otherwise secured at the ends of the twining rows. All things considered, it is easier to twine a fabric in the direction of the weft-yarn twist, but a conscious decision to take the opposite course might be made in order to produce a softer fabric.

It is worth noting that the opposite relationship holds with plied yarns: all over the world, it is far more common to find yarns plied in the reverse direction from that in which the individual elements were spun than in the same direction. Any twisted element will tend to untwist unless it is anchored at both ends; if two yarn elements that were spun in the same direction are placed together without constraint, they will untwist, coiling around each other in a direction opposite to that of their spin. In the case of spinning, this tendency is exploited to make a yarn that will hold together naturally. However, skillful spinners must calculate exactly how much twist to exert while spinning and plying to achieve the desired result.

A fabric's *scale* (fineness or coarseness) is important in determining both its strength and its flexibility. The *density* of a fabric affects its effectiveness as a container, an insulator, a visual screen, or a pad.

The *complexity of a textile* may be due to functional refinements intended to suit it for a very specific purpose, or refinements may be intended primarily for decorative purposes. Examples of functional refinements are braided ties added to the corners of skirts or mantles; weft-faced, braided, or interlooped finishes that secure and reinforce edges; and fine, soft yarns produced for a fabric intended to be worn next to the skin. Examples of decorative refinements are additions that add visual patterns to a fabric, such as geometric patterns of holes formed by transposed warp yarns. Examples of refinements that can add to both utility and visual interest include combinations of structures such as plain twining and oblique interlacing that vary significantly in flexibility. If rows of such structures are alternated, fabrics will bend or stretch along predetermined lines, but they also will contain interesting contrasts in texture and pattern.

Structural consistency within a fabric can be an indicator of functional versus decorative intent. If attributes are the same throughout a textile, or variations are located or shaped to fit points of wear or stress, a utilitarian purpose might be inferred. If, however, shapes or locations of variations in yarns or structures appear to be arbitrarily patterned—as with "stripes" formed by a regular pattern of grouped twining rows, or with geometrically arranged "holes"—a decorative intent would seem likely.

A diverse textile complex, formally computed (e.g., Dickens 1980:34) or informally estimated by noting the ranges of values for particular yarn and fabric attributes, can be an indication that a wide variety of functions was served by individual fabrics within the complex. It could also indicate a relatively great extent of intergroup contact, based on the idea that when different groups come into contact with each other, it is very likely that they also will be coming into contact with new ideas, commodities, and designs, some of which they may adopt or adapt for their own use (Caldwell 1964:135–136; Dickens 1980; see also Braun and Plog 1982).

Considered together with fabric condition, the diversity or similarity of fabrics impressed on a sample of sherds can be used to infer the originally intended function(s) of the textiles. For example, an extremely diverse but relatively unworn assemblage might be representative of fabrics made for many different purposes and still in use for those purposes, being employed occasionally also in the manufacture of pottery. A diverse but damaged assemblage might represent rags, previously used for other purposes. A standardized group of fabrics with a wide range of wear could indicate fabrics made particularly for the pottery-production process that were saved and reused repeatedly for that purpose.

Finally, *edge structures*—fine or bulky, compact or expansive, shaped or straight—can affect both the speed of construction and the functional qualities of an item. For example, the fastest finish for free-hanging yarn ends is a knotted or twined fringe. However, while a garment with long fringes can be a highly effective visual element on a dancer, it could result in disaster for a careless person cooking over an open fire.

DIAGNOSTIC CHARACTERISTICS OF MISSISSIPPIAN TEXTILE ARTIFACTS

To form a framework for determining what might have been the originally intended function(s) of fabrics impressed on pottery at Wickliffe, Mississippian textile artifacts were examined through published accounts, photographs available from museum collections, and personal inspection where possible. The goal was to acquire quantitative attribute data that could be compared objectively to the data obtained from Wickliffe textile impressions. Pictures and early historical descriptions were used to obtain general information about artifact types, dimensions, decorative motifs, and typical usage. Textile structure types, edge finishes, and/or dimensions of artifacts sometimes could be obtained from archaeological site reports, and a few specialized studies actually included additional measured attributes such as yarn diameters or fabric count. If a scaled photograph of an artifact was

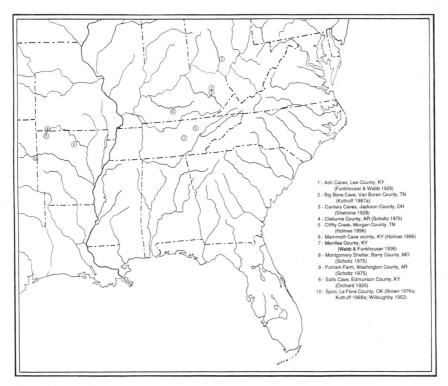

1 - Ash Caves, Lee County, KY
  (Funkhouser & Webb 1929)
2 - Big Bone Cave, Van Buren County, TN
  (Kuttruff 1987a)
3 - Canters Caves, Jackson County, OH
  (Shetrone 1928)
4 - Cleburne County, AR (Scholtz 1975)
5 - Cliffty Creek, Morgan County, TN
  (Holmes 1896)
6 - Mammoth Cave vicinity, KY (Holmes 1896)
7 - Menifee County, KY
  (Webb & Funkhouser 1936)
8 - Montgomery Shelter, Barry County, MO
  (Scholtz 1975)
9 - Putnam Farm, Washington County, AR
  (Scholtz 1975)
6 - Salts Cave, Edmunson County, KY
  (Orchard 1920)
10 - Spiro, Le Flore County, OK (Brown 1976a;
  Kuttruff 1988a; Willoughby 1952)

Figure 12.
Sites yielding published information on Mississippian and related textile artifacts.

available, I measured as many as possible of the same attributes from it that I measured from the impressed fabrics.

Unfortunately, only a small number of complete or near-complete Mississippian textile artifacts have survived. Besides the very few that definitely can be assigned to the Mississippian, a number of well-preserved items have come from southeastern caves and rock-shelters with multicomponent or undated assemblages, possibly assignable to the Mississippian. Some of them are described below. As can be seen in Figure 12, none of the locations from which they came are near Wickliffe, or even within the northern Mississippian region with which it is most closely connected. This, along with the uncertain dating of many of them, must be borne in mind in the comparisons that will follow.

Mississippian textile items were made to the size and shape required, not cut and sewn. Virtually all large items except bags were constructed as flat rectangles, with different functions distinguishable only through relative size, special edge finishes, and particular qualities of yarns and fabric structures. Because some information about bags is pertinent to flat textiles as well, they will be discussed first, followed by garments, mats, burial wrappings, and hunting and fishing nets.

Bags

Bags served a variety of functions in Native American life, and this diversity is reflected in a wide range of sizes and fabric attributes. Many prehistoric and historical examples survive that are 50 centimeters (20 in) or more in their smallest dimension, certainly adequate to encompass the outside surfaces of many "saltpans." Bags definitely assignable to the Mississippian are constructed only from plain and alternate-pair twining, but knotted and linked or looped bags ("knotless netting") also are known from undated prehistoric contexts. Historical examples include a much greater variety of textile structures and design motifs than extant prehistoric artifacts.

Taken as a class, bag fabrics may average somewhat coarser than fabrics for skirts or mantles. However, the primary distinguishing characteristics of bags are found not in their textiles but rather in their edges. Unlike garments and other fabric artifacts, bags characteristically were made as three-dimensional forms with distinctive terminal edges, and positive identification of this artifact type requires the evidence of at least two edges.

The general method of bag manufacture is known from early historical and ethnographic records, confirmed by structural analysis of prehistoric examples. Although some details of the production technique are lacking, we know that Mississippian bags typically were made upside-down, in one continuous three-dimensional piece shaped like a large pocket (Figure 13a) or a tube (Figure 13b). The starting edge eventually became the bottom, while the terminal edge became the rim. Twining might be done in separate circular rows or in a continuous spiral; knotting or looping would continue around the bag in a spiral (e.g., Carter 1933:37–43; Densmore 1929:Plate 67; Douglas et al. 1968; Lyford 1953:77–81; Skinner 1921:Plate 53; J. White 1969:9–10).

If such a bag is laid flat, as in Figure 14, the *side edge* will simply look like a piece of fabric, folded over at right angles to the twining (or knotting or looping) rows. Two different types of *starting edges* are known, depending on whether a bag is constructed as a tube (Figure 13b) or with three closed sides. In the former case, the bottom of the bag will be sewn together after fabric construction has been completed, often with a stitch that simply laces between alternate warp loops. It will look like a starting edge, such as the

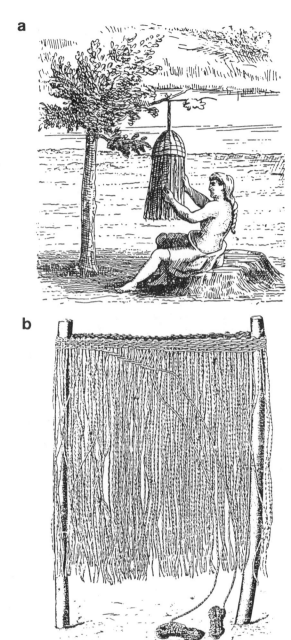

Figure 13.
Examples of twined bag construction on free-hanging warps: *a*, bag- or basket-making with
free-hanging warps (Holmes 1896:Plate 1b), showing the construction of a pocket-shaped
textile made with three closed sides; *b*, starting a twined textile with free warp ends (Lyford
1953:79). The latter shows the beginning of an Ojibway twined bag, made as a tube; when
finished, it would be sewn together at the bottom. In a single-layer fabric, warp elements
would be suspended from a cord or stick, and weft twining rows would travel back and forth
rather than spirally.

Figure 14.
Plain-twined bag from Cliffty Creek Rock-shelter, Morgan County, Tennessee, 51 × 33 centimeters (20 × 13 in). Groups of warp yarns have deteriorated at intervals. (Smithsonian Institution Department of Anthropology Cat. No. 132255, Neg. No. 32546-Z. Used by permission.)

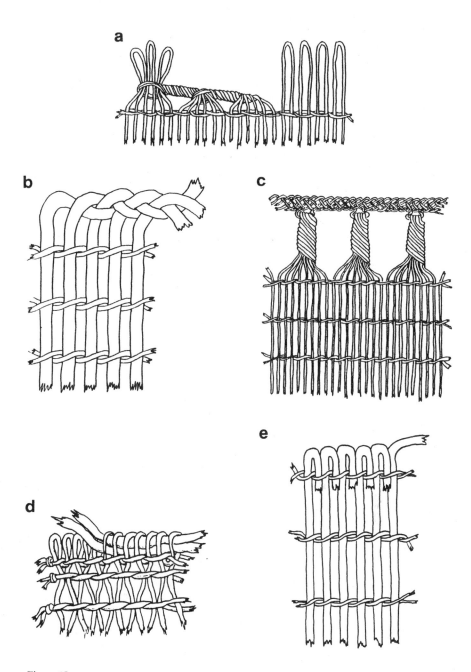

Figure 15.
Edge finishes from prehistoric textiles, including four bag rim finishes: *a*, twisted, interlooped
warp groups (after Douglas et al. 1968:Drawing 7); *b*, braided cut warp ends (after Scholtz
1975:Figure 139); *c*, twisted warp loop groups secured by braid (after Scholtz 1975:Figure
135); *d*, expanded diagram of starting edge of twined garment (Figure 20) and skirt with very
long fringe (after Holmes 1896:Figure 6); *e*, warp ends secured in last row of twining (from
description of small bag, Pu-330 [Scholtz 1975:114]). Structure *d*, in actuality, had no space
between warp yarns. Large yarns at top served as gathering cords and ties. (Structures *a–c*
from Drooker 1990c:Figure 5. Copyright 1990 The Kent State University Press; used by
permission.)

Table 3. Summary of measured textile attributes for specific Mississippian artifact types

Attribute	Prehistoric twined bags					Historic double-faced twined bags				
	min.	mean	max.	s.d.	no. cases	min.	mean	max.	s.d.	no. cases
Width, cm	4.5	27.5	66.0	21.5	8	—	—	—	—	—
Height, cm	6.5	29.9	64.0	20.9	8	—	—	—	—	—
Warp diameter, mm	1.0	3.4	9.0	2.7	7	1.2	1.6	2.0	0.3	6
Weft diameter, mm	1.0	2.6	5.0	1.6	6	0.5	1.0	1.5	0.35	6
Number of warp plies	1.0	1.8	2.0	0.4	6	1.0	1.8	2.0	0.4	6
Number of weft plies	1.0	1.8	2.0	0.5	5	2.0	2.0	2.0	0.0	6
Warp twist category	0.0	2.25	3.0	1.5	4	2.5	2.75	3.0	0.4	2
Warp elements per cm	1.1	4.4	9.0	2.4	8	6.0	8.4	11.0	2.0	6
Weft elements per cm	0.8	1.9	3.0	0.9	8	3.3	4.4	5.6	0.8	6
Fabric count	1.9	6.3	11.8	3.1	8	9.3	12.9	15.6	2.6	6
Warp density	9.0	9.6	10.0	0.5	7	10.8	13.1	16.5	2.0	6
Weft density	0.5	1.7	2.2	0.6	6	1.3	2.2	2.8	0.6	6
Complexity Index No. 1	2.0	4.1	5.0	1.0	8	4.0	5.3	6.0	0.8	6
Complexity Index No. 3	5.0	10.75	13.0	3.9	4	—	—	—	—	—

Note: Prehistoric twined bags include two from Tennessee (Big Bone Cave and Cliffty Creek Rockshelter) and six from the Ozarks (Montgomery and Putnam Farm shelters, and a site in Cleburne County, Arkansas) (Holmes 1896:Plate 5; Kuttruff 1987a, 1988a:Nos. 43, 47; Scholtz 1975:Nos. 45-2, 32-10743, Pu-330, Pu-?; Holmes 1896:Plate 5). Measurements for historic bags (1 Winnebago, 2 Ojibway, and 3 Potawatomi) relate to the central double-faced panel only (Harvard University Peabody Museum Nos. 62237, 62993, 64735, 65063, 80343). Garment fabrics include one oblique 1/1

one in Figure 2a, with an additional element passing through each warp loop. Twined bags made with three closed sides most frequently are started by a single row of twining across the center of the set of warp elements and perpendicular to them. Then the free-hanging warps are folded over a supporting cord or stick, along the row of twining. Construction of the bag then continues in three dimensions, spiraling or circling around the entire bag. When a bag made like this is laid flat (Figure 14), its starting edge looks like a piece of fabric folded parallel to the twining rows. A number of different finishes were employed for *terminal edges* (rim edges). All of them have the virtue of extreme sturdiness, and many are rather bulky.

Prehistoric garments			Etowah burial fabrics		
Spiro		Cliffty Creek			
Interlaced (1)	Alternate-pair (mean of 3)	Alternate-pair (1)	Plain-twined (mean of 6)	Plain-twined (1)	Alternate-pair (1)
146	137	117	—	—	—
—	—	61	—	—	—
2.6	3.1	—	—	0.7	0.5
—	3.1	—	—	0.75	0.5
2.0	2.0	—	2.0	2.0	—
—	2.0	—	1.7	2.0	—
3.0	3.2	—	3.1	3.0	—
3.4	4.1	6.3	3.8	9.0	15.0
—	3.2	2.8	1.8	5.6	32.0
6.8	7.3	9.1	5.6	14.6	47.0
8.8	6.1	—	—	6.3	7.5
—	5.0	—	—	4.2	16.0
3.0	4.7	4.0	2.7	4.0	11.0
8.0	—	—	—	—	—

interlaced and three alternate-pair-twined textiles from Spiro (Kuttruff 1988a:Nos. 62–65; Willoughby 1952) and one alternate-pair-twined textile from Cliffty Creek Rock-shelter, Tennessee (Holmes 1896:Plate 3). Etowah burial fabrics include mean values for six plain-twined textiles measured by Schreffler (1988:155–156), and one plain-twined textile and one alternate-pair-twined textile measured at the R. S. Peabody Foundation.

Some utilized cut warp ends, while others required looped warp ends (Figure 15.a–c).

Textile attributes for eight examples of prehistoric bags with reasonable probability of being assignable to the Mississippian were obtained, including six from Ozark Bluff sites with Caddoan Mississippian components, and two from Tennessee cave or rock-shelter sites (Drooker 1989b:Appendix 4). Each is briefly described below, then the group is discussed as a whole. Attribute data are summarized in Table 3.

The bag shown in Figure 14 came from the undated Cliffty Creek Rock-shelter, Morgan County, Tennessee, along with some skeins of Indian hemp

(Eryngium yuccifolium), a mat, and two garments described below (Holmes 1896:29–35, Plate 5; U.S. National Museum accession cards). This is a good example of a bag constructed as a three-dimensional "pocket" with three closed edges. Its structure is **S**-twisted plain twining, with pairs of weft rows grouped together slightly. Darker warp yarns that formed stripes in groups of two separated by eight elements of lighter color have deteriorated, with the result that the bag now has regularly spaced holes. It is possible that this was caused by the deleterious effect of an acidic dye. The two-ply yarn with final twist in the **S** direction was made from nettle fiber *(Urtica gracilis)*. The rim (terminal edge) was formed by twisting groups of warps together for about five centimeters, then "they are brought together and plaited with remarkable neatness into a string border" (Holmes 1896:34). Holmes's drawing of this edge appears virtually identical to the edge finish in Figure 15c, but the rim may have been constructed with separate warp ends rather than warp loops. Borders with spaced open holes like this sometimes are found with a cord laced through the holes, to use in closing the bag. Dimensions of the Cliffty Creek bag are 20 × 13 inches (51 × 33 cm).

A second bag from Tennessee, analyzed in detail by Kuttruff (1987a), may be Mississippian or Middle Woodland. Two organic samples collected near its findspot in Big Bone Cave, Van Buren County, gave uncorrected radiocarbon dates of A.D. 355 and 1510. The bag is 24 × 18 centimeters (9 × 7 in), plain twined in the **S** direction with regularly spaced rows. Yarns are of several different plant fibers, but all are **S**-twisted and two-ply, with warps and wefts approximately 2.0 and 1.5 millimeters in diameter. The warp is continuous rather than consisting of a set of separate yarns, so that warp loops occur along the rim edge. The rim structure is like that in Figure 15c, except that instead of a braid, a single-element interlooped band (like "a very tight crochet chain") joins twisted groups of warp loops together (Kuttruff 1987:130).

Three larger bags, all wider than long, came from an undated cavern near Mammoth Cave, Kentucky (Holmes 1896:34). Probably all three were of plain twining; one had an edge finish similar to Figure 15c. Their yarn fibers are named as "bast" and hemp, and their dimensions are given as 34 × 15, 22 × 16, and 14 × 9 inches (86 × 38, 56 × 41, and 36 × 23 cm).

A 20 × 17-centimeter (8 × 7-in) alternate-pair-twined bag from a rockshelter in Cleburne County, Arkansas, is the one from which Figure 15c actually was drawn (Scholtz 1975:126–128). Its two-ply **S**-twisted warp yarns, however, are much thicker than shown in the drawing, giving a dense fabric appropriate for its contents, which were seeds and corn. Like the bag from Big Bone Cave, this one could be Mississippian or earlier. Although maize became a staple food in the Southeast during the Mississippian, it was present by at least the Middle Woodland period (Chapman and Crites 1987).

Two incomplete plain-twined bags from the Putnam Farm Shelter, Washington County, Arkansas, contrast in size, one being at least 20 × 52 centimeters (8 × 20 in) with 9-millimeter and 5-millimeter warp and weft, and the other probably not much more than 4.5 × 6.5 centimeters (1.8 × 2.6 in) with 2- and 1-millimeter (0.08- and 0.04-in) warp and weft (Scholtz 1975:116–118). The latter has a rim like that shown in Figure 15e, while the former lacks a rim. In both cases, twining twist was **S**. Scholtz tentatively places this site in the Mississippian because it yielded a twined textile with a pattern formed by manipulated warps.

A wide size range also was found in three bags from Montgomery Shelter 4, Barry County, Missouri, a site judged to be Mississippian by the associated artifacts (Kuttruff 1988a:76). A complete **S**-twisted plain-twined bag, constructed from thick, barely shredded and almost untwisted warp elements, is only 4.5 × 9.0 cm (1.8 × 3.5 in) (Scholtz 1975:116–117). Its rim structure is similar to Figure 15b. Another plain-twined bag is 30 × 40 centimeters (12 × 16 in), with 4-millimeter two-ply **S**-twisted warp and weft. A third, 66 × 64 centimeters (26 × 25 in), is constructed in alternate-pair twining, also with two-ply yarns, but of only 2.5-millimeter diameters. In both cases, twining is in the **S** direction (Kuttruff 1988a:Appendix D).

In spite of the wide range of sizes, these bags have many similarities. Each was twined in a single structural variation (either plain or alternate-pair twining), with spaced twining rows. Warps tended to be close together (mean warp density ranged only between 9 and 10) and generally much thicker than wefts. These are relatively dense, coarse fabrics; for comparison, they have much thicker yarns, higher total density, and lower fabric count than burlap (Table 2). Twining twist was in the **S** direction for all of them, and where final yarn twist is known, it too is "**S**." Most yarns, both warp and weft, are two-ply, and all are of vegetable fibers. In general, yarns and fabric structures united to make a strong, opaque container, with complexity indices averaging higher than for burlap; that is, the bags may be coarse, but they were not particularly simple to make.

All of these artifacts apparently were made as three-dimensional entities, with three closed sides, at least two bags apparently on a set of continuous warps; that is, they had rim edges with looped rather than cut warp ends (e.g., Kuttruff 1987a). Although a variety of finishes were used for terminal edges, twisted groups of warp ends secured by a narrow band occurred in three out of five cases where rim structure was known. Similar edges were very common in historical bags from the Great Lakes and Plains (e.g., Figure 16 below).

It is worth noting that bags from other Ozark Bluffs sites not assignable to the Mississippian incorporated **Z**-twisted twining as well as a higher percentage of unspun yarn elements than those described above (e.g., Scholtz 1975:Figures 119, 124).

Less complex bags are known, as well, from the northeastern periphery of the Mississippian. A rough "pouch" containing bone awls was found with a burial at the Canter's Caves site, Jackson County, Ohio (Shetrone 1928:9, 11; Ohio Historical Society Accession File No. 332). This site, with a single uncorrected radiocarbon date of A.D. 1620 ± 200 (M-467), lies within the Fort Ancient culture area. The hastily made, very open plain-twined bag was constructed from elements described as "flat splint-like fibers" averaging perhaps 3 millimeters in width and spaced at 2.0 per centimeter in the warp. **S**-twisted twining rows are spaced at 0.4 per centimeter. The pouch, fashioned with three closed edges, was approximately 7 inches (18 cm) square. Because the attributes of this artifact are so different from the other archaeological specimens, they were not included in the averages of Table 3.

Other textile structures besides twining probably were used for bags during the Mississippian, but examples have come only from earlier or undated prehistoric sites. Undated caves near Louisville and Mammoth Cave, Kentucky, have yielded two small bags in spaced twining over nonalternating warp pairs (Orchard 1920:17–19). Knotted bags are known at least from pre-Mississippian contexts. Scholz describes a portion of a very small one, only 4.5 centimeters (1.8 in) in diameter, from the Indian Bluff site in northwestern Arkansas (1974:28–29). Made with square knots (Figure 10f), and having approximately one element per centimeter, its cords average 1 millimeter in diameter. Funkhouser and Webb describe another from a cave in Lee County, Kentucky, as having 0.7-centimeter (0.3-in) mesh constructed out of 1-millimeter-diameter cord, knotted with overhand knots (1929: 93–95). If "mesh" is considered to be the number of spaces per linear measurement, an 0.7-centimeter mesh would be equivalent to 1.4 elements per centimeter.

Museum collections and art books contain thousands of examples of historical bags from eastern North America. In post-Contact times, twined bags from the Great Lakes and Plains regions very often incorporated combinations of two or more textile structures, sometimes for utilitarian purposes, but more often to decorate the bags with colored or textured geometric or representational designs. A number of these fabric structures are present in prehistoric textiles impressed on pottery. For example, in Rachlin's opinion, the twined diverted-warp and supplementary warp techniques used by historical Native American groups in these regions, particularly the assemblage of techniques used by the Fox of eastern Iowa to make their bags, have significant similarities to textile structures impressed on pottery at the Angel site in Indiana (Rachlin 1954a:5–8). For this reason, some of these more complex bags are briefly described below.

Bags and pouches described by Swanton from early southeastern historical sources generally were made from animal skins rather than being woven. The two examples he cites as constructed from yarn were made by the Choctaw, described in a passing reference by Adair to a small pouch for shot made during the eighteenth century, and in a mid-nineteenth-century report that "mentions among ancient Choctaw productions 'bags of the bark of trees, twisted and woven by hand'" (1946:480).

Bushnell describes two oblique-interlaced buffalo-hair bags inferred to have come from the Ohio River valley during the early Contact period, and he juxtaposes a photograph of one with that of a textile impression from pottery excavated in Ste. Genevieve County, Missouri, to illustrate their essential similarity in scale and structure (1914:663, Plate 56). One of these bags is 19¾ × 8 inches (50 × 20 cm), made of "twisted cords," and dyed red (1909:403; see also 1906). Additional examples of oblique-interlaced bags are known from the Great Lakes area (e.g., Burnham 1976:360, 363).

Twined bags have been collected from many groups that resided to the north and west of Wickliffe during the eighteenth through the twentieth centuries, including Chippewa, Fox, Menominee, Ojibway, Osage, Ottawa, Potawatomi, Santee Sioux, Sauk, and Winnebago. Plain twining with spaced weft rows and relatively coarse, close warps is a typical combination for bags, often with a rim finish that incorporates a row of twisted and/or braided groups of warps, virtually identical to archaeological specimens described above from the Ozarks, Tennessee, and Kentucky. Warp stripes are a common decoration, or a more complex design may be produced by controlled twisting of two colors in a thick warp, secured by comparatively thin wefts, similar in proportion to the yarns illustrated in Figure 2h (e.g., Whiteford 1977:57). Alternate-pair twining also is found, notably in the Osage bison-hair medicine bundle containers described as "in form, material, and general twining technique . . . similar to prehistoric fabrics" (Whiteford 1978:37). See also Douglas et al. (1968) for an analysis of the construction of another Osage medicine bag, the rim structure of which is depicted in Figure 15a.

Transposed crossed warp structures (Figure 9h), alone or alternating in rows with plain twining, were used for openwork corn-washing and corn-hulling bags (Drooker 1989b:Figure 18.1a; Whiteford 1977:54); this is the most common example of a structural variation related to function in bags. The same structure was used for decoration on denser bags (Figure 16). Whiteford also describes, without specifying its locale, "an unusual technique in which adjacent warps cross and then re-cross each other after each

Figure 16.
Winnebago twined bag of shredded bark with design in transposed crossed warps (see Figure 9h), 51 × 54 centimeters (20 × 21 in). Edge finish consists of slightly twisted groups of warps braided together as in Figure 15b. (Harvard University Peabody Museum Cat. No. 10/65777, copyright President and Fellows of Harvard College 1991. Used by permission.)

row of weft twining" (Whiteford 1977:59)—possibly transposed, interlinked warps (Figure 9i).

The designs on the bag in Figure 17 also were formed by transposed crossed warps, but instead of simply creating a textural contrast, here pairs of crossed warps in two colors have been manipulated so that one color or the other shows on the surface, as diagramed in Figure 9e. This textile structure, based on alternate-pair twining, typically was used on bags for wide central panels with geometric or animal-shaped motifs. Often the rim finish on such bags consists of separate (cut) warp ends doubled back on themselves and enclosed in several rows of close twining, leaving loops at the

Figure 17.

Ojibway double-faced twined bag, with transposed-warp decoration (Ontario, early 1800s), 26 × 20 centimeters (10 × 8 in). See Figure 9e for center panel fabric structure and Figure 15c for a similar edge structure. Plant fiber is "bass wood." Colored yarns on side panels are from unraveled trade blankets, with brown yarn in center panel possibly buffalo hair. (Harvard University Peabody Museum Cat. No. 10/64735, copyright President and Fellows of Harvard College 1991. Photograph by Hillel Burger. Used by permission.)

rim edge of the bag to be twisted in groups. The example in Figure 17 has a separate braid through the tops of its twisted warp loops, similar to Figure 15c. The difference is that on the edge in Figure 15c, the warp ends never were separate. Earlier bags of this type often were made with light-colored plant-fiber yarns plus dark-colored bison-hair yarns (Whiteford 1977:58, 61–62), while later ones sometimes incorporated colored, commercially made yarns into the side-panel designs. Average attributes from the central double-faced panels of a small sample of such bags are included in Table 3. Other techniques used to make colored designs include supplementary diverted warps on a plain-twined background, twined tapestry, and a two-color version of wrapped weft-faced twining (Whiteford 1977, 1978).

Sizes of historical Great Lakes region bags range from about 66 × 46 centimeters (26 × 18 in) for clothes storage or corn processing, down to 10 × 8 centimeters (4 × 3 in) for storing special items; a common size, used for food storage, seems to be about 51 × 38 centimeters (20 × 15 in).

Utilitarian twined bags tended to be made of plant fibers, including processed and unprocessed bark, nettle, and hemp, while the more elaborately patterned bags used hair yarns as well. Wefts ordinarily were spun yarn; warps might be bark strips, unspun fiber "bundles," or spun yarn (Densmore 1929:Plate 72; Skinner 1921:Plate 54; Whiteford 1977, 1978). Extremes of element types likely to be encountered are exemplified in Figures 16 and 17: warps in the former are of bundles of "hard," unspun bark fiber, while those in the latter are of highly processed soft fibers, spun and twisted into two-ply yarns. Also made and used were pliable bags interlaced of thin bark strips (e.g., Densmore 1929:157–158, Plate 64; Lyford 1953:86–87; Skinner 1921:Plate 56).

In summary, bag fabrics most likely to be encountered in Mississippian contexts would be plain twined and constructed of two-ply plant-fiber yarns, with densely packed thick warps held together at intervals by thinner wefts. From the historical evidence, however, finer fabrics and more complex combinations of textile structures should not be ruled out. Relatively elaborate terminal edge finishes can be expected.

Garments

General information on southeastern clothing from early chronicles, later historical and ethnographic accounts, and Misissippian artwork is fairly abundant. Unfortunately, very few relatively complete Mississippian garments have survived, most of them from one special context: high-status burials at a single Caddoan Mississippian ceremonial site. From the written and pictorial record, however, we can get some idea of the dimensions, designs, and materials of men's and women's attire during the Mississippian. Large fabric garments included rectangular mantles and skirts, while smaller items ranged from sandals and slippers to leggings, garters, and sashes. Textiles were worn by both sexes, but women's everyday garb may have included more large cloth items than men's.

According to Swanton (1946:456–465), men's basic clothing item, the breechcloth, usually was of tanned skin rather than cloth. Likewise, most other male garments, including skin and fur robes in winter for all groups and skin garments functioning like shirts for eighteenth-century Natchez and Chickasaw, were nonwoven throughout the post-Contact Southeast.

Another clothing item derived from animal products was the ubiquitous, and apparently gorgeous, feather robes described by the Spanish chroniclers and most other writers up through the eighteenth century (Swanton 1946:454–456). These apparently were worn, at least by high-status individuals, as summer substitutes for equally gorgeous fur robes decorated with beads, copper, or furs of contrasting colors. Often incorporating colored designs in carefully selected feathers from different bird species, they were constructed in one of two ways, either of plant-fiber yarns into which feathers or portions of feathers had been twisted or spun (e.g., Holmes 1896:29, quoting John Haywood's description of an Indian interment discovered in Tennessee), or of feathers attached to both sides of a base fabric of bark or hemp. Adair's account for the eighteenth-century Chickasaw says that the women

> make turkey feather blankets with the long feathers of the neck and breast of that large fowl—they twist the inner end of the feathers very fast into a strong double thread of hemp, or the inner bark of the mulberry tree, of the size and strength of coarse twine, as the fibres are sufficiently fine, and they work it in the manner of fine netting. As the feathers are long and glittering, this sort of blankets is not only very warm, but pleasing to the eye. (1968:423)

Among the Natchez, feather mantles sometimes were made for "the women of the Honored class" by attaching feathers to old fishnets or old mulberry bark mantles (Swanton 1946:455, quoting Le Page du Pratz). Except for an owl- and turkey-feather neckpiece from Kettle Hill Rock-shelter, Fairfield County, Ohio (Shetrone 1928:29–31; Ohio Historical Society Accession No. 854–5), no extant examples are known of techniques in which feathers are attached to a backing (M. E. King, personal communication 1990), but fragments of fabrics woven from yarns with down or feathers twisted into them have been recovered from archaeological sites such as Etowah, Spiro, and Ozark Bluff shelters. Good diagrams of typical feathered yarns can be found in Scholtz's comprehensive volume on Ozark cordage, textiles, and basketry (1975:19–22).

Men described as wearing cloth most often seem to have been observed in ceremonial circumstances. The Gentleman of Elvas (but none of the other chroniclers) says that the Spanish with De Soto saw men wearing woven mantles over the left shoulder with the right arm free (Swanton 1946:458). One of John White's late sixteenth-century watercolors of Virginia Indians, labeled "One of their Religious men," depicts the subject garbed in a short, probably twined, fringeless cloak that covers the left arm while leaving the right one free (Lorant 1946:198); all the other adults from settlements near Roanoke whom White painted, including both women and men, wore leather skirtlike garments. Short tuniclike garments worn over one shoulder were illustrated by Le Page du Pratz for ten Chitimacha men ceremonially offering the *calumet de paix* to four Frenchmen in Louisiana (Swanton 1946:Plate 84); here, some of the garments appear to be skin rather than cloth. Tonti, visiting the main town of the Taensa in northern Louisiana in 1682, observed the chief sitting in his lodge, "while 60 old men, wrapped in white cloaks woven of mulberry-bark, formed his divan"; the chief in turn visited the Frenchmen "clothed in a white robe" (Tonti, in Parkman 1892:281–282). These garments might have resembled the long, togalike robe worn by the leader of an Indian council in a drawing by Lafitau (Holmes 1896:19). Du Ru described a group of Oumas marching with his group of Frenchmen in 1700 to visit the Taensas: "Their chiefs . . . march in front with white blankets on their backs." He also described "cloth or coverings made out of buffalo hair" displayed by one of their chiefs, along with "a sort of dress made out of the bark of trees" (1934:20), but did not tell under what circumstances they were worn. Mantles also were given as ceremonial presents. As Holmes put it, "Everywhere woven shawls were a principal feature of the propitiatory gifts of the natives to the Spaniards" in the sixteenth century (Holmes 1896:25).

In contrast to the white garments worn during formal meetings such as described above, du Ru reported that for games and dances among the early eighteenth-century Bayagoula and Mougoulacha, "The men wear skins and red linen cloth" (1934:21). Throughout the Southeast, white was symbolic of peace (E. White 1987:66–69), and red of war and death; peace chiefs and war chiefs traditionally came from the white moiety and the red moiety, respectively (Hudson 1976:235). The ball game was a fiercely competitive matter akin in many ways to warfare.

Unlike the apparently somewhat limited use of cloth garments by men during historical times, women's garments very often are described by early

European chroniclers as made from various plant and animal fibers, although women of many groups also wore skin garments and fur robes, particularly during cold weather.

Women's basic garment was the wraparound skirt. It usually is described or illustrated as knee length, for instance in eighteenth-century drawings of Mississippi River Indians by De Batz (Swanton 1946:Plates 48 and 3; Harvard University Peabody Museum PM 41-72/16). Le Page du Pratz depicts it as almost ankle length for the eighteenth-century Natchez (Swanton 1946:Plates 69.2, 105); the pictured skirts, however, probably were of trade cloth rather than native-made (Le Page du Pratz 1763:2:230). According to Swanton, native fabric skirts are mentioned by Ranjel for sixteenth-century southwestern Georgia, and by various eighteenth-century writers for the Virginia–North Carolina area (said to be made of "silk grass," with a bottom fringe), Louisiana (mulberry yarn), Chickasaw and eastern Siouans (mulberry), and the Choctaw (bison hair mixed with plant fiber). The last fabric is described by an anonymous early eighteenth-century writer as "double like two-sided handkerchiefs and thick as canvas, half an ell wide and three quarters long [approximately 2 × 3 ft, or 57 × 86 cm]" (Swanton 1918; 1946:450–452).

Unlike men, who seem to have worn mantles as a single tuniclike garment (perhaps over a breechcloth), women always are described as wearing them in combination with a skirt. Like skirts, women's mantles were rectangular. From historical accounts, the two garments seem to be essentially the same size and shape; according to M. E. King, however, mantles were both wider and longer than skirts (personal communication 1990). They were worn fastened over one shoulder, leaving the other arm free. Mantles are mentioned in early Spanish accounts as worn by the Apalachee in northwestern Florida; at Cofitachequi and Ichisi in South Carolina and Georgia, where they were described as "apparently of homespun linen (probably native hemp, nettle, or mulberry) and very thin"; and generally throughout the Southeast (Swanton 1946:450–452, 469–475; Ranjel in Bourne 1904:2:88). Eighteenth-century Natchez mulberry-yarn mantles were "at least an ell [45 in, or 114 cm] square and a line in thickness . . . very white and very neat" (Le Page du Pratz 1763:2:231). Although mulberry-yarn cloth could be thin, as noted above, it could be very sturdy: Catesby, describing fabric made by the eighteenth-century Chickasaw and other groups and used for "petticoats and other habits," said that "its substance and durableness recommends it for floor and table-carpets" (Catesby in Swanton 1946:453). The remnants of the de Soto expedition, building seven brigantines to travel down the Mississippi from Aminoya (eastern Arkansas or Louisiana), demanded and received great numbers of native shawls from which to construct sails; to be effective, they must have been dense enough to catch the wind (Bourne 1904:1:187–191). Mulberry yarn also was used to make very open fabrics. Among the Natchez, women bound their hair "in a kind of net made of mulberry threads" (Le Page du Pratz 1763:2:232). From these varying descriptions, it would seem that southeastern plant-fiber fabrics could vary considerably in their attributes.

Historically, bison hair was used in the Southeast for belts, garters, and other similar small articles, as well as for clothing (Swanton 1946:439; du Ru 1934:20; Adair 1968:222–223). Bushnell quotes from a 1721 source to show that Kaskaskia Indians living in the vicinity of present-day St. Louis were making robes from finespun bison wool manufactured into "stuffs" and dyed yellow, black, or red. Descriptions of other items made of bison hair in Illinois, western Carolina, and the Lower Mississippi Valley from additional late seventeenth- and early eighteenth-century sources also are presented (Bushnell 1906, 1909, 1914:663, Plate 56). Hunter described blankets of bison and other hair yarns made by early nineteenth-century Osage (quoted in Holmes 1896:25–26). From archaeological evidence, the bison was a relative latecomer east of the Mississippi (Neuman 1983; Rostlund 1960); for example, it is not known in the central Ohio River Valley before the fifteenth century (Tankersley 1986; Tankersley and Adams 1989).

Although bison hair may not have been a common yarn fiber during earlier Mississippian times, many other animal fibers were available for spinning. Plant-stem fibers, however, including grasses, hemp, nettle, milkweed, and the inner bark of various trees, seem to be more frequently mentioned by the early chroniclers in regard to cloth-making.

A different range of information about garments can be obtained from Mississippian images of people, including stone statues and effigy pipes (e.g., Emerson 1982, 1989; Fundabark and Foreman, 1957:Plates 97–102; Perryman 1966; Prentice 1986), ceramic statuettes and effigy pots (e.g., Fundabark and Foreman 1957:Plates 119–120), incised designs on shell gorgets and cups (e.g., Duffield 1964; Kneberg 1959; Phillips and Brown 1978; see also Fundabark and Foreman 1957), repoussé designs on copper plates (e.g., Hamilton et al. 1974; Strong 1989), and pictures engraved on stone (Holmes 1891; Parker 1949).

The shell and copper artifacts are primarily ceremonial objects, frequently associated with elite burials. Costumes depicted on them usually are interpreted as associated with particular ritual functions of their wearers, who are almost always male, although C. Brown (1982) argues that some were female. The most elaborate costumes present their wearers as "bird men" (e.g., Strong 1989). Actual counterparts to many of the items depicted, such as fragments of twined tapestry mantles from Spiro with designs in the shape of feathered wings, have been recovered from mortuary contexts (Willoughby 1952; J. Brown, 1976b; King and Gardner 1981; Kuttruff 1988a). Duffield (1964) offers a particularly detailed description and interpretation of ornaments and articles of clothing depicted on engraved shells from Spiro, including sashes and belts, "g-strings," "aprons," skirts, capes, and foot coverings. Phillips and Brown (1978:95, 102) also summarize this information, with some differences in interpretation. Of the larger garments, skirts were knee length, often decorated and usually fringed, and capes extended from shoulder to well below the waist, with many of them decorated in designs of repeated geometric shapes. A tuniclike garment, sometimes but not always depicted as being made of skins, consisted of a very short skirt with a triangular "bib" extending over one shoulder (Duffield 1964:Plates 3–9; Fundabark and Foreman 1957:Plate 25).

The engraved slate "Thruston tablet" from Sumner County, Tennessee, portrays a number of men and perhaps one woman (Thruston 1890; Holmes 1891; Parker 1949) (Figure 18). The possibly feminine figure wears a knee-length, rectangular, unfringed skirt decorated with a border design of circles. Three of the men wear garments bordered by narrow triangular points, probably indicating fringe or fur. Two of the garments are irregularly shaped skirts, while the other appears to cover the entire body from the neck to above the knees, about the same dimensions as worn by the Virginia Indian painted by John White. Because of their shapes and jagged edging, these three garments seem more likely to have been made from skins than from cloth.

Three-dimensional stone and ceramic images depict both men and women, often in much simpler dress than that shown in two-dimensional portrayals. In fact, such figurines often appear to be completely nude, although many are decorated with representations of body paint or tattoos. Some of them are considered to be ancestor figures, while some female figures are linked with fertility symbolism (J. Brown 1985:102–108, 123, 126). The common garment for women is an unfringed rectangular skirt, extending from waist to just above the knees. Examples are known, for instance, on stone figurines from Cahokia (Emerson 1982:Plates 4–6, 1989:Figures 2–6) and Etowah (Fundabark and Foreman 1957:Plate 97; Perryman 1966; R. S. Peabody Foundation, Andover, Massachusetts), and on an effigy pot from Obion, Tennessee (Baldwin, 1966:Plate 43). Some women's skirts may have been longer. At least one female effigy bottle from Cahokia (Coe et al. 1986:56) may be wearing an ankle-length skirt, as may a ceramic figure from a stone grave near Nashville, the body paint of which includes a cross-in-circle design on one shoulder (Figure 19). The Harvard Peabody Museum collection contains at least six more similar figures from Tennessee with

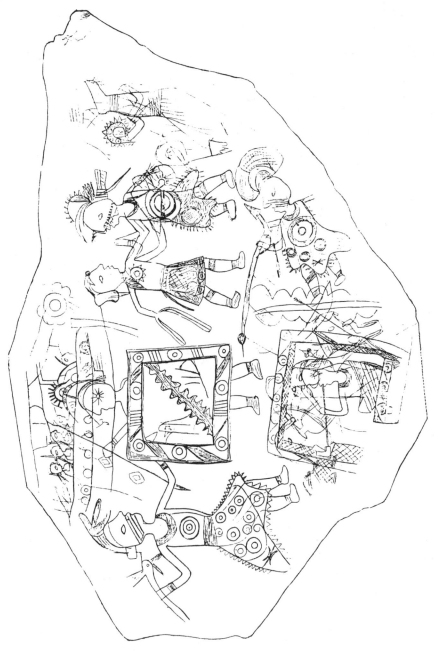

Figure 18.
Depiction of garments on engraved stone "Thruston Tablet" from Sumner County, Tennessee (Holmes 1891:Plate 1).

Figure 19.
Example of "effigy pot" female figure (Phillips 1970:139). From stone grave near Nashville, Tennessee. (Harvard University Peabody Museum No. 84-63-10/32486, copyright 1970 by the President and Fellows of Harvard College. Drawing by Eliza McFadden. Used by permission.)

knee-length or ankle-length skirts and negative-painted designs on the upper body. Such painted designs are not uncommon on female effigy bottles (e.g., Thruston 1890:Plate 9), and may possibly represent decorated openwork mantles rather than body paint or tattoos. A male ceramic effigy bottle from the early Mississippian (ca. 900–1400) site of Cemochechobee, Clay County, Georgia, definitely is wearing a knee-length cloak, adorned with ogee shapes in black and buff (Schnell et al. 1981:75–79).

The garments of many of these Mississippian figures, particularly the men depicted in two-dimensional media, probably represent special ceremonial dress rather than day-to-day clothing. Also probably representing ceremonial dress are all but one of the extant Mississippian garments. These artifacts came from a single location: Spiro, a ceremonial center on the western periphery of the Mississippian (Figure 1) dating to the thirteenth–fourteenth centuries (Brown 1976a:124). The site yielded a very large group of textiles and textile artifacts from elite mortuary contexts, including significant portions of a number of garments in oblique interlacing, plain twining, alternate-pair twining, countered-twined tapestry, and twined featherwork. Fragmentary textiles included the widest range of fabric structures, yarn fibers, and decorative techniques that has come from any Mississippian site (J. Brown 1976b:323–342; Burnett 1945:Plates 88, 91; King and Gardner 1981; Kuttruff 1988a; Drooker 1991c; Willoughby 1952). These will be discussed at more length in Chapter 7.

Only a single prehistoric utilitarian garment, from a burial in the undated Cliffty Creek Rock-shelter, Tennessee (Holmes 1896:31–32, Plate III), was located for analysis (Figure 20). However, it was much more complete than any of the Spiro garments.

From the same burial came a skirt consisting almost entirely of long fringe, with just a few rows of alternate-pair twining at the top (Holmes 1896:Plate 4), perhaps making up a matched set with the more structured garment, as implied in du Ru's account of Bayagoula and Mougoulacha games and dances in the Louisiana of 1700: "The women have on dresses of bark . . . with a fringe of the same material, about their waist, that falls down like the nets which are put on our horses in summer to protect them from flies. These nets reach down to the knees and cover them effectively" (1934:21–22). At least some of the French "nets" for horses consisted solely of fringe (e.g., Gillispie 1959:Plate 470). Such a style is consistent with Le Page du Pratz's report for young Natchez girls (1763:2:231) and for De Bry's portraits of Florida women (Lorant 1946). Similar, deeply fringed garments from Spiro have been described and illustrated (e.g., Willoughby 1952:Plate 149). However, Kuttruff found evidence of additional, now-disintegrated twining wefts on all of the previously reported "fringed skirts" she examined at the National Museum of Natural History and in general for Spiro; that is, those skirts originally may have consisted of spaced twining rather than of long fringe (personal communication 1990). Holmes speculated that the example from Tennessee might have been an unfinished garment, although he considered it improbable (1896:31). In any case, it is unlikely that such unstructured textiles would have been important in the pottery-making process.

All of the skirts or mantles that consist of large pieces of fabric are rectangular, but in only the Tennessee fabric are all four edges present. Its

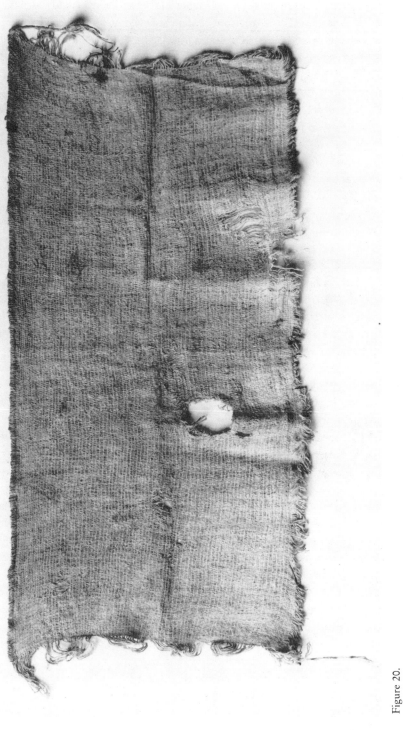

Figure 20.
Alternate-pair-twined garment from Cliffty Creek Rock-shelter, Morgan County, Tennessee, 117 × 61 centimeters (46 × 24 in) (Smithsonian Institution Department of Anthropology Cat. No. 132253, Neg. No. 32547-H. Used by permission.)

dimensions are given as 46 × 24 inches (117 × 61 cm), with alternate-pair twining rows parallel to the long dimension. Of the garments from Spiro, one is constructed of dense oblique interlacing and is 135–145 centimeters (53–57 in) wide (King and Gardner 1981:Figure 4; Willoughby 1952:Plate 148). The other garments from Spiro included in this study are of alternate-pair twining. Two of them have complete dimensions parallel to the weft rows: 133 and 142 centimeters (52 and 56 in). Dimensions perpendicular to twined rows on incomplete fabrics ranged up to 67.5 centimeters (27 in). If worn as a skirt, such a garment would reach well below the knees, even on a tall person.

The garment from Tennessee has ties extending out parallel to the starting edge. They consist of lengths of cord strung through a tube formed by folding back the tops of the looped-over warp yarns and securing them with a row of twining (Figure 15d). The top edge of the garment with long fringes appears to be essentially identical. The side edges of the structured garment are knotted, but then the weft yarns are extended out in wide loops, entering the fabric again as wefts several rows below their original position and forming a sort of scalloped fringe in the process. The terminal edge is fringed, with cut ends secured by the final row of twining.

One of the Spiro garments (Willoughby 1952:Plate 145, bottom) also has ties, but in this case extending perpendicular rather than parallel to the starting edge. I would interpret this as definitely a mantle rather than a skirt, while the Tennessee configuration probably would serve for either. In contrast, M. E. King interprets all seven relatively complete garments from Spiro as skirts (personal communication 1990, 1991; King and Gardner 1981:131). She notes that skirts often are made with perpendicular ties in Peru, and mantles do not necessarily have to be made with ties: they can hang around the shoulders, their corners can be tied together, or some sort of pin can be used to secure the ends together. All historical accounts of southeastern fabric mantles describe them as fastened over one shoulder, but the method of fastening is specified only for the early eighteenth-century Natchez, among whom, according to Le Page du Pratz, mulberry-fiber mantles "are fastened on by means of cords of the same thread, having tassels hanging at each end" (Swanton 1946:453).

Three of the twined garments from Spiro have fringed side edges plus an incomplete terminal edge probably consisting of fringe (M. E. King, personal communication 1991). One of the twined garments is difficult to interpret, at least from photographs (Willoughby 1952:Plate 147). Three edges are present, including two fringed warp edges (Kuttruff 1988a:220); that is, there appears to be no conventional "starting edge" for this fabric. The warpwise dimension is 99–102 centimeters (39–40 in).

Table 3 summarizes textile attribute data for the garment from Tennessee, plus the four garments from Spiro for which the most complete measurements are available (Drooker 1989b: 128–132, Appendix 4). The Oklahoma fabrics are somewhat coarser than the Tennessee garment.

According to Whitford (1941:13; N.M.N.H. catalog cards), both the fabric garment and the skirt of fringe from Tennessee were made of nettle fiber yarns *(Laportea canadensis)*. Fibers used for the Spiro garments were more diverse. Willoughby calls them rabbit hair, apparently from visual inspection alone (1952:114). According to Kuttruff, where fibers can be identified in these seven garments, they are animal rather than vegetal (1988a:258–259). M. E. King, who supervised chemical and microscopic analysis of fibers and dyes from a number of Spiro textiles, reports that the garments contain feather/down and vegetable fiber as well as animal hair (personal communication 1990). Although down made up a large proportion of some yarns, in most Spiro textiles where it occurred it was mixed with vegetable fibers in a matrix consisting mostly of animal hair, usually rabbit or hare (King and Gardner 1981:128).

All seven of the Spiro garments were dyed dark red (Willoughby 1952:115–118). Three of them incorporate very large-scale geometric designs in yellow, either all over or as borders: a crenellated line, concentric circles, and concentric semicircles (Willoughby 1952:Plates 145, 147, 148). These are similar in scale to garment decorations portrayed in the Spiro engravings (Phillips and Brown 1978) and also reminiscent of the cloaked effigy figure from Cemochechobee (Schnell et al. 1981:75–79).

It seems most likely that the Spiro garments were ceremonial and worn by men. Their somewhat coarse texture was offset by comparatively soft yarns (M. E. King, personal communication 1990; J. Kuttruff, personal communication 1990). Their large-scale, colorful designs and their deep fringes could be seen and recognized at a distance, congruent with Wobst's theory of costume as communication (Wobst 1977). In contrast, the Tennessee garment seems appropriate for everyday wear by an ordinary person, male or female. Since the burial from which it came also contained hanks of unspun fiber and bone awls, it may well have belonged to a woman. It clearly was worn over a long period of time, for it has a significant hole near the bottom, perhaps caused by friction where its owner habitually sat or knelt. The off-center location of this hole may point to use of the garment either as a mantle, secured over one shoulder, or as a wraparound skirt, habitually worn in exactly the same position around the wearer's waist.

The only description of any detail that we have of garment construction in the Southeast comes from early eighteenth-century Louisiana. To make mulberry-bark mantles, the Natchez plant two stakes in the ground about a yard and a half asunder, and having stretched a cord from the one to the other, they fasten their threads of bark double to this cord, and then interweave them in a curious manner into a cloak of about a yard square with a wrought border round the edges. (Le Page du Pratz 1763:2:231)

The setup involves the use of free-hanging warps (as in Figure 13b, but a flat fabric rather than a tube), but the edge finish described does not seem to be fringe. Consistent with this description, all but one of the examples that I have seen of relatively complete, large, flat Mississippian textile artifacts include side and terminal edge finishes diagnostic of fabrics made on free-hanging warps. However, the available sample is not large enough to know how common non-free-hanging warps may actually have been in such textiles. If a continuous warp is stretched between two cords or bars, as is done on the backstrap looms of Central and South America and on the frames that were used by southwestern Indians to make twined fur cloaks (Kent 1983:112–116), both the starting and the terminal edges will consist of warp loops. As discussed above, some Mississippian and early historical twined bags were made with a continuous warp (e.g., Kuttruff 1987a:129; Douglas et al. 1968). One way to construct them would be to secure the looped ends rather than letting them hang free, but free-hanging looped ends also could be used. All of these possibilities were kept in mind while analyzing the Wickliffe impressed textiles.

Attributes from one more group of textiles are included in Table 3 because of a fairly high probability that they served as garments. The collection of the R. S. Peabody Foundation, Andover, Massachusetts, contains a number of fragments of comparatively fine fabrics from elite burial contexts at Etowah, Georgia (Figure 1). Several similar fragments of plain twining, excavated from Mound C (Byers 1964; Moorehead 1932:61), appear to be of animal fiber, although they have not been examined under the microscope. The largest is decorated all over with a design of yellow crosses and circles-and-crosses on a brown background; motifs are on the order of 5 centimeters (2 in) across. Because of its prominent symbolic decorations, it is possible that this textile may have been analogous in function to the Spiro garments decorated with yellow geometric motifs. The attribute measurements for this textile can be compared with those for six other significantly coarser plain-twined fragments from outer burials of Mound C obtained by Schreffler (1988:155–156), as summarized in Table 3. Three interlaced textiles all had five elements per centimeter, finer than the Spiro interlaced garment; their yarn diameters were not reported (Schreffler 1988:155). Yarns for all of the plain-twined and interlaced fabrics are **Z**-spun and **S**-plied. The

Peabody Foundation collection also contains a light-colored, very fine alternate-pair-twined fragment, apparently made from vegetable fibers; its measurements are included in Table 3.

To summarize, from Mississippian statues and effigy pots and from early historical accounts, it seems that a knee-length, sometimes ankle-length, wraparound skirt was a common garment for southeastern women during this period. Dimensions of 2 × 4 feet (60 × 120 cm) would be ample, while 18 × 42 inches (46 × 107 cm) would be adequate for an above-the-knee skirt. In addition, a mantle of similar or larger size might be worn over one shoulder by either women or men. For everyday clothing, one would expect flexible, soft, relatively fine fabrics. Alternate-pair twining, fine plain twining, or interlacing could serve the purpose. In the warm Kentucky climate, dense textiles would not be needed year-round but might be employed for winter robes. Such garments would best be constructed of well-processed yarns with good insulating properties but should not be excessively stiff or heavy in weight. From the sparse archaeological record, alternate-pair twining is the most common fabric structure used for garments, while fringed sides and bottom edges are the most common edge finishes. In Mississippian art, women typically wear smooth-edged skirts, and men sometimes wear fringed skirts.

Information such as this will be essential in interpreting the original functions of the Wickliffe impressed textiles. However, as we shall see, it in turn can be greatly extended by means of the much more abundant record of textiles impressed on pottery.

Basketry: Mats and Containers

Basketry items made of nonpliable materials, including flat mats and shaped baskets, constituted a very important class of craft items in the prehistoric and historic Southeast. Both flat and shaped items were made from strips of material in a wide variety of interlaced structures. Impressions from such fabrics do occur on pottery, although far less frequently than impressions of pliable textiles made from spun yarns.

Baskets—used for gathering, processing, and serving food, transporting and storing a wide variety of items, and interring the dead—were constructed in the Southeast primarily by interlacement, often in very complex patterns based on twill structures. Split cane segments and bark strips were the most commonly used materials. Coiled baskets, although found at the western periphery of the Mississippian-influenced culture area (Scholtz

1975:30–44), are not common prehistorically from the Mississippi River eastward.

Mats—used for sitting on, sleeping on, covering the walls of buildings, and wrapping the dead for burial—were interlaced, oblique-interlaced, twined, or sewn together by piercing plant stems with a needle. They were made of palmetto, rushes, reeds, cane, bark, or other plant products, depending on the locale. Like baskets, many were decorated by painting or by weaving geometric patterns in two or more colors (e.g., Baerreis 1947; Fundabark and Foreman 1957: Plate 134; Hoffman 1896:Plates 21–22; Rogers 1983; Webb and McKinney 1975). If made from thin and/or narrow elements, they had the potential for being quite pliable, but they were far more likely to be relatively stiff. An important quality for mats used for sitting and sleeping was smoothness. The variety of attributes that might be encountered in archaeological mats is apparent from this description of artifacts from San Marco, Florida: "Portions of mats, some thick, as though for use as rugs, others enveloping various objects, and others still of shredded bark in strips so thin and flat and closely platted that they might well have served as sails, were frequently discovered" (Swanton 1946:603, quoting Cushing).

The most complete southeastern prehistoric mat that I have located was excavated at Cliffty Creek Rock-shelter, Tennessee (Figure 21). It accompanied a burial, enveloping a bag (Figure 14), two garments (Figure 20), human remains, and other items (Holmes 1896:30–31). Its size, structure, and materials probably are typical of many southeastern mats, although its design is less elaborate than the colored mats with pictorial designs described by early travelers (Swanton 1946:602–603) and recovered in fragments from some archaeological sites (e.g., Webb and McKinney 1975). Made from split cane $3/16$ to $1/3$ inch (5–8 mm) wide, the mat is 78 × 40 inches (198 × 102 cm) in size. Its fabric structure is oblique interlacing, primarily in two different twills, a 3/3 straight twill and a 4/1 broken twill (Figure 10e). Borders of one or more rows of straight twill against a textured background of 4/1 broken twill are common on such mats. Straight twill structures or contrasting sections of broken twill with long floats running perpendicular to each other also were used to make geometric and animal shapes on more elaborate mats (and baskets). Contrasting colors of elements can be used to enhance the effect, as in a frequently illustrated Chitimacha mat from Louisiana (Fundabark and Foreman 1957:Plate 134; Hudson 1976:215; Swanton 1946:Plate 76.1), and in the complex basketry from Spiro (Baerreis 1947). As with an oblique interlaced textile made from yarn, the cane elements meet the selvage at a nonperpendicular angle, then are turned back into the fabric to continue interlacing. The use of a few rows of straight twill at the edge, rather than the broken twill, is typical and makes a neater edge than would a broken twill.

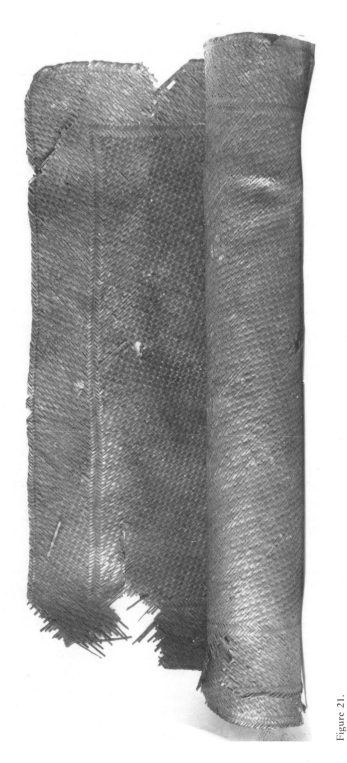

Figure 21.

Interlaced cane mat from Cliffty Creek Rock-shelter, Morgan County, Tennessee, 102 × 198 centimeters (40 × 78 in) (Smithsonian Institution Department of Anthropology Cat. No. 132252, Neg. No. Tennessee 98. Used by permission.)

The starting and side edges of such a mat will be similar to each other, with cut elements apparent only along the terminal edge, which may be finished by interlacing the ends of the elements into the back side of the mat.

While oblique interlacing probably is typical of Mississippian basketry matting, other structures have been used historically within the larger region of eastern North America to make mats. Bark mats in plain and twill interlacing with two sets of elements were made by nineteenth-century Chippewa and Menomini (Hoffman 1896:Plates 20, 22; V. Jones 1948:356; Skinner 1921:Plate 58). Warp-faced, patterned twined and interlaced mats made of rushes also are known from the Great Lakes area (Rogers 1980). To date, no impressions of such structures have been found in Mississippian pottery.

What are the visual characteristics of matting materials? Relatively fresh split cane is easily identifiable: smooth and slightly convex on the "right" side, with sharp edges. The inner surface is slightly rougher than the outer. Flat archaeological basketry fragments (pieces of mats or baskets) from the Ozarks had cane elements between 3 and 7 millimeters (0.1 and 0.3 in), wide, with 4–6 millimeters most common (Scholtz 1975). Elaborately decorated matting fragments from the Mounds Plantation site (tenth–thirteenth centuries), Caddo Parish, Louisiana, had splints of southern cane *(Arundinaria gigantica)* from 3.5 to 5.2 millimeters (0.14 to 0.20 in) wide, with 4 millimeters most common; they are described as "paper thin, 0.3 to 0.35 mm" (Webb and McKinney 1975:107). Equally complex twill basketry from Spiro, interpreted as almost all matting rather than containers, used 5-millimeter (0.2-in) cane strips (Baerreis 1947:6). Frayed elements are more likely to be bark than cane, but cane can deteriorate and fray as well (e.g., Brain 1979:253). From ethnographic evidence, elements in bark mats might fall within a wider range of widths than in cane mats. An Ojibway twill-interlaced mat used ¼-inch (6-mm) cedar-bark strips and was said to be relatively flexible (Lyford 1953:92–93), while a Chippewa mat interlaced with two sets of elements was made from bark strips that were ⅛ inch (3 mm) thick and ½–¾ inch (13–19 mm) wide (V. Jones 1948:356). A frequent width for bark strips used to make Ozark Bluffs containers was 4 millimeters (0.16 in) (Scholtz 1975:68). Rushes, used in relatively recent Great Lakes mats (Rogers 1980), are less consistent in width and thickness than cane because they are flexible enough to balloon out between interlacements. Typically, they will have linear indentations parallel to their length.

How can mats be distinguished from baskets, with evidence from impressions alone? Both baskets and mats can be fine or coarse. Because far more archaeological fragments can be identified definitely as baskets than as mats, it does not seem feasible to try to distinguish containers from flat basketry statistically by material or size of element. Nor is it easy at this time to make a definitive statement as to whether certain structures are more typical of baskets than of mats. Interlaced basketry from Ozarks Bluff sites, much of it in the form of containers, was classified into almost two dozen different fabric structures, including the 3/3 and 4/1 twill structures typical of many mats (Scholtz 1975:149). It is quite possible that prehistoric southeastern basket structures may be more varied than mat structures, but quantitative evidence is lacking. Baskets can be open or dense; mats, however, are always dense.

Unlike flat mats, shaped containers often have elements that do not meet each other at right angles; sometimes "warp" elements are added within the body of the basket at an angle to previous elements (the appearance may be similar to a gore in tailored clothing), and "warp" spacing can vary as the shape of the container expands or contracts. Baskets often have bulky rims, made from added elements. Mat edges tend to be simpler and flatter. Since basket rims are all terminal edges, an edge—or, even better, a corner—of oblique interlacing constructed of continuous elements (no cut ends) would be diagnostic of a mat.

Other Large, Flat Fabrics: Burial Wrappings and "Bedding"

In addition to rectangular fabrics with ties or cords that were clearly intended to be worn as garments, a number of other large textiles have survived that may or may not have been used as garments. Some have come from mortuary contexts, others from less formal settings. None can be assigned to the Mississippian with any certainty, but information about their construction and dimensions can be a useful supplement to data from better-provenienced artifacts.

Some very large textiles have been discovered serving the purpose of burial wrappings. They may have been made specifically for that function or might have been used previously as bedding by the deceased or others. Drawings showing reconstructions of two such burials from Tennessee and Missouri can be found in Lewis and Kneberg (1970:Plate 102) and Fundabark and Foreman (1957:Plate 134).

An example of a mummified body of an adolescent boy recovered from a cavern in Kentucky in the early nineteenth century serves to illustrate how many different kinds of wrappings might be included with a single person:

> Several human bodies were found wrapped carefully in skins and cloths . . . inhumed below the floor of the cave. . . .
> The outer envelope of the body is a deer skin, probably dried in the usual

way, and perhaps softened before its application, by rubbing. The next covering is a deer skin, whose hair had been cut away by a sharp instrument,
resembling . . . a sheared pelt of beaver. The next wrapper is of cloth, made of
twine doubled and twisted [plied]. But the thread does not appear to have been
formed by the wheel, nor the web by the loom. The warp and filling seem to
have been crossed and knotted by an operation like that of the fabricks of the
northwest coast, and of the Sandwich islands [twining]. Such a botanist as the
lamented Muhlenburgh, could determine the plant which furnished the fibrous
material.

The innermost tegument is a mantle of cloth like the preceding; but furnished with large brown feathers, arranged and fastened with great art, so as to
be capable of guarding the living wearer from wet and cold. The plumage is
distinct and entire, and the whole bears a near similitude to the feathery cloaks
now worn by the nations of the northwestern coast of America. (Mitchell
1820:318–319)

Holmes quoted a series of early nineteenth-century manuscripts describing mortuary fabrics discovered in caves in Warren County, Tennessee, and
Barren County, Kentucky, that also included twined feathered robes. One of
these, wrapped around a woman, was 3 feet wide and 6–7 feet long (91 ×
183–213 cm). An additional Tennessee cave yielded two bodies wrapped in
"a kind of blanket, supposed to have been manufactured of the lint of nettles,
afterwards with dressed skins, and then a mat of nearly 60 yards in length"
(Holmes 1896:29, 21 [quotation from Brackenridge]).

Dallas focus (Late Mississippian) village burials in eastern Tennessee at
least sometimes had burial wrappings, occasionally "a coarse textile," but
"usually made of coarse twilled-plaited matting" (Lewis and Kneberg
1946:144).

In Hopewell mortuary contexts, textile canopies, an elaborately beaded
twined "blanket," and twined and interlaced bags enclosing ceremonial artifacts such as copper celts and breastplates have been identified (Hinkle
1984; E. White 1987), but no such usages are certain for Mississippian interments.

Southeastern prehistoric burials have yielded a range of textile types, some
of them unique and unusual, that cannot be recognized as specific artifacts
because they have survived only in small fragments. Representative examples
will be discussed on a site-by-site basis in Chapter 7.

A number of researchers working with materials from eastern North
America have shown that textile differences in mortuary contexts—like
differences in types and amounts of other grave offerings such as shell
ornaments or metal artifacts—can be correlated with hierarchical status differences. Schreffler analyzed and compared yarns and textiles from differing

elite burial contexts at Etowah, finding that the structural complexity of the fabrics did "appear to be related to status differences" (1988:2). In comparing textiles from high-status burials at Spiro with textiles from low-status burials in Ozark rock-shelters in Missouri and Arkansas, Kuttruff found that textiles of greater average complexity (higher Textile Production Complexity Index numbers) were associated more with higher-status burials than with lower-status burials. Attributes associated with higher-status as opposed to lower-status textiles included dyed colors, geometric and figural designs, greater number of patterning techniques, spun animal fibers, stitched and fringed edge finishes, and higher fabric counts (Kuttruff 1988a:139–140, 152–155).

Some types of textiles encountered as burial wrappings may have served originally as bedding materials for the living. Is there any way in which these might be distinguished from either garments or specially made mortuary fabrics?

Mats and furs are mentioned by early historical observers as bench covers and bedding in southeastern dwellings (e.g., Swanton 1946:422), but few additional details are offered. A pre-Mississippian Kentucky rock-shelter affords some evidence that twined textiles may also have been used for this purpose (Webb and Funkhouser 1936:116–123). At the Newt Kash shelter, twined fabrics up to 3 × 4 feet (91 × 122 centimeters) in size were heaped together, possibly to serve as bedding. They are described as heavy and strong; all those illustrated seem to be of plain twining with spaced weft rows and fairly thick warps, although no scale is included in the photographs. The textiles all had been damaged to some extent, although at least one of them had been repaired to extend its usefulness. The authors envision them as originally functioning as garments or possibly a very large bag, rather than having been made specifically to sleep upon. In fact, one has a braided edge finish that appears very similar to a bag rim. It is quite possible that large garments could have been worn during the day, then used as blankets at night. Certainly, worn-out garments could have been employed as cushioning to sleep on, but a coarse, bumpy fabric would not be ideal for the purpose.

Probably because of its scale, Orchard interpreted a piece of coarse weft-faced, interlaced fabric that he found in a Kentucky cave as a blanket. Both warp and weft consisted of six- or eight-ply yarns, and he estimated that when new, the fabric was ¼ inch (6 mm) thick (1920:17, Plate 5). The yarns, then, might be on the order of 3 millimeters in diameter. Such a fabric would have been a heavy covering but probably a good insulator. Because of its smoothness, it would have been comfortable to lie upon as well.

In summary, it is possible that some textiles were made especially for use as burial wrappings or bedding. One earmark of such a function might be a larger size than would be convenient to wear. Another might be a heavier fabric. In some cases, burial fabrics—either clothing or wrappings—for elite interments might be finer and characterized by more complex structures and decorations than those accompanying nonelite burials. Utilitarian village fabrics of whatever function might be expected to be more similar to the latter than the former.

Hunting and Fishing Nets

No artifacts that can be identified definitely as hunting or fishing nets have been recovered from Mississippian contexts, only relatively small fragments of knotted netting. However, attributes are available for prehistoric and early historic hunting and fishing paraphernalia from the Southwest and Great Lakes regions. Since attributes of these artifacts should be highly correlated to function, it seems permissible to consider this evidence for application to the Wickliffe impressed textiles, even though it comes from beyond the periphery of the southeastern region and is not limited to the Mississippian time period.

During the historical period, bark and grass of various sorts commonly were used for rope and strong cords rather than yarns spun from animal hair (Swanton 1946:450). Fish nets and bird nets, among other items, were made from such yarns. If their structure is described at all, usually such nets are said to be "like ours," that is, of knotted netting (Cleland 1982:762; Holmes 1896:26; Le Page du Pratz 1763:2:229; Swanton 1946:336–337). Cleland has summarized archaeological and early historical information on fishing nets used in and around the Great Lakes. He says that seine nets used in shallow water would be finer than gill nets used in deep water (1982:774). Gill nets used at Mackinac around 1687 are described as being made from relatively fine yarn: "although they only make them of ordinary sewing thread, they will nevertheless stop fish weighing over ten pounds" (Joutel in Cleland 1982:762).

Although few prehistoric fishing nets have survived, one, with sinkers attached, was recovered from a site in Ontario County, New York, dating from the seventh or sixth century B.C., where fish bones, particularly of the brown bullhead, a shallow-water catfish, were found in abundance. Thus, this most likely should be considered a seine net. It is described as being made of "apparently Indian-hemp fiber, twisted into a cord of small diameter, which was woven into a net with about two-inch [5 cm] mesh," but whether the fiber identification is more than simply visual is not indicated (Cleland 1982:769, quoting W. A. Ritchie). This mesh size would be equivalent to 0.2 elements per centimeter. Petersen, Hamilton, Adovasio, and McPherron employed the information compiled by Cleland to interpret net impressions on pottery from the Late Woodland Jutunen site at the Straits of Mackinac in the upper Great Lakes, all of which exhibited a mesh of less than 2–3 centimeters (0.3–0.5 elements per centimeter), as seine nets (Petersen et al. 1984:204–205, 210–211).

Large prehistoric nets from Hinds Cave, Val Verde County, Texas, interpreted as small game nets, averaged 1.82 millimeters in yarn diameter and 2.9 millimeters (0.11 in) in "mesh diameter" (Frison et al. 1986:355). This would be equivalent to 3.4 elements per centimeter if mesh diameter is measured from center to center of the cords that define it, but 2.1 elements per centimeter if this "diameter" simply measures the interior width of a hole in the netting. Some rabbit nets from still farther afield, in New Mexico and Arizona, have much larger mesh (2.5-inch mesh width, or 0.16 element per cm) (Kent 1983:56). Large Caddoan and Fort Ancient knotted netting fragments of unknown function (but probably not from bags) were fashioned from two-ply vegetable-fiber yarn ranging from 1 to 2 millimeters in diameter, spaced 1.0 to 0.5 elements per centimeter (Scholtz 1975:28–30; Shetrone 1928:13, 15, 16; Ohio Historical Society Accession No. 332/23).

From this sparse evidence, it seems that fishing nets most likely would have been made of rather thin but strong two-ply vegetable-fiber yarn. Since a heavy sewing thread (mentioned in the historical accounts) might be approximately 1 millimeter in diameter, that could be used as a lower limit for yarn size. Shallow-water seine nets might be expected to have on the order of 0.2 or more elements per centimeter, while gill nets would have fewer. Hunting nets might use larger yarns, perhaps as much as 2 millimeters in diameter, with mesh size perhaps ranging from a very close 2–3 elements per centimeter up to fewer than 0.2 per centimeter.

Fabrics Designed as Manufacturing Tools

Textiles designed to do specific manufacturing jobs typically exhibit a very narrow range of attributes. A familiar modern example is fine, open cheesecloth, used to drain and wrap cheeses. During the Hopewell period in the Southeast, fine oblique-interlaced fabrics were used to manufacture copper artifacts (E. White 1987:88–89). Their invariant interlaced structure and the restricted range of yarn diameter and fabric scale provide an unequivocal example of specialization. Through replication studies, White demonstrated that production of such fabrics would have been very time consuming, but she reasoned that such a time expenditure was justified because the copper earspools, celts, and other artifacts with which the fabrics were associated were so highly valued by Hopewellian society (1987:90).

Drying and lifting functions have been proposed for textiles used to make Mississippian "saltpans." Either function would be best served by textiles with a fairly narrow range of attributes. It has been postulated that such fabrics should be relatively simple (Kuttruff 1987b; Kuttruff and Kuttruff 1986)—why spend any more time than necessary on such a utilitarian fabric? If lifting heavy "saltpans" was important, the textiles should be relatively strong; if helping to even out the drying cycle was important, they should be relatively dense but formed from soft rather than hard fibers. In both cases, an optimum range of yarn and textile attributes could be obtained easily through experimentation.

Thus, textiles constructed specifically to be used in pottery-making could be expected to be relatively simple, incorporating a balance between strength and speed of manufacture. Standardization for a specific function should result in each measured attribute, such as yarn size and numbers of elements per centimeter, encompassing only a limited range.

Table 4 summarizes information on textile structures and minimum dimensions for various artifact categories. All occur in large enough sizes to envelop at least medium-diameter "saltpans." The tabulation does not represent the complete range of textiles that have been excavated from mortuary contexts, because in many cases the intended functions of small fragments were unknown. Functions of weft-faced fabrics remain speculative; sandals and slippers are the only prehistoric artifacts that are known with certainty to have been made in such structures.

The most diverse functional category appears to be historical twined bags. Is this simply because the sample size is much larger than for other categories? If not, how might such differences be explained? Do the presumably utilitarian fabrics impressed on pottery at Wickliffe conform to the textile types found in extant Mississippian utilitarian artifacts? After looking at the Wickliffe impressed textiles in the next chapter, we will return to questions such as these, attempting to answer them by means of quantitative and qualitative comparisons between the attributes of Wickliffe impressed fabrics and those of Mississippian textile artifacts.

Table 4. Fabric structures and dimensions associated with types of southeastern artifacts known from the archaeological record

Artifact	Twining					(Oblique) interlacing			Weft-faced	Knotted netting	Featherwork	Estimated range of smaller dimension, cm
	Plain	Alternate-pair	Banded	Transposed warps	Tapestry	Plain	Twill[a]	Transposed warps				
Mantle											x	60–90
Skirt or mantle	x	x				x						45–60
"Bedding"	x								x			90
Bag												
Prehistoric	x	x										4–60+
Historical	x	x	x		x	x or x				x		4–60+
Hunting/fishing net										x		100
Basketry matting							+					100–150
Mortuary wrapping	x or x						+				x	90–150

[a] Here + = made of cane or bark strips, not yarn.

CHAPTER 5

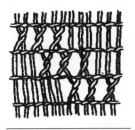

CHARACTERISTICS OF WICKLIFFE TEXTILES IMPRESSED ON "SALTPAN" POTTERY

On the basis of the data described in Chapter 4, my working hypothesis was that the fabrics impressed on pottery at Wickliffe originally were constructed for other purposes than simply to serve as aids in pottery-making—specifically, that they had been relatively large pieces of cloth originally serving as skirts, mantles, and/or blankets. In order to test this hypothesis, it was necessary to analyze in some detail the textile fragments "preserved" on pottery at Wickliffe.

This chapter describes the data base obtained from Wickliffe fabric-impressed sherds. First, the entire population and the selected sample of fabric-impressed sherds used in the study are delineated. Results of the analysis of Wickliffe textiles impressed on pottery are presented, including their structures, decoration, and finishing details, as well as statistical summaries of numerical indicators of fabric scale, density, and complexity. Textile characteristics relative to the characteristics of the vessels on which they were impressed, such as their position with respect to vessel form, are outlined. Finally, the evidence for textile and "saltpan" variation over time and between different portions of the Wickliffe site is briefly discussed.

DEFINITION OF SHERD SAMPLE

As summarized in Chapter 3, archaeological excavation at Wickliffe has included all major mounds plus several additional locations. Textile-impressed pottery has been recovered from virtually all components of the site. Unfortunately, however, documentation and labeling of artifacts excavated in the 1930s from Mounds A, B, and C was poor to nonexistent, and it is not clear what portion of excavated items remain on site. Likewise, the whereabouts of a collection of ceramics from the north end of Mound D that was shipped to the University of Chicago are unknown. Criteria for retaining artifacts differed between the 1930s and 1980s excavations. For instance, the ceramic sherds collected during the 1930s are significantly larger on average than those from more recent excavations. Because of factors such as these, it is difficult to estimate accurately the total population of recovered artifacts, let alone what this represents in terms of the total site artifact population.

Of the textile-impressed sherds currently located at the Wickliffe Mounds Research Center, all recovered during the 1983–1988 excavation seasons were examined. The major collections of provenienced artifacts excavated in the 1930s and still housed at the center are from Mounds D, E, and F. All of the textile-impressed sherds from Mound D were analyzed, with the exception of three categories: disturbed areas, unknown provenience within Mound D, and surface finds. These categories represent approximately 10% of the sherds. From Mounds E and F, sherds from alternating rows of excavation grid squares were examined (Drooker 1989b:90–93). For Mound E, approximately 53% of the available sherds were analyzed, and for Mound F, approximately 57%. Unprovenienced sherds from Mounds E and F and an additional group of unprovenienced Wickliffe ceramics from surface collection and unknown locations were not examined. Roughly estimated, approximately 65% of the textile-impressed sherds retained at Wickliffe from the 1930s excavations were examined in all, representing about 82% of the provenienced sherds from that time, along with 100% of the sherds excavated during the 1980s.

Two lots of ceramics from the 1930s excavations were sent by King to the University of Chicago and the University of Michigan. The whereabouts of the former are presently unknown, while the original numbers of the latter have been reduced from 13,775 (plus two uncounted "lots") to 3,114, with the discarded artifacts presumed to have been undecorated body sherds (Wesler 1988:4). Most of the ceramics in the University of Michigan collection came from the north end of Mound D, but some were from Mound C and general surface collecting. All of the textile-impressed sherds from Wickliffe in the University of Michigan collection were included in this study.

Approximately 14% of the sherds were too small or had impressions too faint to analyze the impressed fabric. Analyzed sherds ranged from approxi-

Table 5. Numbers of Wickliffe textile-impressed sherds analyzed

	Sherds examined	Sherds analyzed
Mound A	87	69
Mound C	8	8
Mound D and vicinity	947	816
Mound E	225	187
Mound F	338	298
North Village	154	125
Other	61	56
Total	1,820	1,559

mately 1 × 2 centimeters (0.4 × 0.8 in) to approximately 15 × 20 (6 × 8 in) centimeters in size. Table 5 summarizes the numbers of sherds examined and analyzed. Of the 1,559 sherds analyzed, 15 had two clearly discernable fabrics impressed upon them, so the total number of textile fragments analyzed was 1,574.

ATTRIBUTES OF WICKLIFFE TEXTILES IMPRESSED ON POTTERY

Attributes of fabrics impressed on pottery at Wickliffe encompass a remarkably wide range. Yarns vary from almost unprocessed to highly processed, textile scale extends from very coarse to extremely fine, and fabric structures run the gamut from simple to relatively complex. Only a small percentage of Wickliffe textile impressions contain combinations of two or more structures, but among these are fabrics intricate enough to hint at a truly sophisticated textile complex.

The following paragraphs describe Wickliffe textile attributes as preserved on pottery, including structures, yarns, scale, and complexity. Significant differences in attributes between major structural groups, as well as clustering of attributes within these groups, are delineated. In addition to fabric structure per se, characteristics of structural designs and fabric edges are illustrated and analyzed.

Table 6 summarizes the measured and computed attributes of all Wickliffe textile impressions analyzed. As has been mentioned previously, not all

Table 6. Summary of attributes for all Wickliffe impressed textiles

Attribute	min.	mean	max.	s.d.	no. cases
Warp diameter, mm	0.50	1.53	6.00	0.75	1,457
Weft diameter, mm	0.50	1.66	5.00	0.70	1,481
Avg. yarn diameter, mm	0.50	1.55	4.00	0.65	1,371
Number of warp plies	1.00	1.66	4.00	0.48	1,471
Number of weft plies	1.00	1.40	2.00	0.49	1,486
Warp twist category	0.00	2.41	4.00	0.68	629
Weft twist category	0.00	1.98	3.00	1.11	27
Warp elements per cm	0.60	4.17	12.00	1.92	1,520
Weft elements per cm	0.60	3.24	21.00	2.10	1,343
Weft rows per cm	0.30	1.62	10.50	1.07	1,327
Fabric count	1.66	7.59	31.00	3.33	1,325
Warp density	0.90	5.70	13.60	1.78	1,411
Weft density	0.46	2.54	12.45	2.02	1,314
Total density	1.85	7.92	20.40	2.40	1,215
Complexity Index No. 1	2.00	3.11	8.00	0.79	1,323
Complexity Index No. 2	3.00	4.62	9.00	0.84	1,242
Complexity Index No. 3	3.00	7.10	10.50	1.07	549

attributes could be measured for each textile. (For a complete listing of attribute data for all sherds with the exception of those from the 1988 excavations, see Drooker 1989b:Appendix 3; 1988 textile attributes are listed in Drooker 1990a.)

To give perspective on the significance of these numbers, they can be compared with the same attributes measured for a modern, machine-made burlap fabric (Table 2). On average the Wickliffe textiles are somewhat coarser than burlap, having larger mean yarn diameters and smaller mean fabric count. Their average complexity, however, is higher than the modern fabric, because burlap yarns are only single-ply, and the fabric consists of only one textile structure—plain interlacing. For additional perspective, it is worth noting that most modern handweavers would regard fabrics finer than 5–8 warp elements per centimeter as requiring particular skill to construct.

Individual textile attributes and their variation within major structural categories—plain twining, alternate-pair twining, weft-faced structures, knotting, and interlacing—are discussed separately below. First, though, the textile structures themselves, as found at Wickliffe, are described and illustrated.

Textile Structures

Some 89% of the textiles analyzed were twined, with approximately two-thirds plain twining and one-third alternate-pair twining. The next-largest category was weft-faced, probably including both plain twined and plain interlaced textiles but primarily, if not almost entirely, the former. One twill-interlaced fabric, constructed of flat elements rather than yarns, and nine examples of knotting also were present. Lumped together into a catchall category were textile impressions that were too faint or too small for classification of the fabric structure, along with impressions that consisted primarily of yarns with no recognizable fabric structure. Table 7 lists the frequencies of occurrence of fabrics in each structural category and subcategory. Descriptions and examples of each textile structure or combination of structures are presented below.

With but a few exceptions, all of the twined textiles had weft pairs twisted together in the **S** direction. In six cases, very faint impressions of **Z**-twisted structures occurred, which could have been either weft-faced twining or parallel **Z**-twisted yarns. The latter interpretation seems likely for most of the cases, and they are discussed below under "Yarns." Two to four examples of **Z**-twisted twining (probably representing one face of a three-strand braided twining structure) occur in combination with **S**-twining within groups of closely spaced twining rows in an otherwise open-twined fabric. This combination may be typical of edge structures and will be discussed below in the subsection "Edges and Joins." The single instance found of **Z**-twist twining (or three-strand braided twining) within a fabric is described later in this section.

Figure 22 may give some idea of the diversity of simple plain-twined textiles at Wickliffe. Although the fabric structures are topologically identical, the other attributes obviously cover a wide range.

From Figure 23, it can be seen that the same attribute diversity occurs within the category of alternate-pair twining. Differences in density are particularly noticeable in these textiles because open fabrics exhibit a zigzag appearance that is decorative in and of itself. Both the finest and the densest fabrics analyzed from Wickliffe were alternate-pair twining, even though the average density of weft-faced fabrics was greater.

One possible example was found of wrapped twining, in which one of the two twining elements remains on one side of the fabric, while the second makes a complete twist around it between each warp.

Two fabrics were classified as twining over nonalternating paired warps (Drooker 1989b:Figure 23). This may or may not be a correct designation. A case easily could be made that this actually is plain twining over warp ele-

Table 7. Textile structure frequencies of occurrence at Wickliffe

Textile structure	Count	Percentage of total
Twining		
Twining structure unknown	6	0.38
Plain twining, alone	830	52.73
Plain twining with warp yarn "stripes"	3	0.19
Plain twining combined with:		
Grouped twining rows	32	2.03
Diagonally diverted warps	23	1.46
Transposed, crossed warps	4	0.25
Transposed, interlinked warps	14	0.89
Oblique interlacing	2	0.13
Wrapped twining over single warps	1	0.06
Twining over nonalternating paired warps	3	0.19
Alternate-pair twining, alone	450	28.59
Alt.-pair twining with warp yarn "stripes"	3	0.19
Alt.-pair twining combined with:		
Grouped twining rows	5	0.32
Twining over nonalternating paired warps	1	0.06
Transposed, crossed warps	1	0.06
Transposed, interlinked warps	1	0.06
Total	1,379	87.59
Weft-faced		
Weft-faced, structure unknown	82	5.21
Weft-faced, probably twining	15	0.95
Weft-faced, probably interlacing	12	0.76
Total	109	6.92
Knotting		
Knotting, structure unknown	5	0.32
Knotting, square knot	3	0.19
Knotting, sheet bend or fishnet knot	1	0.06
Total	9	0.57
Interlacing		
Interlacing, 3/3 twill	1	0.06
Structure unknown		
Completely indecipherable	8	0.51
Parallel yarns	51	3.24
Nonparallel yarns	17	1.08
Total	76	4.83
Grand total	1,574	99.97

Figure 22.
Examples of Wickliffe plain-twined textiles. (Drooker 1990c:Figure 6. Copyright 1990 The Kent State University Press; used by permission.)

Figure 23.
Examples of Wickliffe alternate-pair-twined textiles. (Drooker 1990c:Figure 7. Copyright 1990 The Kent State University Press; used by permission.)

ments consisting of two loosely plied two-ply yarns. The fragments were not large enough to be certain either way.

Several types of structural variations and combinations occurred within the larger categories of plain twining and alternate-pair twining. Together, they make up 5.3% of the total fabrics analyzed, but as a group this is a diverse lot indeed. All of the combinations resulted in designs that served a decorative purpose; that is, differing fabric structures were combined in lines and shapes with potential visual interest. Some of the combinations may have served functional purposes as well. The group includes banded designs formed by the grouping of twining rows, combinations of plain twining and oblique interlacing, and designs formed by diagonally diverted warp elements, by crossed warps, by interlinked warps, and by extra weft twining twists.

Not in a separate textile structure category but deserving of mention are the few fabrics with warpwise "stripe" designs formed by planned variations in yarn diameter and structure. Examples occurred in both plain and alternate-pair twining, usually with one very thick yarn separated by eight or more thinner yarns, as illustrated in Figure 24.

Another type of "striped" (banded) pattern was formed by grouping weft twining rows together. This might be in a very regular sequence, most commonly with two very close rows separated by open spaces, or it might be in a more complex pattern. With small sherds it was not always possible to discern the entire sequence, or, indeed, to be certain that the observed pattern was a planned design rather than sloppy construction or worn and missing weft rows. All "possibles" were put into this category, however. Just as for warpwise "stripes" due to yarn variation, these grouped-twining-row bands occurred on both plain-twined and alternate-pair-twined textiles, although only 16% of them were alternate pair. Some examples are included in Figure 24. Of the 37 sherds in this category, 11 (30%) probably came from a single textile on a single vessel. Including both plain and alternate-pair twining, this structural variation makes up 2.4% of the textiles analyzed, making it the largest category of structural decoration.

The next-largest tabulated category, plain twining with diagonally diverted warps, is a structural variation that can be thought of as a combination of plain and alternate-pair twining. When I first encountered it, I thought it was a mistake, formed when the weaver accidentally twined two warps together instead of one in a plain-twined fabric. However, in many of these fabrics a consistent pattern could be recognized: wefts twined around two warps at regular intervals within rows of otherwise-plain twining, resulting in an apparent diagonal line passing through the warp elements (Figure 25, top). In some of the examples a single warp thread could have been carried

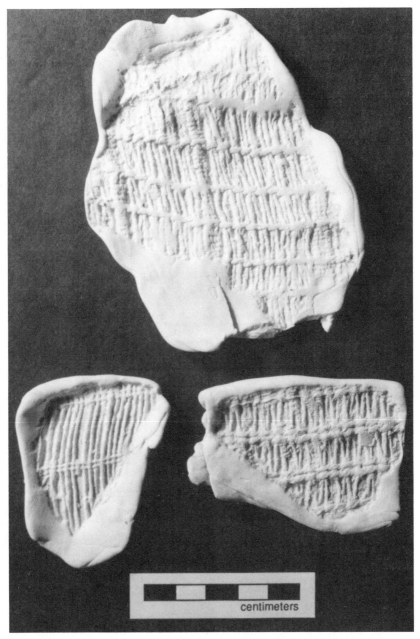

Figure 24.
Examples of Wickliffe "striped" textiles: *top*, warpwise "stripes" formed by variation in yarn diameter and structure; *bottom*, bands formed by regularly grouped weft twining rows.

along that diagonal. In one case, the diverted thread describes a zigzag line rather than a diagonal and could be considered to be a supplementary warp element rather than an essential part of the fabric structure. In these instances, the design could have been emphasized by coloring the pattern yarn, as was done by Native Americans of the Great Lakes and Plains regions in the bags they produced during historical times.

In most cases, the "diagonal line" was formed by diverting adjacent warps in a regular, stepwise sequence. Other than serving as a subtle design element, this structure could have functioned like pleats, making regularly spaced pliable lines in an otherwise relatively stiff plain-twined fabric.

As a whole, the group of fabrics designated as "plain twining with diverted warps" is problematic because it includes all possible cases. The majority of these came from very small sherds, so in 16 out of 23 examples it was not possible to be certain that the "diverted warps" were not caused by random mistakes. Two (possibly three) of the good examples resemble each other enough that they could have come from the same fabric, and in fact they were excavated from proveniences in Mound D that were not widely separated.

If diverted warps are interchanged in a reciprocal relationship, they are "transposed." Wickliffe twined textiles containing sections of transposed warps are of two general types, crossed warp and interlinked warp (Figures 9h, 9i). When added to spaced plain twining, these transpositions result in textural contrasts and/or prominent "holes" that can be grouped to form decorative designs. As with diagonally diverted warps, some of these designs could have been made more visually prominent by the addition of color to selected yarns.

Transposed crossed warps combined with plain twining were found in four examples. Although most crosses were in the **Z** direction, one textile included crosses in both directions (Figure 25, bottom). Its structure, but not its yarns, is like that used to decorate some historical twined bags from the Great Lakes region, such as the Winnebago bag illustrated in Figure 16. In at least some of the Wickliffe fabrics with crossed warps, individual warp elements continue in long diagonals across the fabric rather than simply zigzagging back and forth between two positions. The maker could have emphasized such yarns with a color contrast, but their textural contrast against the plain twining would have been a decorative element by itself. All four of the fabrics were damaged, and their impressions are not completely clear, so it is difficult to analyze the design shapes formed by groups of crosses. On one textile, they may simply have been arranged in weftwise rows, but the others probably were organized in more complex geometric shapes. Indeed, the fragment pictured in Figure 25 is consistent with a design

Figure 25.
Examples of Wickliffe twined
textiles with diverted and
crossed warps: *top,* diagonal
lines formed by diverting
adjacent warps in a regular,
stepwise sequence, in a
combination of plain and
alternate-pair twining;
righthand example has two
parallel diagonal lines (see
Figure 9f for diagram of
structure); *bottom,*
transposed crossed warps,
with some individual warp
elements diverted away from
their original positions (see
Figure 9h for diagram of
structure).

similar to the diamond shapes in the historical Winnebago bag (Figure 16),
although it is difficult to see because of the variations in yarn tension. All of
the examples included at least some plain twining over vertical warps.

The single instance of alternate-pair twining with crossed warps is clearly
visible but tantalizingly small in size (Figure 26, upper portion of textile).
Unlike the plain-twined crossed-warp textiles, this structure is dense, with
no decorative "holes." At the center of the crossed-warp section of the fabric
the crosses are consistently in the **Z** direction, while two small areas at lower
right and upper left consist of **S**-direction crosses. These would produce a
visual contrast in texture, but if the warps were in two contrasting colors
corresponding to their physical structure, the design contrast could be
prominent indeed, as diagramed in Figure 9d. As far as I am aware, this
structure has not previously been reported for Mississippian fabrics. It could
have been used to produce the same types of two-color designs found on
historical bags constructed with the crossed-warp structure illustrated in
Figure 17.

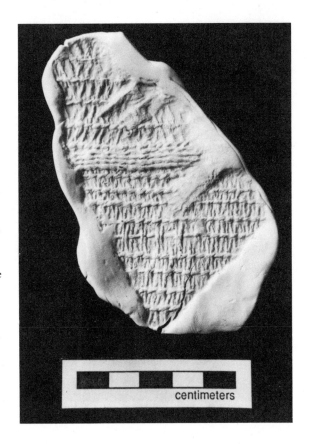

Figure 26.
Example of Wickliffe
alternate-pair-twined textile
with crossed warps (upper
portion of fragment). This
structure has the potential to
create double-faced designs
in two colors (Figure 9d).
Other structures on the same
fabric include alternate-pair
twining with some wefts
missing (lower portion) and
four rows of close three-
strand twining (center)
(Figures 9c, 9b). (Drooker
1990c:Figure 17. Copyright
1990 The Kent State
University Press; used by
permission.)

This particular textile is notable in another way. When I first analyzed it, I thought that the linear section of weft-faced twining was an edge, overlapping a second, separate fabric. Upon counting and tracing individual yarns, I found this not to be so. Rather, the sherd probably contains a single textile with multiple structures. If so, this fabric would be the only clearly discernable example seen so far from Wickliffe in which two different fabric structures (here, simple alternate-pair twining and alternate-pair twining with crossed warps) are used within separate areas with a third structure (here, weft-faced twining over two warps) used to partition them off from each other. Moreover, the weft-faced section contains both **S**-twisted and **Z**-twisted twining, the only instance where twining in the **Z** direction has been found other than in edge finishes. It is probable that, in this case at least, the **Z**-twining actually consists of a three-strand braided twining structure (Figure 10c), but this is difficult to confirm on a pottery impresssion, where only one side of the fabric is visible.

To the modern eye, the most visually interesting textiles in this study un-

Figure 27.
Examples of Wickliffe plain-twined textiles with transposed, interlinked warps. See Figure 9i for diagram of structure. (Drooker 1990c:Figure 15. Copyright 1990 The Kent State University Press; used by permission.)

centimeters

doubtedly are those designated "octagonal openwork" by early twentieth-century researchers, in which designs were created by interlinking warp yarns to form prominent "holes" in the fabric (Figure 9i). Only one such fabric was found at Wickliffe in which the base structure was alternate-pair twining. This is understandable, because the decorative holes are much more clearly visible within the less-pliable and less-dense plain-twined structure.

Plain twining plus transposed, interlinked warps occurred in 14 examples, almost 1% of all textiles analyzed. Some, but by no means all, are extremely fine and delicate-appearing. Those illustrated in Figure 27 represent the complete range of yarn and textile scale. Although two of the impressions included no vertically aligned warps, most of them incorporated contrasting areas of vertical warps and interlinked warps. All of the interlinked twists were in the **Z** direction and involved two warp yarns. In two cases the interlinked warp pairs always occurred between the same two warps (e.g., Figure 28). Generally, though, the linking alternated between warp pairs, so that the holes formed were staggered rather than aligned. As would be

Figure 28.
Example of Wickliffe textile
with transposed, interlinked
warps plus extra weft twists,
exaggerating the size of the
"holes" in the plain-twined
background. Unlike the
structure in Figure 27, where
interlinking is between
alternating pairs of warp
elements, here interlinking
consistently is done between
the same pair of warp
elements. (Drooker
1990c:Figure 16. Copyright
1990 The Kent State
University Press; used by
permission.)

centimeters

natural with such a structure, designs are made up of diagonally shifting groups of "holes." Unfortunately, no fragment was large enough to discern entire shapes of motifs. Given the fine scale of some of these textiles, it would be possible to create fairly intricate shapes in this structure if the makers were so inclined.

Another type of fabric structure in which designs are created by deliberately formed "holes" consists of warps forced farther apart than usual by means of extra twists in the weft twining elements. By this technique, it is possible to divert warp threads and produce complex geometric patterns consisting of rectangular and triangular "holes" (e.g., Figure 2f). However, rectangular openings also can result accidentally if warp yarns are pulled out of a plain-twined fabric (see Figure 24, bottom left). Altogether, six examples of plain-twined fabrics with rectangular holes, but without obviously torn-out warp yarns, were found. However, five of them occurred in obviously worn fabrics, and all *could* have been formed by accidental removal of warp threads, as happened with the bag in Figure 14. For this reason, these five textiles were not classified as a separate decorative type.

The only extra-weft-twist fabrics I found that certainly were formed de-

Figure 29.
Examples of Wickliffe textiles combining plain twining and oblique interlacing. See Figure 9g for diagram. (Drooker 1990c:Figure 13. Copyright 1990 The Kent State University Press; used by permission.)

liberately were two textiles that combined both transposed, interlinked warps and extra weft twists with plain twining (Figure 28). Transpositions always occurred between the same warp pairs. This combination of structures results in especially large "holes," emphasized in one of these fabrics by the use of very thin yarns. I have not found any published depiction or description of this structural combination in textiles from other southeastern sites.

Finally, two fabrics were found that seem to consist of plain twining plus oblique interlacing, a combination of structures also not previously described in the literature (Figure 29). Both impressions are extremely faint and difficult to interpret. The bottom fabric seems to consist of sections of oblique interlacing stabilized at intervals of about 1 centimeter (0.4 in) by rows of plain twining. On the top fabric only one row of twining is visible, but the structure does seem similar to that of the first. In addition, it incorporates a feature of great interest: the oblique interlaced elements merge into vertical plied yarns of larger size. Either these larger warp yarns were unplied and the smaller strands then interlaced, or the smaller elements were

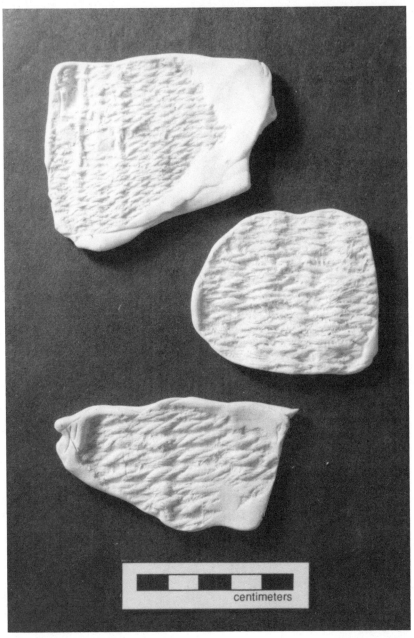

centimeters

Figure 30.
Examples of Wickliffe weft-faced textiles. The bottom example definitely is weft-faced plain twining. Most fabrics classified as "weft-faced" probably are twined, but many could be interlaced; because of the typical two-ply weft yarn, analysis is difficult.

twisted into larger yarns after being interlaced diagonally in the oblique section. It was not possible to be sure whether two strands or more than two were combined into each larger yarn.

In contrast to twined textiles, the other major categories lacked combinations of multiple structures. Of course, their numbers were far smaller than those of plain- and alternate-pair-twined fabrics, so that the absence of decorative elements in the weft-faced, knotted, and interlaced textiles could be due to small sample size.

The outstanding characteristic of weft-faced fabrics is their density. In Mississippian examples, wefts generally are packed so tightly together that it is difficult if not impossible to tell whether the textile structure is plain twining or plain interlacing. Adding to the confusion is the fact that both the twining twist and the final twist of the predominantly two-ply weft yarn are almost invariably in the **S** direction, making it difficult to separate individual weft yarns visually in order to analyze the structure. Only when some of the weft threads have been worn away or have slipped apart, and not always then, is there a chance to determine the fabric structure. For example, in the weft-faced textile at the bottom of Figure 30, the clustering of the weft rows strongly indicates a twined structure.

In two of the weft-faced textiles, it appeared that thin, single-ply yarns had been sewn through or under individual weft strands, approximately parallel to the warp. They could have been used to attach ornaments such as beads to the fabric surface or for some more utilitarian purpose.

The weft-faced fabrics do appear to have had at least some flexibility. For instance, an impression of one of them was found under an everted vessel rim, bent sharply back parallel to the warp.

All nine of the knotted textiles examined can be described as knotted netting (Figure 31)—mesh with knots spaced at intervals—although one of them is relatively dense. In two examples, the structure definitely could be identified as a square knot; for a third, the square knot designation was more tentative. One example might have incorporated crossed elements such as in the sheetbend or fishnet knots, two might have been constructed of overhand knots, and the remainder had knot structures that were completely unidentifiable.

The single example of non-weft-faced interlacing had a 3/3 twill structure and was constructed of flat rather than rounded elements, one of which was missing (Figure 32).

There were significant differences in textile attributes between structure groups. In Table 8, attributes are summarized for plain-twined, alternate-pair-twined, weft-faced, and knotted fabrics. The table also includes comparable data for the two most significant categories of decorated fabrics—those

Figure 31.
Examples of Wickliffe
knotted textiles, both with
square knots. (Drooker
1990c:Figure 10. Copyright
1990 The Kent State
University Press; used by
permission.)

with grouped-weft-row banding, and those combining plain twining and interlinked warps. The latter two groups are statistically redundant, because their members are included within either plain-twined or alternate-pair-twined textiles, depending on their basic background fabric structure. They are part of the table so that their attributes can be discussed in comparison with those of the larger, inclusive groups. For ease of comparison, Figure 33 presents mean attribute values in the form of bar charts.

Yarns

Almost all of the yarns analyzed were single- or double-ply, with final twist in the **S** direction. In size and in amount of processing, however, they exhibit considerable diversity, as can be seen in the previous and following photographs.

With a mean diameter of 1.53 millimeters, warp yarns averaged somewhat smaller than the 1.66-millimeter mean for weft yarns (Table 6). As well, warps covered a somewhat broader size range than wefts. Both had minima

Figure 32.
Example of Wickliffe 3/3 twill-interlaced basketry fabric. (Drooker 1990c:Figure 9. Copyright 1990 The Kent State University Press; used by permission.)

of 0.5 millimeters, but warps ranged up to 6 millimeters, or 1 millimeter larger than wefts. For both warps and wefts, over 80% of the yarns were no larger than 2 millimeters. Warp and weft diameter frequency distributions are graphed in Figure 34. The clustering of values at 1.0, 1.5, 2.0, 2.5, and 3.0 is due to the visual averaging process used in measuring the yarns.

Whereas 61% of the warps could be seen to consist of two plies, this was true for only 38% of the wefts, and the average warp ply and weft ply values reflect this (Table 6). Where spin or twist of the single-ply yarns that made up **S**-plied double-ply yarns could be discerned, it invariably was in the **Z** direction. Three textile impressions contained yarns that possibly consisted of two two-ply yarns re-plied together.

For only 27 sets of weft yarns could final twist angle be measured, not a large enough sample to draw any conclusions. Of the 629 warp yarns in which twist angle could be discerned, over 60% had an angle from approximately 25 to 45 degrees (Category 3 in Figure 11); this represents 24% of all warp yarns (Figure 34). Only 1% of all fabrics analyzed had warp yarns twisted at 45 degrees or more.

Table 8. Summary of Wickliffe fabric attributes by textile structure category

Textile structure	min.	mean	max	s.d.	no. cases
Plain twining, including all decorative variations (919 cases)					
Warp diameter, mm	0.50	1.52	5.00	0.73	907
Weft diameter, mm	0.50	1.52	4.00	0.63	903
Avg. yarn diameter, mm	0.50	1.52	4.00	0.63	895
Number of warp plies	1.00	1.71	2.00	0.46	909
Number of weft plies	1.00	1.29	2.00	0.46	909
Warp twist category	0.00	2.38	4.00	0.67	444
Weft twist category	0.00	1.08	3.00	1.36	6
Warp elements per cm	0.77	3.89	11.00	1.46	911
Weft elements per cm	0.60	2.44	9.00	1.16	794
Weft rows per cm	0.30	1.23	8.30	0.62	794
Fabric count	1.66	6.44	19.00	2.42	791
Warp density	0.96	5.23	10.50	1.53	901
Weft density	0.47	1.67	12.45	0.81	784
Total density	1.85	6.90	15.45	1.84	774
Fabric count category	1.00	1.81	4.00	0.58	791
Complexity Index No. 1	2.00	2.92	6.00	0.70	790
Complexity Index No. 2	3.00	4.43	7.50	0.78	784
Complexity Index No. 3	3.00	7.02	10.50	1.05	395
Alternate-pair twining, including all decorative variations (460 cases)					
Warp diameter, mm	0.50	1.37	4.00	0.64	446
Weft diameter, mm	0.50	1.69	4.00	0.66	458
Avg. yarn diameter, mm	0.55	1.53	4.00	1.61	444
Number of warp plies	1.00	1.55	2.00	0.50	451
Number of weft plies	1.00	1.50	2.00	0.50	458
Warp twist category	0.00	2.51	4.00	0.64	160
Weft twist category	2.50	2.50	2.50	—	1
Warp elements per cm	1.20	5.58	12.00	1.83	458
Weft elements per cm	0.80	3.94	21.00	2.41	442
Weft rows per cm	0.40	1.97	10.50	1.21	442
Fabric count	2.30	9.59	31.00	3.93	440
Warp density	2.50	6.75	13.60	1.71	444

Table 8. *Continued*

Textile structure	min.	mean	max	s.d.	no. cases
Weft density	0.60	2.91	10.50	1.44	441
Total density	3.60	9.61	20.40	2.13	425
Fabric count category	1.00	2.42	7.00	0.87	440
Complexity Index No. 1	2.00	3.45	8.00	0.88	440
Complexity Index No. 2	3.00	4.97	9.00	0.85	430
Complexity Index No. 3	3.50	7.34	10.50	1.04	152
Weft-faced (109 cases)					
Warp diameter, mm	1.34	2.95	5.00	0.83	25
Weft diameter, mm	1.00	2.61	4.00	0.67	105
Avg. yarn diameter, mm	1.42	2.83	4.00	0.66	25
Number of warp plies	1.00	1.31	2.00	0.47	29
Number of weft plies	1.00	1.86	2.00	0.35	106
Warp twist category	1.00	1.00	1.00	—	1
Weft twist category	0.00	2.12	3.00	0.85	13
Warp elements per cm	0.60	1.18	4.00	0.41	100
Weft elements per cm	3.40	6.74	16.00	1.89	97
Weft rows per cm	1.70	3.46	8.00	0.95	88
Fabric count	4.34	7.90	20.00	2.16	92
Warp density	0.90	3.74	10.00	2.06	24
Weft density	3.06	8.45	12.25	1.55	87
Total density	6.90	11.98	18.00	2.74	14
Fabric count category	1.00	2.11	5.00	0.48	92
Complexity Index No. 1	2.00	3.11	6.00	0.48	92
Complexity Index No. 2	3.50	4.67	7.50	0.72	27
Complexity Index No. 3	5.00	5.00	5.00	—	1
Knotting (9 cases)					
Avg. yarn diameter, mm	1.00	1.64	2.00	0.44	8
Number of yarn plies	2.00	2.00	2.00	0.00	8
Yarn twist category	2.00	2.83	3.00	0.41	6
Elements per cm	0.80	1.19	1.65	0.25	8
Fabric count	1.60	2.39	3.30	0.50	8
Element density	1.10	1.90	2.60	0.47	8
Total density	2.20	3.81	5.20	0.94	8
Fabric count category	1.00	1.00	1.00	0.00	8
Index No. 1	2.00	2.00	2.00	0.00	8

Table 8. *Continued*

Textile structure	min.	mean	max	s.d.	no. cases
Index No. 2	4.00	4.00	4.00	0.00	8
Index No. 3	6.00	6.83	7.00	0.41	6
Grouped-weft-row bands, both plain twined and alternate-pair twined (37 cases)					
Warp diameter, mm	0.70	1.18	2.30	0.28	37
Weft diameter, mm	0.80	1.30	4.00	0.64	37
Avg. yarn diameter, mm	0.85	1.24	2.65	0.40	37
Number of warp plies	1.00	1.81	2.00	0.40	37
Number of weft plies	1.00	1.49	2.00	0.51	37
Warp twist category	2.00	2.83	3.00	0.32	24
Warp elements per cm	1.70	4.84	8.00	1.39	37
Weft elements per cm	1.00	2.94	6.00	1.14	34
Weft rows per cm	0.50	1.47	3.00	0.57	34
Fabric count	2.70	7.75	11.00	2.14	34
Warp density	2.60	5.55	8.28	1.58	37
Weft density	0.78	1.79	3.75	0.74	34
Total density	3.38	7.34	9.98	1.72	34
Fabric count category	1.00	2.00	3.00	0.49	34
Complexity Index No. 1	3.00	3.94	5.00	0.55	34
Complexity Index No. 2	4.00	5.60	7.00	0.66	34
Complexity Index No. 3	6.50	8.65	10.00	0.73	24
Plain twining combined with interlinked warps (14 cases)					
Warp diameter, mm	0.50	0.89	1.60	0.35	14
Weft diameter, mm	0.50	0.89	1.50	0.32	14
Avg. yarn diameter, mm	0.50	0.89	1.50	0.30	14
Number of warp plies	1.00	1.57	2.00	0.51	14
Number of weft plies	1.00	1.21	2.00	0.43	14
Warp twist category	3.00	3.00	3.00	0.00	4
Warp elements per cm	4.00	5.93	11.00	1.88	14
Weft elements per cm	2.50	4.28	8.00	1.33	14
Weft rows per cm	1.25	2.18	4.00	0.63	14

Table 8. *Continued*

Textile structure	min.	mean	max	s.d.	no. cases
Fabric count	6.60	10.21	19.00	3.08	14
Warp density	3.50	4.92	8.00	1.40	14
Weft density	1.00	1.81	2.30	0.46	14
Total density	4.65	6.73	9.28	1.40	14
Fabric count category	2.00	2.57	4.00	0.65	14
Complexity Index No. 1	3.00	4.57	6.00	0.76	14
Complexity Index No. 2	5.00	5.96	7.00	0.63	14
Complexity Index No. 3	8.50	9.25	10.50	0.87	4

Yarn characteristics varied significantly among textile structure groups (Table 8). The upper left bar chart in Figure 33 illustrates yarn diameter differences among the major structural categories and the two most important decorative categories.

Warp and weft yarns in plain-twined fabrics average almost the same diameter. Yarns in alternate-pair twined textiles are similar on average to those in plain-twined textiles but tend to have larger wefts and smaller warps. Both warp and weft yarns of weft-faced fabrics are almost twice as large as those of the other two categories. Yarn diameters in knotted textiles fall slightly above plain- and alternate-pair-twined fabrics but well below the average for weft-faced fabrics. Weft-row banded textiles had yarn diameters averaging somewhat below those of undecorated twined fabrics (1.24 mm), while interlinked-warp textiles were constructed of significantly thinner yarns (mean = 0.89 mm).

Without exception, all knotted yarns were two-ply. In weft-faced fabrics, 83% of the wefts were two-ply, while 70% of the plain-twined warps but only 53% of the alternate-pair-twined warps could be discerned as two-ply. Whereas 50% of alternate-pair-twined wefts were double-ply, only 29% of plain-twined wefts could be seen to have two plies. Final yarn twist angle averaged highest for knotted yarns, lower but very similar for plain- and alternate-pair-twined warps on which twist could be discerned, and still lower for wefts in weft-faced fabrics.

Figure 35 (top) shows three sizes of well-twisted, well-processed two-ply yarns. Many of the previous figures include additional examples; for instance, the knotted fabrics in Figure 31 all were made from strong, well-twisted two-ply yarn. Visible long fibers within the component strands have been thoroughly shredded. Many of the very coarse plain-twined or

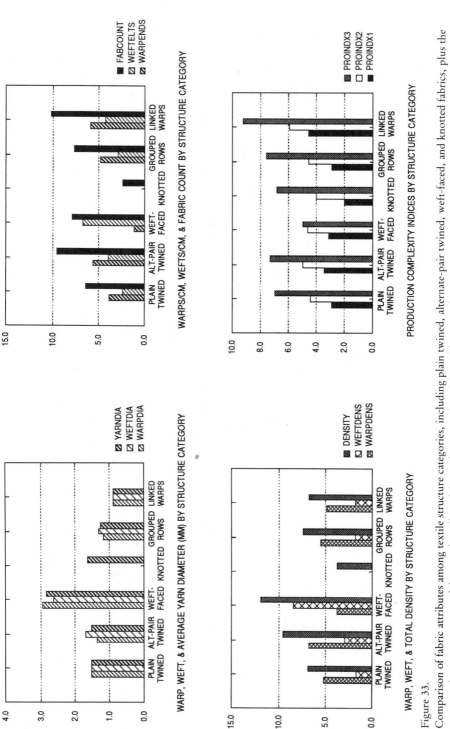

Figure 33.

Comparison of fabric attributes among textile structure categories, including plain twined, alternate-pair twined, weft-faced, and knotted fabrics, plus the two most important groups of decorated textiles: plain or alternate-pair twining with grouped-twining-row bands and plain twining plus transposed interlinked warps. Bar charts represent mean values of measured textile attributes and computed indices for yarn diameter, fabric scale, fabric density, and fabric complexity within each structure category. Note that knotting is a single-element textile structure and thus has no warp or weft per se.

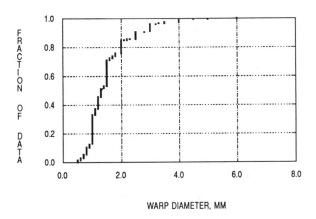

WARP DIAMETER, MM

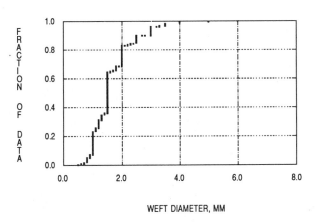

WEFT DIAMETER, MM

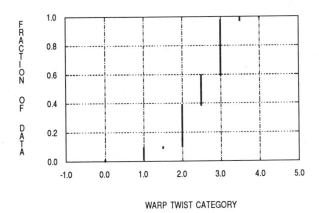

WARP TWIST CATEGORY

Figure 34.
Yarn diameter and final twist angle frequency distributions for Wickliffe textiles. Warp twist categories are as diagramed in Figure 11.

Figure 35.
Examples of well-processed and less well-processed yarns from Wickliffe: *top*, well-processed two-ply yarns; *center*, highly processed, soft yarns; *bottom*, less-processed, hard-fiber yarns.

alternate-pair-twined textiles were constructed of yarns similar to the largest-diameter ones in Figure 35, and they also are representative of weft yarns in coarse weft-faced fabrics (as in Figure 30). In other words, the yarns in these coarse fabrics were thick, but by no means poorly made.

Figure 35 (center) illustrates two types of yarns particularly typical of fine-to medium-scale alternate-pair twining at Wickliffe, both of which have the appearance of softness and pliability. When individual fibers in such yarns can be discerned, they always are very fine, implying that the yarns were highly processed. If these yarns were to be named descriptively, "fluffy" would be an appropriate designation for the first of the two. In alternate-pair-twined textiles it often occurs as weft in combination with much smaller warp yarns. The example shown here is comparatively coarse, but see Figure 23 for finer fabrics constructed with similar yarns.

At the bottom of Figure 35 are examples of less completely processed yarns, including yarns probably consisting of unprocessed fibers twisted together and a relatively thin two-ply yarn exhibiting almost no twist. Another relatively unprocessed yarn, consisting of twisted or braided bundles of unspun fibers, is shown at the bottom of Figure 36. Warps like this, which may have been braided as illustrated in Figure 2h, showed up on three sherds, always in combination with comparatively thin wefts.

The most unusual yarns encountered were thick and almost chenillelike in appearance (Figure 36, top left). It was not possible to determine exactly what was involved in this structure, but it may have been constructed by spirally wrapping a thin, two-ply yarn around a core yarn. A medium-diameter yarn, slightly to the right of the thick yarn, appears to be wrapped spirally with a thinner, single-ply yarn, but this may simply be a two-ply yarn that was twisted together using differently sized strands. The large yarn was found in two impressions of alternate-pair-twined textiles, combined in the warp with thinner, more orthodox yarns (see Figure 24 for the second example). Both sherds came from the north end of Mound D, and the impressions are not inconsistent with the possibility of a single source fabric. Probably these fancy yarns represent a large investment of time, and this may be the reason why no fabrics have been found with warps consisting entirely of this type of yarn.

Another less ambiguous example of a wrapped yarn serves as warp in a very different sort of fabric (Figure 36, top right). Here, a medium-diameter core yarn has been wrapped spirally with a thin, single-strand thread. The thin strand is difficult to see, but it seems to occur consistently on all of the warp yarns in this textile.

Five possible instances were found of yarns with final twist in the **Z** direction: one a single warp yarn in a plain-twined textile otherwise consist-

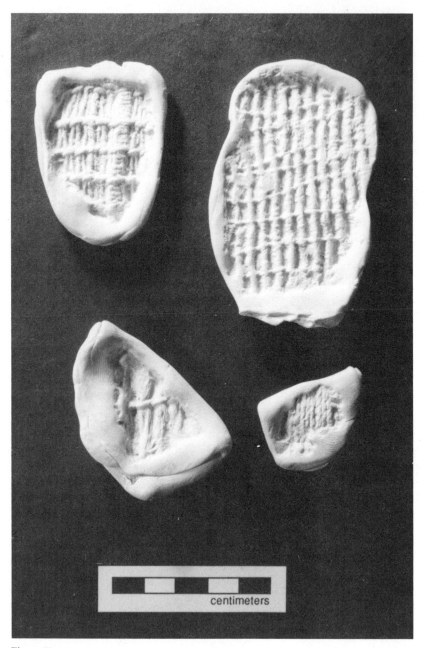

Figure 36.
Examples of unusual yarns from Wickliffe: *top,* wrapped yarns; *bottom left,* bundles of unspun fibers, possibly braided; *bottom right,* **Z**-twisted yarns.

ing of **S**-twisted yarns, and the others sets of parallel cords (Figure 36, bottom right). All but one of these four impressions were very faint, and no perpendicular yarns could be seen, so that it was impossible to tell whether they might rather be examples of **Z**-twisted weft-faced twining similar to that encountered on some edge structures, or even of cord-marking.

The flat elements woven together to make the twill-interlaced fabric (Figure 32) averaged 4 millimeters wide in one direction and 5 millimeters in the other, and were approximately 0.5 millimeter thick.

Fabric Count and Density

Fabric count and density are indicative of the manner in which yarns are combined into a given fabric. It will be remembered that fabric count measures numbers of yarns per square centimeter, while density in addition takes into account their diameters, indicating the amount of space in the fabric actually taken up by yarns. For instance, a warp density of 10 means that there are no empty spaces between warp yarns. A high fabric count can indicate either a very fine fabric with approximately equal numbers of warp and weft yarns per centimeter, or a warp-faced or weft-faced fabric.

As has been obvious from the photographs, fabric count and density vary widely among Wickliffe textiles, from fine, open plain-twined textiles with transposed, interlinked yarns (Figures 27 and 28), to fine, dense alternate-pair-twined cloth (Figure 23, top), to coarse, open knotted netting (Figure 31), to coarse, dense weft-faced fabrics (Figure 30).

Table 6 includes summary statistical information about warps per centimeter, wefts per centimeter, fabric count, warp density, weft density, and total density for all Wickliffe textiles analyzed. Distributions of these data are plotted in Figures 37 and 38.

Fabric count as a whole shows a rather regular distribution, slightly skewed from the normal (Figure 37). Some very fine textiles, with fabric counts greater than 15, do occur, but more than 80% of fabric counts are less than 10. (For comparison, the fabric count of burlap is 9.6.)

From Figure 37, it can be seen that warp and weft elements per centimeter do not show the same patterns of variation. Although they fall within similar ranges, with only a very few fabrics having more than 10 warp or weft elements per centimeter, on average there are more warps than wefts per centimeter (4.2 vs. 3.2). Weft values are skewed to lower numbers: more than 60% of cases fall below the mean. In comparison, warp values are more evenly distributed about the mean. Since the wefts are concentrated in twined pairs, the visual contrast between warp elements per centimeter and

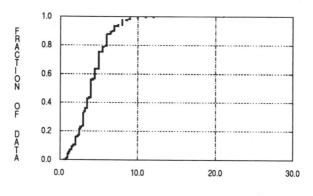

WARP ELEMENTS PER CENTIMETER

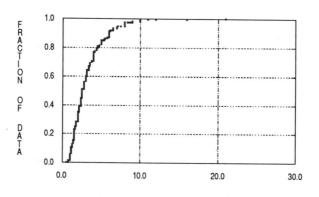

WEFT ELEMENTS PER CENTIMETER

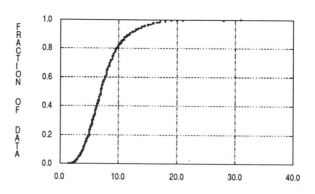

FABRIC COUNT (WARPS/CM + WEFTS/CM)

Figure 37.
Frequency distributions of fabric scale parameters for Wickliffe textiles.

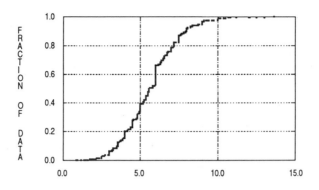

WARP DENSITY (WARP DIAMETER IN MM X ELEMENTS/CM)

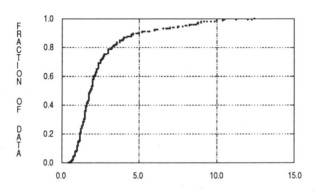

WEFT DENSITY (WEFT DIAMETER IN MM X WEFT ROWS/CM)

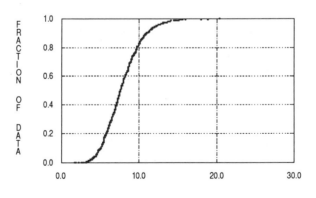

TOTAL DENSITY (WARP DENSITY + WEFT DENSITY)

Figure 38.
Frequency distributions of density parameters for Wickliffe textiles.

weft rows per centimeter is even greater than implied by average elements per centimeter.

When yarn diameter is taken into account, the contrast between warp and weft distributions is even greater. The mean warp density is more than twice the mean weft density (5.7 vs. 2.5), and weft distribution is significantly skewed toward the lower values (Figure 38). Total density, with a mean value of 7.9, is just slightly skewed to lower values. A total density value of 10 may be taken as a very rough indication of complete visual opacity; fewer than 20% of all fabrics fall into this category.

Just as differences between variation in warp and weft element count and density are obscured when fabric count and total density are considered as entities, differences among textile structure categories are submerged when average values for all fabrics are presented. In fact, fabric count and density characteristics varied significantly among fabric structure groups (Table 8, Figure 33).

In terms of elements per centimeter, it can be seen that alternate-pair-twined fabrics are much finer than plain-twined textiles, with both types of textiles containing more warp than weft elements per centimeter. Weft-faced fabrics have a high fabric count, approaching that of alternate-pair twining, but it is due almost entirely to a very high number of weft elements per centimeter. Knotted textiles have comparatively few yarns per centimeter.

For both plain- and alternate-pair-twined textiles, warp density is much greater than weft density. Of these two categories, plain twining is demonstrably less dense. In significant contrast are weft-faced fabrics. For them, relative values of warp and weft densities are reversed compared to the other two categories, and mean total density is far higher. Knotted textiles are relatively low in density.

Twined textiles with banded patterns formed by grouped weft rows do not differ greatly from plain- and alternate-pair-twined textiles as a whole, although they are indeed somewhat finer. Of these, 86% are plain twined, and average density is just slightly above that of all plain-twined textiles. However, their warp count, weft count, and fabric count are noticeably higher than the mean for all plain-twined textiles, because, on average, they contain *greater numbers* of *thinner* yarns than plain-twined textiles as a whole. The disparity is even greater for structurally decorated fabrics consisting of plain twining plus interlinked warps. Their density is very similar to that for all plain-twined fabrics (slightly closer weft rows, slightly more open warp spacing), but their average fabric count is more than one and a half times that of all plain-twined textiles. These fabrics are noteworthy not only by being decorated but also by being significantly finer than their undecorated cousins.

Textile Production Complexity Indices

The Modified Textile Production Complexity Indexes employed in this study consist of the sums of index numbers indicative of steps added to the production process of a given textile. The more components, the more refined can be the differentiation among textiles. However, it was not possible to measure all index components on all fabrics, so several different modifications of indexes were computed. Modification No. 1 utilized fabric count (scaled to an ordinal number) plus number of textile structures present, No. 2 added the average yarn ply number, and No. 3 added the amount of warp yarn twist (by category). These indexes could be computed for 1,323, 1,242, and 549 textiles, respectively.

The frequency distributions plotted in Figure 39 are indicative of the increasingly refined differentiation provided by successive versions of the index. Nevertheless, the general picture remains the same: a large group of textiles of moderate complexity, a small group of somewhat lesser complexity, and a slightly smaller group of greater and more diverse complexity at the top end of the scale. The mean index values for Wickliffe textiles of 3.1, 4.6, and 7.1, respectively (Table 6), signify that they are slightly more complex on average than modern burlap, the index values for which are 3, 4, and 6 (Table 2).

Among major structure categories, these indexes do indicate some differences. The bar charts (Figure 33) include all three of the modified indexes, plus the scaled value for fabric count alone (see Table 8 for statistical summaries by textile structure category). Differences among categories are in the same direction for all four indicators but are exaggerated as additional components are added to the indexes.

The textiles involving the least production complexity are the knotted fabrics. However, when warp twist is taken into account, with Index No. 3, they approach the complexity of plain-twined fabrics. This indicates that, compared with the other textile categories, the effort that went into yarn construction averaged higher, while the effort that went into fabric construction averaged lower. Weft-faced textiles are very slightly higher in complexity than plain-twined textiles, except with Index No. 3. Actually that value is not meaningful, as it is based on only one measurement of warp twist. If weft twist could have been included, the complexity index profile for weft-faced fabrics would have been very similar to that for plain twining. Alternate-pair fabrics, primarily because of their greater fineness, average slightly higher in complexity index values than the other three primary structure categories. As would be expected from their relative fineness and from the fact that they combine more than one fabric structure, the struc-

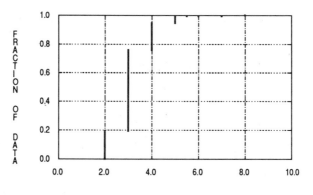

MODIFIED TEXTILE PRODUCTION COMPLEXITY INDEX NO. 1

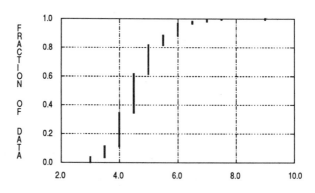

MODIFIED TEXTILE PRODUCTION COMPLEXITY INDEX NO. 2

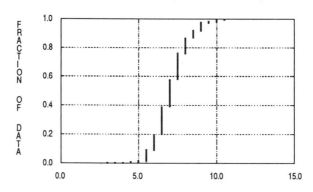

MODIFIED TEXTILE PRODUCTION COMPLEXITY INDEX NO. 3

Figure 39.
Frequency distributions of Modified Textile Production Complexity Indices for Wickliffe textiles.

turally decorated textiles are distinguished by notably higher complexity index values.

What this means in terms of textile production is that the decorated textiles absorb more time and more mental effort than Wickliffe fabrics as a whole. In contrast, the basic single-structure categories of plain-twined, alternate-pair-twined, weft-faced, and knotted textiles do not differ very much from each other in average production complexity.

Inter- and Intragroup Comparisons

From the above comparisons of individual attributes among textile structure groups, it should be manifest that real physical differences do exist among them but that these are fully apparent only when several different attributes are taken into account. As can be seen when Figure 33 is viewed as an entity, it is the combination of variation in warp diameter, weft diameter, warps per centimeter, wefts per centimeter, fabric count, and density, together with a priori differences in textile structure, that distinguish Wickliffe plain twining, alternate-pair twining, weft-faced fabrics, knotting, and decorated textiles from each other, not differences in only one or two variables.

Because there is a wide range of these attributes within the major structure groups as well as between them, and because textile function could well be correlated to finer-tuned variations of these attributes than occurred between groups, a search was made for clusters of attributes within structure categories. To divide the plain-twined, alternate-pair-twined, and weft-faced textiles into subgroups, the CLUSTER module of the SYSTAT program (Wilkinson 1987) was utilized, employing the k-means procedure, a nonhierarchical methodology that splits sets into groups by maximizing between-cluster versus within-cluster variation. Only a preliminary analysis was carried out, dividing textiles of each major structure into no more than five groups. Nevertheless, it was helpful in objectively sorting textiles on the basis of some half-dozen attributes, including number of structures, warp and weft diameter, warp and weft ply, and warp and weft elements per centimeter (Drooker 1989b:206–216).

Fabric scale (fabric count together with yarn size) dominated as the distinguishing factor among cluster groups. Examples representative of plain-twined fabrics in group 1 (coarsest), group 3, and group 4 can be seen, respectively, in Figure 22 bottom (2 examples), top right (2), and top left (1), while the finest textile in Figure 27 is representative of group 5, which contains the smallest-scale fabrics. For alternate-pair-twined textiles, representative examples of groups 1 (coarsest) through 5 (finest) can be seen in

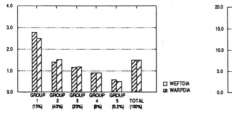

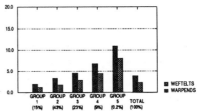

WARP & WEFT DIAMETER (MM) BY PLAIN TWINED CLUSTER GROUP

WARPS/CM & WEFTS/CM BY PLAIN-TWINED CLUSTER GROUP

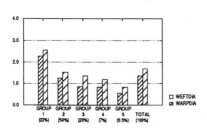

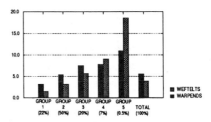

WARP & WEFT DIAMETER (MM) BY ALTERNATE-PAIR TWINED CLUSTER GROUP

WARPS/CM & WEFTS/CM BY ALTERNATE-PAIR TWINED CLUSTER GROUP

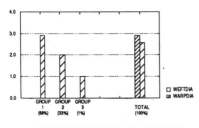

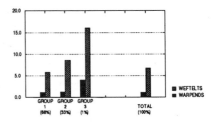

WARP & WEFT DIAMETER (MM) BY WEFT-FACED CLUSTER GROUP

WARPS/CM & WEFTS/CM BY WEFT-FACED CLUSTER GROUP

Figure 40.
Comparisons of yarn diameters and elements per centimeter for cluster groups within major
structure categories. For each graph, the bars at the far left represent mean attributes for the
coarsest cluster group (no. 1) within the structure category, and the bars at the far right
represent mean attributes for the structure category as a whole. Percentages indicate the size of
each cluster group relative to the entire structure category. (Warp diameter was not used as an
attribute in determining weft-faced cluster groups because so few examples could be
measured.)

Figure 23 bottom right, bottom left, middle right, top right, and top left, respectively. There were three cluster groups within the weft-faced fabric structure category. Groups 1 and 2 are exemplified by the two textiles in Figure 30, while group 3 (finest) effectively includes but one fabric, which is illustrated at the bottom of Figure 43, below.

Graphic comparisons of average warp and weft diameters and average numbers of warp and weft elements per centimeter among cluster groups and for the structure group as a whole are shown in Figure 40. It should be kept in mind that for all three structure groups, the cluster groups containing the finest fabrics were much smaller in number than those with coarser fabrics. Their percentage representation is indicated on each bar chart. The plain-twined cluster groups differed among themselves primarily in fabric scale: yarn diameters decreased and numbers of yarn elements per centimeter increased consistently from group 1 to group 5. Alternate-pair-twined textiles decreased in scale in the same way, but in addition, there was a tendency for them to become progressively more weft-faced from group 1 to group 5; that is, the ratio of weft elements to warp elements per centimeter increased as the fabrics became finer. This is the opposite relationship to what would hold if weft-faced fabrics were all taken as plain twined and combined with them into a single group: the ratio of weft count to warp count would increase at the coarser end of the scale. In other words, there may well be an extreme dichotomy between fine weft-faced alternate-pair-twined textiles and coarse weft-faced plain-twined textiles. For weft-faced textiles, warp spacing remained the same for groups 1 and 2, but group 2 weft yarns were smaller in diameter and more numerous per centimeter than those of group 1.

Edges and Joins

Comparatively few complete edges were found: eight starting edges, two or three side edges, and three terminal edges.

All of the clearly identifiable starting edges were structured as in Figure 41a. Figure 42 illustrates the clearest example of this, which unfortunately occurred on a very small sherd. It is typical in having two twined rows close together just below the warp loops.

Six of the eight starting edges were found in pairs, joined together by yarns laced spirally through the two sets of warp loops (Figure 41b). An example of two textiles with warp loops joined together is given in Figure 42. Here, the joined fabrics, one of which has been torn, are virtually identical. In each one, there are two close rows of plain twining immediately adjacent

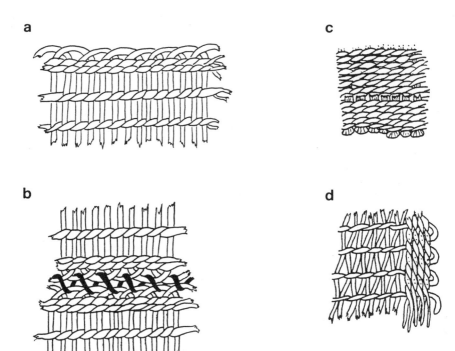

Figure 41.
Diagrams of edge structures from Wickliffe textiles: *a,* typical starting edge structure; *b,* two starting edges laced together; *c,* terminal edge structure in which warp ends are turned back toward the fabric and secured with several rows of closely spaced twining; *d,* side edge structure in which weft (twining) ends are turned back toward the fabric and secured with several rows of closely spaced twining parallel to the warp. (Drooker 1990c:Figure 19. Copyright 1990 The Kent State University Press; used by permission.)

to the warp loops. The lacing or overcasting between warp loops of the two fabrics can be seen as diagonal lines slanting down to the right.

The three examples of joined starting edges are the only sewn-together textiles that were identified on Wickliffe pottery impressions. All three occurred between two very similar fabrics, conceivably between two sets of warp loops in a bag constructed as a tube (Figure 13b).

Unlike the starting edges, the few examples of terminal and side edges were of diverse types.

Because an ordinary twined row can provide a secure finish for a fringed terminal edge, it is quite possible that some impressions of edges such as this were overlooked. Few of the sherds were very large, and it was difficult to know whether a given twining row was the "last" one on a fabric and whether warps that appeared to be hanging free from the edge of a textile

Figure 42.
Examples of starting edge *(top)* and join *(bottom)* on Wickliffe textiles. An overcast stitch (slanting down from left to right) was used to sew together the two plain-twined fabrics, with the sewing yarn alternating between starting-edge warp loops of each fabric. One of the two fabrics has been extensively damaged. See Figures 41a and 41b for diagrams.

were intended as fringe or were simply the result of worn and unraveled twining rows. Figure 43 (top) illustrates one of the few textiles that could be identified with any certainty at all as having a fringed terminal edge held in place by an ordinary twining row. The bottom of Figure 45, below, shows another example that was *not* classified as an edge because it appeared more likely to be a damaged fabric: two weft yarns appear to cross through the "fringe" and continue as twining elements in a torn bit of the same fabric at the left side of the cast.

One faint impression of a possible knotted terminal edge was found. The fabric appeared to consist of a weftwise row of transposed, interlinked warps at the edge of an alternate-pair-twined textile, directly "below" which the warp ends were knotted in pairs. Because of the extreme faintness of the impression, though, this is only a tentative description.

A more complex terminal edge is illustrated in Figure 43 (bottom). This edge overlies a second, separate fabric, a medium-scale alternate-pair-twined textile at a slight angle to the one on top of it. The sherd as a whole included quite a large section of the underlying fabric, but this portion is all that was visible of the top one. As diagramed in Figure 41c, the yarns perpendicular

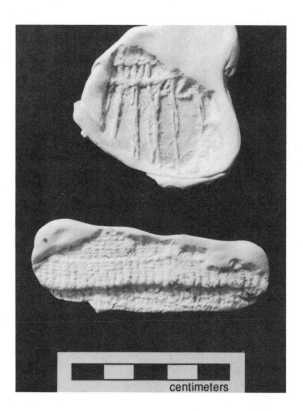

Figure 43.
Examples of terminal edges
on Wickliffe textiles: *top,*
simple fringe, secured by
final row of twining; *bottom,*
weft-faced edge with warp
ends turned back into fabric
and secured by last few rows
of twining. See Figure 41c for
diagram.

centimeters

to the closely spaced twining rows in the top fabric have been folded back into the last six rows of twining; that is, these few rows of twining occurred around doubled-over yarns. This formed a visible ridge in the fabric: the textile is thicker close to its edge than farther away from it. Probably this is a terminal edge, but it could conceivably represent a side edge, in which case the twining would be warpwise.

In Figure 44 is illustrated an edge that definitely is perpendicular to the alternate-pair-twined rows of its fabric yet appears to be bordered by four rows of closely spaced twining in the warpwise direction. On the outside edge of the closely spaced vertical elements can be seen "loops" where the weft yarns turn 180 degrees and reenter the fabric. These weft yarns do not, however, become the next row of weft twining but are cut off. This most likely was a side edge, in which the ends of the twining wefts were inserted back into the textile for about ½ centimeter, then secured by four pairs of warpwise yarns twining around them. It is similar to the "terminal edge" described above, except that in that edge, the yarns appeared to be doubled back into the same place from which they emerged, which is not the case here.

Figure 44.
Examples of side edges on Wickliffe textiles: *left*, side edge bordered by four rows of close-spaced warp twining (see Figure 41d for diagram); *right*, twisted edge on fine alternate-pair-twined fabric overlaying a very coarse alternate-pair-twined fabric.

The construction sequence for the side edge would be as follows. Twine a weft row to the edge of the fabric. Twine the four pairs of close-spaced warps vertically around the two weft yarns. Turn the weft yarns so that they are parallel to and below the just-completed row of weft twining. Twine the four pairs of close-spaced warps around the weft yarns in this position. Proceed to the next weft twining row. It would be most logical to carry out the warp twining after all of the weft twining rows had been completed.

Of the three examples classified as side edges, one may well be simply a torn, unraveled edge (Drooker 1989b:Figure 52b). One of the pairs of twining wefts, about one-third of the way up from the bottom of the cast, appears to be knotted, possibly a remnant of a line of knots that once secured all of the weft rows. However, the impression is unclear, so it is impossible to be certain about this.

The third side edge (Figure 44) also occurs on a fairly fine alternate-pair-twined textile overlying a second fabric, a very coarse example of alternate-pair twining. It seems to be a small-scale cousin to the types of terminal edge finish illustrated in Figures 15a, 15c, and 16b. Pairs of yarns from individual weft twining rows appear to extend, still twisting around each other, for a short distance beyond the last warp yarn, then to turn 90 degrees and enter into a twisted (not braided) selvage parallel to the warp direction.

Twelve additional possible edges were identified, most consisting of several very closely twined rows just at the broken edge of a sherd. Two, possibly four, of them included **Z**-twisted twining rows, either exclusively or along with **S**-twisted rows. These could represent braided three-strand twining (Figure 10c) rather than **Z**-twisted two-strand twining. The notion that three or more close-twined rows on an otherwise open twined fabric probably are indicative of a starting edge, and that such an edge might contain **Z**-twined rows, came primarily from the Kimmswick texile impressions I examined prior to analyzing those from Wickliffe (Figure 50, below). However, I did not find any clear-cut examples of starting edges at Wickliffe that were bordered by more than two close-twined rows. Furthermore, I did find a number of instances of several close-twined rows embedded within a textile, either as part of a grouped-weft-row sequence (Figure 24) or as a separator between two fabric sections of differing construction (Figure 26). The latter example included some **Z**-twisted rows as well. In the absence of additional corroborating evidence, no conclusion can be made as to whether or not these twelve "possibles" might have been edges.

No large starting-edge loops such as those that enclosed drawstrings on the two garments from the Tennessee rock-shelter (Figure 15d) were found, nor were any woven-on ties, such as were incorporated into the corners of at least one garment from Spiro. Neither were any edges discovered with the appearance of folded fabric, which might have been interpreted as bag side edges.

Fabric Condition

Few of the Wickliffe textiles appeared to be in pristine condition. For instance, yarns often seemed to be abraded or somewhat damaged without actually having been ripped apart. If a textile was torn or had missing yarns, it was designated as "worn." At the extreme end of this designation, making up 1% of the total, were impressions that seemed to consist entirely of masses of jumbled, unraveling yarns, with no recognizable fabric structure.

In all, 21% of Wickliffe textile impressions consisted of "worn" fabrics. Some examples have been included in the photographs of textiles, for instance, in Figure 24 and Figure 46, below.

No correlation was found between fabric condition and fabric scale; that is, fine fabrics were no more or less worn than coarse textiles constructed of more massive yarns. However, fabric condition did show a statistically significant correlation with fabric structure (Drooker 1989b:Table 17, for artifacts excavated through 1987). Of twined textiles, 19% of single-structure plain twining and 23% of single-structure alternate-pair twining were defined as "worn," while 36% of textiles combining two or more structures exhibited this quality. Only 8% of weft-faced fabrics were "worn."

No instances of repaired fabrics were found.

RELEVANT ATTRIBUTES OF WICKLIFFE TEXTILE-IMPRESSED POTTERY

To determine the original function(s) of textiles pressed into wet clay by pottery makers at Wickliffe, not only fabric attributes but also characteristics of the fabric-impressed vessels themselves must be taken into account. For example, vessel size and shape can be helpful in estimating the dimensions of impressed textiles, and the positions of textiles relative to vessel form may give clues as to how fabrics were used in the pottery-making process and whether their impressions on the vessel were primarily decorative or functional.

Vessel Form

Estimations of Wickliffe "saltpan" sizes and shapes were discussed in Chapter 3. Probably they averaged on the order of 40–80 centimeters in (16–31 in) diameter. For a shallow form with gradually sloping sides (Figure 3c) such as may be representative of Wickliffe pans, the diameter would not be much shorter than the distance along the vessel wall from rim to rim (less than 5% difference).

Position of Textile Impressions on Vessels

Most textile impressions were on vessel exteriors. Although 12% of rims had wide smoothed edges, in the large majority of rim sherds, fabric impressions were continuous almost to the lip.

Orientation of fabric relative to rim was recorded for 180 sherds, and results are summarized in Figure 45. As would be expected if vessels were

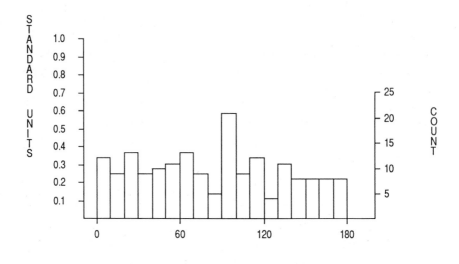

ANGLE OF WEFT ROWS TO RIM EDGE, DEGREES

Figure 45.
Orientation of textiles relative to "saltpan" rims (angle of twined rows to rim, counterclockwise from 0 to 179 degrees).

formed on top of a rectangular fabric laid in a mold, these angles were rather uniformly distributed. The primary exception was the 90-degree orientation, which occurred 11.7% of the time rather than the 5.6% expected for a completely uniform distribution. The somewhat higher prevalence of weft rows perpendicular to the rim may be due to a tendency on my part to estimate the 90-degree angle visually rather than measuring it with a protractor, or it may be an actual phenomenon, related to "saltpan" manufacturing methods. Its significance will be considered in Chapter 6.

On 141 sherds, or 9.0% of the total, two overlaid or joined fabrics could be seen (Figure 46). For 125 of them, the top fabric completely covered the bottom one. On 15 sherds, all with complete overlays, these textiles were oriented so as to be almost coinciding. Their warp and weft rows were aligned, and the characteristics of top and bottom fabric were so similar that they might well represent a bag or a folded piece of the same fabric. In 30 cases (22 of which were complete overlays), fabrics lay at a slight angle to each other, and may or may not have been similar in scale, while in 39 cases (35 of which were complete overlays), they were oriented at a significant angle. The remainder of complete overlays could not be interpreted with certainty.

Since complete overlays could be identified only when the top fabric was relatively open, many cases may have been overlooked. For instance, some

Figure 46.
Examples of overlaid fabrics impressed on pottery at Wickliffe.

textiles were identified that appeared to lie in ridges (Drooker 1989b:Figure 55c). Such a configuration certainly could have been caused by an underlying, very coarse fabric, but there is no way to tell for sure.

In contrast with the fairly high percentages of doubled fabrics found impressed on vessel exteriors, relatively few examples were discovered of two fabrics coexisting on the surface of a vessel, either overlapped or joined. Several of those with finished, rather than torn, edges have been illustrated above (Figures 43 and 44). A more ragged example is included in Figure 46. A total of 15 examples, including 3 joins and 12 overlaps, were found. Two-thirds of the overlapped fabrics were oriented at an oblique angle to each other. Of the 12 overlays where two fabrics overlapped and the edge of one showed, 8 of the overlapping fabrics (67%) were alternate-pair-twined textiles, and 4 (33%) were plain-twined—the reverse proportion of the occurrence of these fabric structures in all Wickliffe impressed textiles. None were weft-faced.

Examples of fabric designs or edges oriented so as to coordinate with vessel form were postulated as possible indicators of a decorative intent on the part of the maker. For instance, in pre-Mississippian cord-marked vessels, markings often were perpendicular to or otherwise related to the rim of the pot on which they occurred. However, no such relationships could be determined for Wickliffe "saltpan" vessels. Except for a few examples of grouped-weft-row banding, no fabrics containing more than one structure occurred on rim sherds, nor were any incontrovertible examples of fabric edges found on rim sherds.

Correlations between Vessel and Textile Characteristics

Ordinary, thick Kimmswick Fabric Impressed sherds from Wickliffe might be marked by fabrics of any scale, from the finest to the coarsest. However, a more restricted set of fabric characteristics occurred on the 10 thin (0.3–0.5-cm thick) textile-impressed sherds that were found. Except for one impression consisting of parallel yarns, all of the impressed fabrics were plain twined; one also incorporated interlinked warps. Eight of them were relatively fine (cluster group 3 or 4), and six were made of well-twisted two-ply yarns (Drooker 1989b:Table 18), lending a distinctive textured pattern to the sherds. One of these is illustrated in Figure 22, top left.

The two fabrics on Bell Plain interiors both were of relatively fine alternate-pair twining, falling into cluster groups 3 and 4.

Although an attempt was made to find statistical correlations between vessel diameter and textile characteristics—warp diameter, weft diameter, warp count, weft count, fabric count, warp density, weft density, and Modified Textile Production Complexity Index No. 1—none were discovered. Likewise, no correlations could be found between rim form and impressed fabric characteristics.

SPATIAL AND TEMPORAL VARIATION OF WICKLIFFE TEXTILES AND POTTERY

The spatial distribution of artifacts available for this study was rather lopsided. As can be computed from Table 5, the majority of textile impressions analyzed (52%) come from sherds excavated in and around Mound D, with no more than 19% from any other single location. Sherds from domestic locations represent only a very small fraction of the total, most of which was recovered from mound fill. Since dirt for building mounds would have been transported from elsewhere, it is unlikely that more than a small minority of the sherds were excavated from their original point of deposition. For these reasons, the site was treated as a single spatial unit in this study.

A similar problem exists with regard to temporal variation. Only a small percentage of the sherds analyzed were excavated from other than Late Wickliffe or unknown/disturbed proveniences (Table 9). However, by combining time categories, it is possible to obtain large enough samples for at least a tentative comparison between earlier and later Wickliffe fabrics and textile-impressed pottery. For this purpose, artifacts from Early, Early-Middle, and Middle Wickliffe contexts were designated "Early," and those from Middle-Late and Late Wickliffe were designated "Late."

The most striking difference in textiles of the two periods is the fact that no complex fabrics—that is, textiles combining two or more structures—have been excavated from "Early" contexts (Table 10, Figure 47). Also strik-

Table 9. Numbers of textiles analyzed per time period

Time Period	Textile count	Percentage
Early Wickliffe	45	2.9
Early-Middle Wickliffe	11	0.7
Middle Wickliffe	17	1.1
Middle-Late Wickliffe	8	0.5
Late Wickliffe	997	63.3
Unknown or disturbed	496	31.5
Total	1,574	100.0

Table 10. Frequency of occurrence of different textile structures in Early Wickliffe and Late Wickliffe contexts

Textile structure	"Early"		"Late"	
	Number	Percentage	Number	Percentage
Plain twining alone	38	52	521	52
Alternate-pair twining alone	14	19	308	31
Weft-faced	11	15	71	7
Knotted	2	3	5	<1
Decorated (combinations of structures)	0	0	61	6
Structure unknown	8	11	39	4
Total	73	100	1,005	100

ing is the 50% decrease in representation of weft-faced fabrics, from 15% to 7%, and the corresponding rise in representation of alternate-pair fabrics.

Textile attributes did differ between the two time periods. For example, mean yarn diameters were larger and densities were somewhat higher for the earlier fabrics (warp = 1.87 mm and weft = 1.83 mm, vs. warp = 1.52 mm and weft = 1.66 mm; total density = 8.30 vs. 8.0), possibly due to the higher incidence of weft-faced textiles. However, detailed comparisons must wait until a larger sample of "Early" textiles is available.

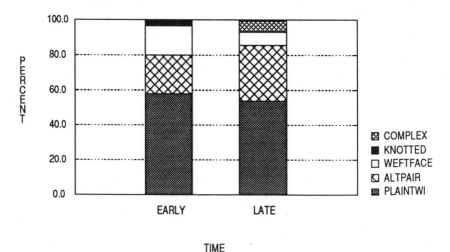

Figure 47.
Comparison of fabric structure variation in "Early" and "Late" Wickliffe contexts (see Table 10). Complex fabrics include all those combining two or more structures.

No textile-impressed pottery with wide smoothed rims came from "Early" Wickliffe contexts. This is consistent with Williams's findings at Crosno, Missouri, where that rim form was associated with later strata (1954:220). Eight of the ten thin-wall sherds were "Late" Wickliffe, and the other two were of unknown date.

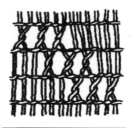

CHAPTER 6

TEXTILE PRODUCTION
AND USE AT WICKLIFFE

From the attribute data collected from Wickliffe impressed textiles, it has been possible to describe statistically a fairly broad range of presumably utilitarian fabrics that were made and used in this Mississippian village. Fabric description, however, was only an intermediate step en route to a broader objective: description of the functions for which Wickliffe impressed fabrics originally were made, the technology involved in their production, and the place of textiles in the Wickliffe socioeconomic structure. These problems are discussed below, in the form of a series of questions, hypotheses, and responses based on the data at hand.

ORIGINAL FUNCTIONS OF WICKLIFFE TEXTILES
IMPRESSED ON POTTERY

My working hypothesis in studying the textiles impressed into "saltpans" at Wickliffe was that they originally were constructed for purposes other than to serve as aids to pottery-making: specifically, that they consisted of relatively large pieces of cloth that originally functioned as skirts, mantles, and/or blankets. In testing this idea, three first-order questions were addressed:

1. Were the textiles impressed on ceramics at Wickliffe constructed specifically for a specialized purpose(s) in the pottery manufacturing process?

2. Did textile impressions on pottery at Wickliffe serve any purpose related to vessel use or to visual enhancement of the "saltpans"?

3. If not intended exclusively for pottery manufacture, then for what function or functions were Wickliffe impressed textiles originally constructed?

Below, these questions are addressed in turn. The first two relate to textiles vis-à-vis pottery at Wickliffe, and the last to textiles per se.

Textiles in the Manufacturing and Use of Pottery at Wickliffe

If textiles impressed onto pottery vessels at Wickliffe had been manufactured specifically to function in the pottery-making process, positive answers would be expected to the following questions.

Was the level of time and labor invested in them no greater than that invested in other aspects of ceramic vessel manufacture? In fact, even Wickliffe fabrics of relatively moderate scale and low complexity, comparable to the garment from the Tennessee rock-shelter (Figure 20), represent a much higher investment in time and labor than do the vessels on which they are impressed (see the subsection " 'Saltpan' Production" in Chapter 2, and the section "Labor Investment and Specialization in Textile Production," below). Hands-on time in textile construction is a matter of weeks, whereas for molded ceramic vessel construction it is a matter of hours. In both cases, of course, elapsed time to completion considerably exceeds actual working time.

Were the fabrics standardized? Were they simple? The fabrics were not standardized, varying quite widely in textile structure, yarn size, fabric count, and density within the sample (Figure 33). They also varied widely in complexity. Although the overwhelming majority consisted of single rather than multiple textile structures, many of the fabrics were comparatively fine, with high numbers of warps and/or wefts per centimeter. In addition, many of the yarns were relatively highly processed, adding to the time and skill invested in the textiles.

Were the textiles consistently sturdy, implying a requirement of strength? Did fabric strength correlate with vessel size in any way? Many of the Wickliffe textiles were indeed sturdy, incorporating relatively large-diameter, plied yarns into their firmly twined structures. About three-quarters of them had fabric counts equal to or coarser than burlap. However, a significant number were relatively fine, constructed of delicate yarns. Moreover, a good 21% of the fabrics were damaged to the extent of having torn or missing threads, or even gaping holes or jumbled masses of separate yarns. Such well-worn textiles would not be as strong as undamaged ones. No significant correlation was found between vessel diameter and yarn size or fabric count or density.

Were the textiles consistently flexible? Did flexibility correlate with vessel shape in any way? Although the observed diversity in textile structure and scale would lead to significant differences in flexibility among Wickliffe textiles impressed on pottery, even the largest-scale weft-faced fabric was flexible enough to bend under an excurvate rim.

The entire range of "saltpan" shapes at Wickliffe is unknown. However, the gradually sloping, rounded shape indicated by sherds like that in Figure 7b could easily be enveloped by a textile of no great flexibility. Usage of weft-faced fabrics apparently did decline with time, and their lesser flexibility compared with other textiles may have been a factor in this.

The two fabrics impressed on Bell Plain interiors were both quite fine and thus quite flexible, as were most of the textiles on sherds that were 3–5 millimeters thick. In fact, many of the coarser textiles made at Wickliffe actually would have been thicker than those thin ceramics and might have punched right through the vessel walls if used to line molds in which they were made.

Were the fabrics consistent in density, such that, if wrapped around wet clay vessels, each would afford a similar amount of protection against too-rapid drying? The textiles encompassed a wide range of both density and yarn characteristics. However, many of the very open fabrics were overlaid one on top of another. This would enhance their ability to moderate the drying process.

Were cloth structures and materials consistent with easy removal from the clay surface and with reuse? Most of the fabrics probably could have been removed fairly easily from dry or partially dry ceramic surfaces. In general, textiles did not seem particularly fuzzy, and no impressions of fur or feather fabrics were found. However, some of the fine fabrics did have yarns that might tend to cling to wet clay (e.g., Figure 23, upper right), as would the damaged textiles with torn yarn strands.

Depth of indentation varied greatly, but many of the knotted and coarse twined textiles were very deeply impressed into the clay surface, so deeply that it was difficult to obtain complete casts from their impressions. Without experimentation with regard to ceramic shrinkage during the drying process, it is impossible to tell how easy it would have been to remove textiles under those circumstances, but the coarse knotted textiles in particular would seem to have been less than ideal for easy removal.

Were the textiles consistently at least as large as the outside surface of the

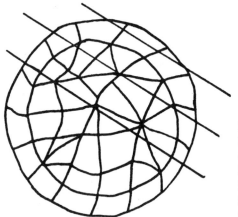

Figure 48.
Position of overlap edge relative to number of sherds containing impressions of edge. For fabric overlap at center of vessel, $n = 10$ (23%); for overlap near edge of vessel, $n = 3$ (7%); for overlap between these positions, $n = 8$ (18%).

vessel on which they were impressed? Most textiles apparently were large enough to cover the entire surface of a "saltpan" vessel. Only 15 examples of two fabrics coexisting on the surface of a vessel were found (3 joins and 12 overlaps). They represent less than 1% of the sherds analyzed. A larger percentage would be expected if vessels consistently were impressed by more than one textile, each narrower than the vessel surface diameter.

For perspective, Figure 48 illustrates possible patterns of occurrence of fabric edges on a vessel broken into 44 pieces. If two fabrics were overlaid halfway across the vessel, the overlap would be visible on 23% of the sherds. For an overlap position near the vessel edge, 7% of the sherds would be marked, and for a position midway between the two, 18% of the sherds would show the overlap. Vessels broken into greater numbers of smaller sherds still should show similar percentages. Of course, breakage might tend to occur along prominent fabric edges rather than across them. Nevertheless, from the small number of fabric edges actually observed, it does seem that the majority of fabric-impressed "saltpan" vessels probably were completely encompassed by a single textile, even if two or more textiles were overlaid in a double layer on the surface.

In 8% of the sherds, two layers of fabrics could be recognized, even though the edge of the top fabric was not visible. Most of the recognizable overlapping with no textile edges present was of two fairly open fabrics. If textiles functioned primarily either to separate vessels from their molds or to slow down the drying process, large structural holes in them would be undesirable, and two layers of nondense fabric might serve the purpose better than one. However, much more overlapping certainly could have occurred than was discernible in the pottery impressions, in cases where the top fabric was too dense to see through.

Did cloth orientation give any clues to manufacturing techniques? Orientation of fabric structures relative to vessel rims did show a greater-than-expected percentage of twining rows perpendicular to the rim (Figure 45). If this discrepancy is indeed real, there are several possible explanations. Some vessels might have been wrapped around their circumference with a long piece of fabric, carefully oriented so that warp yarns were parallel to the rim, or two pieces of fabric with widths about half the vessel diameter might have been laid in the mold at 90 degrees to each other. These scenarios are unlikely because so few impressions of textile edges have been found.

Alternatively, if a large piece of fabric was grasped at the side edges and tugged to straighten it in the mold before clay was pressed down to form the vessel, weft rows might show up as perpendicular to the rim over a wider area than if the fabric had been under no tension. Lifting or suspending a wet vessel by means of the ends of a rectangular fabric is less likely to result in such a pattern, because the fabric markings would have been made while the vessel still was in the mold, prior to lifting.

From the above information, it seems highly unlikely that textiles impressed on "saltpans" at Wickliffe were made specifically to be used in pottery manufacturing. They were not standardized, and many of them represented a large investment of time. The fabrics, however, do seem to have been selected with certain criteria in mind. For thin-walled vessels and the interiors of vessels (possibly bottles), flexible, fine textiles were chosen. Large-sized textiles definitely were preferred, but they did not have to be consistently sturdy. From this, it seems more likely that the primary functions of fabrics in the pottery-making process were to help separate vessels from molds and perhaps to moderate the drying process, rather than to actually lift the heavy "saltpans" from their molds. The tentatively identified decline in use of weft-faced and knotted fabrics over time (Table 10, Figure 47) could be related to the potentially greater difficulty in removing them from the ceramic surface, compared with less highly textured textiles.

Questions related to vessel function are less easily answered from the data collected in this study. They include the following.

How were textile-impressed "saltpans" used at the Wickliffe site? What vessel form(s) were present? Are sherds consistently smoke-blackened? Not enough information was garnered to describe completely the size and shape(s) of Wickliffe "saltpans." Average diameters probably fall between 40 and 80 centimeters (16–31 in), and one common form may have been similar to the gradually curving shapes from Kimmswick and Kincaid illustrated in Figure 3. No formal tabulation of smoke-marking was made, but it was not notably common.

Because Wickliffe is not a saline site, a vessel function other than that of evaporating mineralized water to make salt is likely. Large, relatively shallow vessels unmarked by smoke would be consistent with use as large platters for food consumption, but the bigger the size, the more difficult they would be to carry. Use as a bread oven is possible, but if this were the only use for these vessels, more smoke marking might be expected. The display in the Mound D excavation shelter of sherds from a smooth-surfaced, rounded-form "saltpan"-type vessel within a depression in the ground might indicate its use for heating liquids by means of hot rocks, or as a basin for holding water.

Could textile impressions have enhanced vessel function? The impressions apparently extend around the entire bottom of the Wickliffe "saltpans" and thus could increase heating-surface area if the vessels were used in cooking. They also could retard slippage if such pots tended to be balanced on precarious surfaces. Those vessels in which fabric-marking extends close to the lip (about 87% of rim sherds) would have increased "gripability" where fabric impressions were moderate in depth but could be uncomfortable to lift and hold for any extended period of time if textile impressions were deep and coarse. These observations are not inconsistent with a use-related function for the textile impressions, but they are of no real help in proving its existence or establishing its exact nature.

If textile impressions were intended as decorative rather than primarily functional, positive responses would be expected to the following questions.

Were the impressions visible? If vessels were relatively shallow with gradually sloping sides and used primarily at ground level, textile markings ordinarily would not be visible except in the case of bread ovens. This would be even more the case for the "saltpans" with wide smoothed rims.

Were the textiles neatly applied? Were they oriented so as to complement the form of the vessel? In general, no. The fairly high proportion (21%) of damaged fabrics and the careless alignment of most overlapped edges argues against "neatness" as a criterion in applying textiles to these vessels. Except for the slightly higher than expected percentage of fabrics oriented perpendicular to the vessel rim, no correlation was found between vessel form and fabric orientation.

As noted above, the aberrant perpendicular orientation could have been due to measurement method, to weftwise tension on the fabric during manufacture, to the use of two overlapped textiles, or to wrapping of the vessel around its circumference with a long fabric. As to the last possibility, no fabric edges were found parallel to vessel rims, as would occur if a narrow fabric were used for such wrapping, nor any significant bunching of fabric on nonrim sherds, as would occur if a wide fabric were used and had to be gathered together under the vessel.

Do textile attributes and/or visibility, neatness, and orientation of textile impressions correlate with some selected vessel form(s) but not with others? The only such possible correlation I found was between thin sherds and fine plain-twined textiles made with well-twisted warp yarns.

In total, it seems very unlikely that textile markings were intended as decoration on Wickliffe "saltpan" vessels.

To summarize, the textile impressions on "saltpans" at Wickliffe probably are evidence of a utilitarian rather than a decorative purpose. Although it is possible that the impressions served some function in vessel use, in my opinion the impressed fabrics most likely were employed primarily to separate the clay vessel from its mold and to help moderate the drying process. However, they were not constructed specifically for these purposes.

Textile Functions at Wickliffe

For what purposes, then, were these fabrics made? Some tentative identifications can be made by comparing their characteristics with those of items of known function, as detailed in Chapter 4. Size, shape, edge finishes, and internal characteristics such as textile structure and fabric scale all can provide clues.

What was the size range of textiles impressed on pottery at Wickliffe? As discussed above, it seems likely that many of the fabrics were as wide as the vessels on which they were impressed, measuring at least 40–80 centimeters (16–31 in) along their smaller dimension. No sherds containing impressions of two opposite textile edges were found; that is, there was no evidence for the use of very narrow fabrics.

For the few examples where the overlap or join between two fabrics was visible, the frequency of occurrence of fabrics representing the major textile structure categories differed from their frequency in the sample as a whole. No weft-faced fabrics from cluster groups 1 and 2 were represented. Those two groups in effect include all weft-faced fabrics except for one very fine example, a twined edge, which could have bordered a textile of more open construction (Figure 43). All three of the joins were between plain-twined fabrics, while the remainder of the over- and underlapping textiles included 9 plain-twined and 13 alternate-pair-twined fabrics.

If the fine weft-faced edge is omitted, then, 54% of fabrics involved in joins or edge overlaps were plain twined, and 46% were alternate-pair twined. This compares with 7% weft faced, 58% plain twined, 29% alternate-pair twined, and 6% knotted, interlaced, or unknown in the sample as a whole. This discrepancy is statistically significant at the 0.10 level, so there does appear to be a real difference among textile structure categories. From this information, it is probable that weft-faced fabrics were the largest used and that alternate-pair-twined textiles averaged the smallest in size.

What were the shapes of Wickliffe impressed textiles? There is no evidence for any shape other than rectangular. All nondamaged edges were straight. No appendages, such as woven or braided ties, were found.

Although many of the overlaid fabrics differed significantly from each other, at least 24 examples (1.5% of total sherds) were close enough in appearance that they could have come from the same textile. This situation could occur either in the case of a bag or in the case of a folded fabric. In no case could three layers be distinguished, as would occur in a pleated fold such as might come about if a rectangular fabric were fitted into a deep, steep-sided circular mold. Neither was any recognizable evidence found of fabric bunching such as might occur at the corners of a large rectangular bag if a rounded ceramic vessel were formed inside of it. From this, it seems likely that if bags were used in the pottery-making process, they were used double rather than having a vessel formed inside of them.

What are the attributes of textiles impressed on pottery at Wickliffe? Can these textiles be sorted into groups on the basis of structural characteristics? Do such groups correlate with textile attributes of known artifacts? Wickliffe fabric attributes and textile-structure groups were discussed at length in Chapter 5. What can be said about their characteristics as compared with those of actual textile artifacts?

Mantles and skirts for which I have measurements ranged up to 142 centimeters (56 in) wide and 67.5 centimeters (27 in) high, twined fabrics interpreted as bedding were as large as 122 × 91 centimeters (48 × 36 in), cane mats were at least 100 centimeters (40 in) wide, and bags had dimensions up to 66 × 64 centimeters (26 × 25 in) (Tables 3 and 4). Any of these could completely cover at least a medium-sized Wickliffe "saltpan," and they all are good candidates for the purpose. How might the Wickliffe fabrics fit into these categories?

Textile attributes of the ceremonial garments from Spiro fall within the parameters of Wickliffe's coarsest alternate-pair-twined cluster group, except that the weft rows are more closely spaced than any of the fabrics within that group. Attributes of the garment from Tennessee (Figure 20) fall within the second-coarsest cluster group. Most of the Wickliffe alternate-pair-twined textiles falling within all but the coarsest cluster group (e.g., Figure 23, top), except for some with yarns that appear uncomfortably hard, would seem to be suitable for garments. For winter months, the denser fabrics made of "fluffy" yarns would be particularly appropriate (e.g., Figure 35, center right).

The smaller-scale plain-twined fabrics of the three finest cluster groups (e.g., Figure 22, top) likely would be fine and supple enough to serve comfortably as garments. Even some of the group 2 textiles might work adequately in this capacity. Weft-faced fabrics of all but the coarsest cluster group (e.g., Figure 30, top) also could be candidates for very heavy garments. Although they might be somewhat stiff, their density is consistent with several early historical depictions of garments: the de Soto expedition's use of "shawls" for sails (Bourne 1904:188–191), the eighteenth-century Choctaw skirts that were "thick as canvas" (Swanton 1946:450), the eighteenth-century Chickasaw "petticoats and other habits" with "substance and durableness [that] recommends it for floor and table-carpets" (Catesby, quoted in Swanton 1946:453), and the eighteenth-century sketches by A. De Batz of Indian women near New Orleans, almost all of whom wear short skirts that stick out from the body rather than draping in folds (Swanton 1946:Plate 3; Harvard Peabody Museum collection, PM 41-72/16). None of the large weft-faced textiles impressed on pottery were as fine as the bone-bead-decorated weft-faced "sash" (Figure 6, Table 1). It is comparable in scale only to the fine weft-faced edge structure illustrated in Figure 43.

My inclination is to designate almost all of the complex fabrics (Figures 24–29) as garments. Although some of them were coarse enough to be included in plain-twined cluster group 2, the majority were finer. Most of the textiles with transposed, interlinked warps were made from rather fine yarns and perhaps would be more suitable for mantles than for wraparound skirts, if showing off the openwork designs was a prime consideration: they would not be readily visible if two layers of fabric were overlapped. Although Le Page du Pratz does mention the use of hair nets among the Natchez, and many of these fabrics would be very suitable for such use, hair-net dimensions probably would not be as large as the "saltpans." Openwork fabrics with manipulated warps all were much finer than the openwork bag in Figure 16, which had 5-millimeter warps and a fabric count of only 4.9.

The alternate-pair-twined fabric with transposed, crossed warps (Figures 26, 9d) is similar in scale to historical bags with central panels incorporating two-color, often representational, designs that were made using a comparable, double-faced textile structure (Figures 17, 9e). For instance, the Wickliffe fabric has 7 warps and 3.2 wefts per centimeter compared with an average of 8.4 warps (range = 6.0–11.0) and 4.4 wefts per centimeter (range = 3.3–5.6) for six Potawatomi, Winnebago, and Ojibway bags in the collection of the Harvard Peabody Museum (Table 3). However, the Wickliffe textile is less dense than the average for these double-faced bags because its warp yarns are smaller in diameter (1.1 vs. 1.6 mm). Thus, if it did incorporate bicolored designs, they would be less distinct and well defined than those on the figured bags. Decorated bags like that in Figure 17 traditionally were made of bast and buffalo or moose hair (Whiteford 1977:59, 61). So was the Choctaw skirt fabric mentioned above as "thick as canvas"; the anonymous eighteenth-century writer also characterized this fabric as "double like two-sided handkerchiefs" (quoted in Swanton 1946:450). Likewise, the Chickasaw "petticoat" fabric described by Catesby was "adorned with figures of animals represented in colours" (quoted in Swanton 1946:453). The Wickliffe fabric thus could have been a bag or a garment, incorporating a two-colored design. Its comparatively low density (and thus higher flexibility) may make it more suitable for the latter than the former. Yarns in the Wickliffe textile all seem to be of the same fiber rather than consisting of both hair and vegetable fiber, but they could have been dyed different colors.

Some of the relatively coarse plain- and alternate-pair-twined fabrics assigned to cluster groups 1 and 2 would be suitable for bags. The cluster group mean values for yarn size and warps and wefts per centimeter fall within the range for Mississippian and related bags (Table 3; Drooker 1989b:Tables 13–14). However, the warp densities of these textiles were far less, on average, than those measured from bags (averaging 6.75 and 7.3 for the two alternate-pair cluster groups and 5.4 and 5.6 for the two plain-twined groups, vs. the range of 9 to 10 for the bags). A notable exception are the few fragments of plain twining with relatively thin wefts and thick, possibly braided warps (e.g., Figure 36, bottom left); their scale is consistent with that of many historical-period storage bags (e.g., Whiteford 1977:Figures 3–6). No large-scale, bulky terminal edges with twisted warp groups nor any "folded" side or bottom edges typical of bags have been found in the Wickliffe impressions, although the impressions of joins (Figures 41b, 42) are consistent with joined bottom edges of historical bags (Figure 13b). If these joins connected the warp loops of a bag made as a tube, however, the pottery vessel would have had to have been formed inside the bag rather than on top of both layers, because overlaid fabrics appear on none of the sherds with impressions of joins.

A plain-twined fabric fragment from Wickliffe that seems to be part of a textile interpreted by B. King as a bag (Kuttruff 1990) was finer than most of the eight bags whose measured attributes are summarized in Table 3. Its yarn diameters are equal to the minimum for the sample of bags, its weft elements are spaced closer together than those of any bag in the sample, and it has a higher fabric count than the sample average (Table 1). Its attributes are closest in scale to plain-twined fabrics in cluster group 3. This textile was associated with a quantity of corn, perhaps enclosing it as a burial offering.

Because of the presence of possible side edges, Kuttruff has interpreted the fabric as a wrapping rather than a bag (1990:9–10). Its attribute measurements bear out this interpretation.

For the coarse, open plain-twined fabrics (e.g., Figure 22, bottom), I have found no good parallels. They are much less dense than Mississippian or historical storage bags, and not dense enough to have been used as blankets. Because of their coarseness, they probably would be uncomfortable to sit on and thus unsuitable for garments or mats. One possible function is that of a corn-hulling bag, historical examples of which are made of very open fabrics, but the coarse, open plain-twined fabrics that were produced at Wickliffe are too numerous and diverse for all of them to have served this function.

The coarse weft-faced fabrics, however (Figure 30, bottom), could well have served as blankets. Although the weft yarns are mostly two-ply, not multi-ply like those in the "blanket" fabric illustrated by Orchard (1920:Plate 5), their appearance and size are comparable (a mean weft diameter of 2.9 mm for fabrics in Cluster Group 1, vs. on the order of 3 mm for the Kentucky "blanket" fabric), and they generally are well processed enough to have good insulating properties. Furthermore, these fabrics probably had somewhat larger dimensions than the plain- and alternate-pair-twined textiles, which would be consistent with their use as a covering rather than as a garment. Other possible functions would be mats, bags, or specialized garments. However, I have found no published descriptions of any prehistoric weft-faced artifacts of these types from the Southeast. The only ethnographic weft-faced or warp-faced mats about which I found information, made by Great Lakes peoples about a century ago, were fashioned of rushes, not of spun and plied yarns like the Wickliffe textiles (Rogers 1983). Other possible candidates for mats would be the plain-twined textiles with large-diameter, possibly braided warps and small-diameter wefts (Figure 36, bottom), which would provide relatively smooth surfaces on which to sit or lie. Again, however, there is no artifactual evidence that mats ever actually were made from such fabrics.

All of the fabric side edges and terminal edges impressed on Wickliffe pottery would be suitable finishes for garments. The side edge diagrammed in Figure 41d seems similar or identical to narrow warp-twined bands that occurred along the side edges of three of the Spiro garments (Kuttruff 1988a:97). The textile on which it appeared was an alternate-pair-twined fabric, considerably finer than the alternate-pair-twined fabrics of the Spiro garments but with a similar density. The terminal edge illustrated at the bottom of Figure 43 is similar to the edge finish on the Wickliffe textile fragment that may have been part of a bag (Table 1), except for the fact that its structure is two-element rather than three-element twining. No examples were found of the terminal edge type that seems to be most typical of bags—twisted groups of warp loops secured by a band (Figures 15c, 17).

The single example of twill interlacing probably came from a mat. The sharp edges, flat surfaces, and dimensions of its elements are consistent with attributes of either bark strips or cane strips. The elements are fairly thin and lack a prominent convex surface that would definitely mark them as cane. Their widths tend toward the middle range of matting examples cited in Chapter 4 and should give a somewhat flexible fabric that could be used to line a relatively shallow mold. From Wickliffe pottery impressions there is no evidence whatsoever of "saltpans" being molded inside baskets.

The nine Wickliffe knotted fabrics include both dense and fairly open examples. All of them could have been hunting or fishing nets. Two utilized comparatively fine yarn, but in all cases the yarn was two-ply, well made and strong. The typical small mesh size (0.80–1.65 elements per cm) would fit within the known parameters for hunting and fishing (seine) nets (0.2–3.4 elements per cm), as would the yarn sizes (1–2 mm). The finer, more open knotted fabrics were closest to measurements given for fishing nets, but all had smaller mesh sizes than the upper limit for seine nets. The denser fabrics were more nearly like the Texas hunting net, with its 0.29-centimeter "mesh diameter" and 1.8-millimeter yarn.

The one published example that I found of a prehistoric knotted bag of any size had a fabric similar in scale to the Wickliffe knotted netting (1.4 elements per centimeter, 1-millimeter yarn), but it is perhaps more likely that nets rather than bags would be large enough to cover a "saltpan" vessel. The fact that no impressions were found of knotted fabrics with large mesh sizes could be because open netting is not functionally suitable for pottery-making, rather than because such nets were not made at Wickliffe. Only one of the nine knotted fabrics impressed on Wickliffe sherds—the most open one—was doubled over, as would occur with a rectangular bag laid flat (as in Figures 14 and 16). This is about the same proportion—11% of knotted fabrics—as the proportion of overlaid textiles on all Wickliffe sherds (9%).

If decorative designs are present, where are they placed relative to finished textile edges? What are their shapes and sizes? Structural differences probably designed for visual effect included "stripes" formed by contrasts in warp yarn diameter, grouped weft rows, and alternating sequences of plain twining and oblique interlacing, as well as geometric designs formed by diverted or transposed warps within twined fabrics. Whereas several textiles impressed on pottery from other Mississippian sites included decorative border "stripes" along starting or terminal edges (see Chapter 7), at Wickliffe no designs other than two to five close-spaced twining rows were found on fabrics with edges present.

It was not possible to determine the shapes of design motifs. The largest sherd containing a geometric design formed by transposed, interlinked warps (Figure 27, bottom) was only 6 centimeters (2.4 in) across. As it also was the coarsest example of this type of textile, the shape of its design motifs was no more apparent than those from smaller sherds containing finer fabric impressions. (Fabric count for these textiles ranged from 8.2 to 19, exemplified in Figures 27 and 28.) If the shape at the bottom of the largest sherd in Figure 27 is the top of an octagonal or circular motif, that motif would be at least 5 centimeters (2.0 in) across.

There is no reason why this textile structure could not have been used to form intricate, even representational, forms, but no evidence exists of any such motifs. All that can be said is that designs are composed of geometric shapes made up of straight and diagonal lines formed by rows of "holes" in the fabric. Unlike examples from other sites, no designs consisting solely of horizontal rows of "holes" formed by interlinked warps were found at Wickliffe. The design formed by transposed, crossed warps on an alternate-pair-twined base structure (Figure 26) also probably is geometric, but the fragment is too small to trace any part of its shape.

To summarize, the textiles impressed on pottery at Wickliffe probably are representative of the range of utilitarian large-sized textile items made and used in the village, including skirts and mantles of fine plain twining, fine to medium-coarse alternate-pair twining, and possibly fine to medium-coarse weft-faced fabric; decorated garments of plain twining with "striped" and transposed-warp designs; blankets of coarse weft-faced fabric; possibly large bags of coarse to medium plain and alternate-pair twining; hunting or fishing nets of knotted mesh; and mats of interlaced cane or bark elements. The extent of diversity and expertise that is displayed in Wickliffe fabrics impressed on pottery argues for an extensive, sophisticated total textile complex, with a significant place in the village economy. This is corroborated by computations of production time, discussed below.

SPINNING AND FABRIC PRODUCTION TECHNOLOGY

What evidence on how yarns and textiles were made in the Southeast can be mustered from the archaeological record and early historical accounts? Archaeological evidence of southeastern textile technology in the form of actual tools is extremely rare. No recognizable looms or support structures for making textiles have been recovered from Mississippian or earlier contexts in the Southeast. Bone needles and awls are not infrequently found, but other implements are difficult to pinpoint.

At Tolu, Kentucky, just east of Kincaid (Figure 1), one female was buried with what were interpreted as possible weaving implements—two highly polished, spatula-shaped pieces of bone—in contact with her right arm (Webb and Funkhouser 1931:343–346). A plant-stem shuttle—beveled at one end with yarn wrapped around the other—was recovered from the probably Mississippian Putnam Farm shelter in northwestern Arkansas, and a small bundle of what were interpreted as warp threads with attached plant-stem weights came from the Whitney shelter in the same area (Scholtz 1975:143–144). The burial at Cliffty Creek Rock-shelter, Tennessee, included bone awls and skeins of processed but untwisted vegetable fiber said to be wild hemp *(Cannabis sativa)*, but no recognizable spinning tools (Holmes 1896:30–34).

Definite evidence of spinning or twisting implements is difficult to come by. Although stone and pottery "discoidals" are common at many Mississippian sites, many of them do not have center holes, as would be necessary for a spindle. The Angel site (Figure 1) did include a high percentage of centrally perforated disks (46% of the 452 nearly complete ceramic disks), one interpretation of which was that they were used as spindle whorls (Black 1967:457). A centrally perforated, decorated ceramic disk from Cahokia is believed to be a spindle whorl (Iseminger 1983; J. Brown 1989:196–197), as is a nondecorated perforated disk from Stone, Tennessee (Coe and Fischer 1959:58, 70). None of these perforated disks has been found with a spindle shaft in place.

Early accounts of spinning techniques most frequently mention "thigh spinning." It is specifically described by eyewitnesses John Smith (quoted in Swanton 1946:448) for sixteenth-century Virginia Indians processing bark, grass, and deer sinew; by Charles Wooley for seventeenth-century residents of New Amsterdam and Long Island (quoted in Browning 1974:95); by Peter Kalm for the eighteenth-century Iroquois of New York (quoted in Holmes 1896:23); and by Raudot for the early eighteenth-century western Great Lakes region (quoted in Cleland 1982:762).

J. White (1969:9) portrays the process of thigh spinning a two-ply yarn by twentieth-century Eastern Woodlands Indians as follows:

A quantity of the fiber is held in the left hand, while the right hand gathers enough fiber to allow for the thickness desired in the thread. This is then divided into two parts, still attached at the left end to the main hank of the fiber. These two parts are then rolled with the right hand against the thigh, away from the body, and when tightly twisted are brought together and rolled back towards the body.

He states that although the sequence becomes automatic, its pace is no match for the spinning wheel. The process as described would give a **Z**-plied yarn of two **S**-twisted elements (this can be verified easily by experimentation), and Whiteford confirms this structure for plant-fiber yarn used in twined bags of the Great Lakes Indians from the eighteenth–nineteenth centuries (1977:58).

Dumont de Montigny reported the early eighteenth-century Natchez of Mississippi as spinning without wheel or distaff (fiber-holding device) (quoted in Swanton 1946:449). Le Page du Pratz simply mentions the Natchez as spinning yarn, without describing the process (1763:2:231); likewise for du Ru discussing the Ouma (1934:29). Adair, however, describes mid-eighteenth-century spinners farther to the northeast as using "distaffs, with wooden machines, having some clay on the middle of them [spindles?], to hasten the motion" (1968:422), and a 1693 Spanish group reconnoitering Pensacola Bay found spindles in baskets together with animal hair: "many small crosses, the sight of which delighted them, although they recognised soon that those were spindles on which the Indian women spun the wool of the bison" (Barcia Carballidoy Zuniga, quoted in Swanton 1922:149).

As we already have seen, what little description there is of southeastern textile production techniques through the early eighteenth century generally corroborates the use of free-hanging warps. The picture of a late sixteenth-century Virginia native making a bag or basket upside down (Figure 13a) is probably the earliest depiction of this technique, and Le Page du Pratz's account, quoted in Chapter 4, of the Natchez method of constructing a mulberry-thread cloak on warps hung from a cord strung between two posts very clearly describes a similar process (1763:2:231). An almost-identical setup is depicted in an 1838 painting of a Menominee village in Wisconsin, where a woman stands in front of warps hanging from a branch held up by two forked limbs about six feet in height. She is twining a patterned fabric four or five feet wide, using two wefts (Tanner 1986:8).

Only one relatively late account describes a different process for making large textiles, Adair's portrayal of mid-eighteenth-century Muskogeans weaving "carpets" [mats?] of hemp (1968:422):

"When the coarse thread is prepared, they put it into a frame about six feet square, and instead of a shuttle, they thrust through the thread with a long cane, having a large string through the web, which they shift at every second course of the thread. . . . J. W——t, Esq., a most skilful linguist in the Muskohge dialect, assures me, that time out of mind they passed the woof with a shuttle; and they have a couple of threddles [cords tied to alternate warp threads to aid in lifting them for the passage of the shuttle], which they move with the hand so as to enable them to make good dispatch, something after our manner of weaving.

This definitely would be a description of two-element interlacing rather than twining, most likely on a warp fixed at both ends rather than free-hanging. In spite of the protestations of Adair's informant, however, there is no proof that this weaving method predated European contact.

Still later, and farther west, Hunter (a not-always-reliable witness [I. Brown 1980:31]) described the manufacture of two-element interlaced blankets woven by early nineteenth-century Osage on what might be a horizontal ground loom: warp stretched horizontally between two parallel sticks supported by forked sticks (quoted in Holmes 1896:25–26).

What yarn-spinning and fabric-production tools and methods most likely were used to produce the Wickliffe textiles studied? It seems that more than one possibility exists for both yarn- and textile-production technology at Wickliffe. How can the most likely methods be determined? Attribute data from Wickliffe yarns and textiles can be very useful for this purpose.

In general, yarns at Wickliffe were made of fairly well-processed fibers, with a preponderance of two-ply construction. From historical evidence, both thigh spinning, practiced by peoples to the east and north of the former Mississippian "heartland," and spindle spinning, practiced by peoples to its south, could be candidates for use at Wickliffe. According to modern practitioners of thigh spinning, however, this method would not be suitable for producing very fine yarns, such as the approximately 30% of Wickliffe yarns with diameters between 0.5 and 1.0 centimeter.

In conjunction with experimental replication of Wickliffe yarns (see below), Ella Baker, a spinner with many decades of experience in using a variety of hand-spinning tools, found that fine-yarn production by means of thigh spinning was extremely difficult and time consuming compared with other methods that employ some sort of weight, such as hooked sticks or drop spindles (sticks with disks or smaller weights at one end). This was due, among other things, to the necessity of working with very small amounts of fiber to circumvent tangling problems (personal communication 1989). In corroboration of her experience, she quotes Alena Samuel, who has studied and practiced Northwest Coast type thigh spinning for ten years (A. Samuel 1985), as saying: "Fine yarns, regardless of fiber, cannot be done by thigh spinning." Although Hoffman reported that nineteenth-century Menomini used thigh spinning to produce "all fiber twisting, even to the finest nettle thread" (1896:261), he did not specify the minimum diameter of this "thread."

The Wickliffe penchant for producing yarns with a final twist in the **S** direction for both single- and double-ply yarns also must be considered in inferring the spinning technology employed. Most commonly, the two-ply yarns produced by thigh spinning are **S**-twisted, then **Z**-plied, involving a two-step process of pushing individual strands along the right thigh away from the body, then plying them together by pushing them, together, back toward the body. It certainly is possible to reverse the process in order to produce an **S** ply, but it is somewhat less "natural" to proceed in that direction. Simply because it would require some effort and concentration to learn, such a practice, once established, could account for the extreme consistency of ply direction in Mississippian yarns. However, such a scenario would not account for the equally-consistent **S** twist in unplied yarns. Since, whenever they were visible, the individual elements of **S**-plied yarns at Wickliffe consistently were **Z**-spun or **Z**-twisted, the use of **S**-twisting or **S**-spinning in singles yarns clearly represents a conscious decision to produce a consistent final twist in both single-ply and double-ply yarns. Compared with thigh spinning, in spindle spinning the production of twist direction does not become so deeply ingrained in motor habits, and it is relatively easy to switch back and forth between spinning directions.

For some fibers, one direction of initial twist works better than another because it conforms to the natural twist of the fiber. Thus, there was a distinction in the Old World between **Z**-spun woolen yarns from Gaul, Britain, and Persia, and **S**-spun linen yarns from Egypt and the eastern Mediterranean (Wild 1970:44–53). It is conceivable that some similar distinction was at work in the prehistoric Southeast, with certain specific vegetable fibers being used for **Z**-spun, **S**-plied yarns, while others were used for **S**-twisted single yarns. For the North American Southwest, Maslowski makes the distinction between soft fibers like cotton and retted yucca and hard fibers like agave and unprocessed yucca, noting that within the Southwest the former tend to have an initial **Z** spin while the latter have an initial **S** spin (implying the predominance of a final **Z** twist) (Maslowski 1984:51), but this may be a technological difference (spindle spinning vs. thigh spinning) rather than one predicated on natural fiber twist. Not only direction of twist but also amount of twist sometimes can be related to fiber type, with greater twist being required to secure relatively smoother and shorter fibers. In contrast, conscious decisions based on technological considerations, decorative purposes, or social norms can determine twist direction, as in Roman woolens constructed with **Z**-spun warp and **S**-spun weft "to produce a firmer cloth, closely interlocked" (Wild 1970:44) or in Peruvian counterspun yarns, intended to avert black magic (Kerner 1963). Additional research could be fruitful here, for instance to determine any possible links between twist direction and yarn fiber type in southeastern yarns.

My opinion is that some sort of tool or weight, if not "the spindle" as we know it, probably was used in the production of at least the finer Wickliffe yarns. If twist direction was not automatically determined by technology, there would have had to have been some socially sanctioned, learned "rule" constraining the way yarns were made.

Likewise, the prevalence of **S**-twisted twining begs for explanation. Although in vertical twining there may well be a tendency for right-handed craftspeople to twine in the **S** direction, there is no overwhelming physical reason why one twist direction would be preferred over another by a weaver working horizontally. However, once either the **S**-twining or **S**-spinning direction became prevalent, they could reinforce each other, because it is easier and more efficient to twine in the same direction as the yarn twist. If this is not done, it is possible for twining yarns to untwist and become difficult to work with. It is of interest that in both New Zealand and the Northwest Coast of North America, **Z**-plied yarns produced by thigh spinning were twined in the **Z** direction (J. Smith 1975:32, 40, 89; C. Samuel 1982:86–87).

In my experience, countered twining, in which twining rows alternate direction, tends to occur naturally when a weaver's warp is not attached to a fixed frame, so that she can easily turn her work in progress upside-down at the end of a twining row in order to work always either left-to-right or right-to-left. If she continues the twining twist in the same direction with her work in the new position, countering will result. Thus, small twined items from the southeastern archaeological record, such as sandals, frequently include countering (e.g., J. Miller 1988).

Countering does not occur in Wickliffe textiles impressed on pottery except for the rare instances of **Z**-twisted rows within weft-faced borders that probably represent braided twining. This, along with historical descriptions and pictures of fabric production and bag-making on warps attached at least at one end to a string or stick (e.g., Figure 13), leads me to believe that weaving at Wickliffe was done on such a setup rather than detached from any support. The presence of terminal edges in which individual warp ends are separate (Figure 43), along with some of the structural variations in the fabrics, make me think that free-hanging, separate warp yarns, rather than fixed, continuous warps, were the rule.

Many of the combinations of twining plus transposed warps or oblique interlacing are most easily accomplished with free-hanging warp ends, although it is possible to produce a number of them in fixed-warp setups. For instance, hammocks with bicolored designs as in Figure 10d are constructed on fixed-warp frame looms by the Colombian Guajiro people (Cardale-Schrimpff 1972:633–637). However, widely diverted warps or large areas of transposed, interlinked warps can produce major tension problems if attempted on fixed warps (Rogers 1980:44). They are far more likely to have been constructed using a setup with free-hanging warp ends than one with fixed warp ends.

In experimenting with twining horizontally on free-hanging warp ends, I found that if the warps were too long, they tended to tangle and slow down the weaving process. This factor may have constrained the dimensions of fabrics produced, particularly those in which warps did not remain vertical in the same position throughout the twining process. As a right-handed person, I also found it virtually impossible to produce plain twining plus transposed, interlinked warps other than in a left-to-right direction. When working on a fixed warp, the solution to this problem would be either to end each twining row on the right and start again at the left side, or, if using wefts that continue from row to row, to shift around to the other side of the fabric for the next level of twining. In effect, the latter method was used by bag makers working "in the round," whose twining rows encircled or spiraled around their work (Figure 13). Neither method would change the twist direction of twining rows or warp interlinks. The few side edges found on Wickliffe pottery (e.g., Figure 44) would be consistent with the former method.

Although most Wickliffe textiles probably were constructed on free-hanging warps attached at one end to a support, textile construction on fixed warps also may have occurred. Kuttruff is of the opinion that the narrow "sash" from Wickliffe that she analyzed must have been woven on such a setup (personal communication 1990, 1991). Because of the downward-overlapping bone beads that most likely were inserted into the fabric as the weaving progressed, the textile almost certainly was woven from the bottom up. Further evidence comes from the fabric structure itself: the interlacing would have been prone to slip downward along the warp if it had been woven from the top down, particularly on a free-hanging warp. Such a warp is entirely suitable for twining, but less so for two-element interlacing on widely spaced warp elements.

LABOR INVESTMENT AND SPECIALIZATION IN TEXTILE PRODUCTION

The relative amount of time and effort expended on textile production at Wickliffe can be important in illuminating both economic and social relationships within the society. With cheap, abundant yard goods readily available in the modern world, we easily forget how much time and creativity can go into the hand production of textiles. Choices made by peoples of various cultures as to where and how to "invest" their craft production hours can provide valuable clues as to their economic subsistence level, physical mobility, and social structure. Economically oriented questions raised about textile production at Wickliffe include the following.

How much time would have been required to produce the different types of textiles in evidence at Wickliffe? Published information on production times for southeastern utilitarian textiles is quite meager, so in order to assess the actual labor time invested in production of textiles at Wickliffe, additional data about fiber-processing times, spinning times, and fabric-production times were gathered to aid in the determination of how many person-hours it might take to produce a given amount of fabric of a specified structure and scale.

Ethnographic and early historical descriptions of the processing of vegetable fibers used to make bags and mantles in the Southeast depict a procedure very similar to that of processing flax, a bast fiber, to make linen yarn (Adair 1968:422; Le Page du Pratz 1763:2:231; Swanton 1946:454; J. White 1969:9; summaries in Drooker 1989b:50–51). These processing steps include rotting, beating, peeling (in the case of bark fibers), combing, and drying. For linen, a significant amount of elapsed time is required, including harvesting, turning fiber bundles daily as they "ret" in water for a week or more, plus fairly long periods of drying, before the combing operations can begin. Using two accounts by modern experimenters who grew and processed their own flax (Chase 1982; S. Miller 1982), my very rough estimate is that one to two people-days of work should be allowed for processing a pound of fiber. In machine-manufactured linen yarn, a pound is equivalent to 3,000 yards of approximately 1-millimeter-diameter two-ply yarn (designated size "20/2" in the industry) or 1,500 yards of 1.5-millimeter two-ply yarn (size "10/2").

As discussed above, historical descriptions of Native American yarn spinning pointed to either thigh spinning (in which fibers are rolled along the thigh to twist them together) or the use of some kind of spindle for making yarn. Extensive experimentation was carried out by handspinner Ella Baker to determine the time required to spin yarn using a variety of possible techniques. For fine yarns, thigh spinning was significantly slower than other methods. Using this technique, Baker produced less than two yards of two-ply, 0.8-millimeter-diameter linen yarn in 2½ hours. Four yards of two-ply, 2-millimeter-diameter wool yarn took 30 minutes. Using a hooked stick to aid rotation, she spun 8 yards of single-ply, 0.5-millimeter diameter linen yarn in 35 minutes; using a bead whorl spindle, she spun 10 yards of similar-size cotton yarn in 15 minutes. (Bead whorl spindles consisting of bamboo stick plus clay weight were used to spin extremely fine cotton yarns in India.) Finger-plying the cotton singles into 10 yards of loosely twisted two-ply yarn took 5 minutes; plying with a bead whorl took longer.

Estimation of twining times is based on my own experience of making twined hammocks in the South American manner (twining vertically on a fixed horizontal warp), plus making small samples of horizontal twining over free-hanging warp ends. Setting up a continuous horizontal warp of 1,026 elements, 3 yards (274 cm) long took 2 hours. A discontinuous set of warp ends undoubtedly would require more time to set up. Twining time per row varied from 155 to 100 minutes, as I gained speed with practice. The twining pattern included twining over both single warps and pairs of warps, for a total of 634 twists per row, giving an average time per twining twist of 0.158 minute for the fastest row. In a small sample of horizontal plain twining, my average time per row was 0.146 minute per twist. A row of transposed, interlinked warps secured by plain twining took twice that time.

Based on this information, how long would it take to make a fabric similar to the utilitarian garment from Cliffty Creek rock-shelter (Figure 20, Table 3)? As far as can be determined from its photograph, it has 6.3 warps per centimeter and 1.4 twining rows per centimeter. This would place it within cluster group 2 of Wickliffe alternate-pair-twined textiles. Based on mean values for the cluster group, compatible yarns would average 1.4 millimeters in diameter, with half of them two-ply (say, the weft) and half single-ply (say, the warp). There are approximately 86 rows in the 61-centimeter length of the garment, and approximately 730 warps in the 117-centimeter width. Omitting the looped weft ends from the calculations and allowing an extra 33% for take-up in twining, the garment would require approximately 270 meters (295 yd) of weft yarn and 450 (492 yd) meters of warp yarn (about ½ pound of fiber). A total of approximately 31,400 twining twists would hold the fabric together.

Assuming use of a spindle weight rather than thigh spinning, and allowing spinning and plying time of 10 meters per hour for two-ply and 10 meters per 45 minutes for single-ply bast yarn, it would take about 61 hours to spin the yarn, in addition to a very rough estimate of 6 hours for processing the fiber. Twining, at 4 hours to set up the warp and 0.14 minute per twist, would take 77 hours. Total time, then, for a fairly large, medium-coarse textile would be 144 hours. Assuming no more than four hours per day devoted to spinning and weaving, elapsed time for those two processes would be some 35 days.

Plain twining rather than alternate-pair twining and/or finer fabrics using larger numbers of yarn elements would require correspondingly longer to make. For example, a 60 × 120 centimeter (24 × 47 in) textile equivalent to the very fine, dense one illustrated in Figure 23, upper right, with 9 warp elements and 4.5 weft rows per centimeter, would require more than twice as much yarn and 460% more twining twists to produce—on the order of 530 hours for fiber processing, spinning, and weaving.

Some additional data on production times for various types of fabrics are available from the literature. According to V. Jones (1948), who observed Chippewa Indians near Sault Ste. Marie, Michigan, it took two people-days to spin cord for a mat, not counting gathering the components of the cordage, and 20 hours to gather and process materials and construct an interlaced bark mat, 100 warps by 46 wefts. J. Miller (1988) experimentally replicated some Early Woodland weft-faced twined slippers, finding that a pair could be twined in four to eight hours, depending on the experience of the maker.

Church attempted to calculate the labor input costs associated with a group of fine, presumably high-status Hopewellian mortuary textiles. Using information from V. Jones and J. White and from personal experimentation, she determined that it would take well over 2,000 hours to make the yarn and construct a fabric of approximately 46 × 92 centimeters (18 × 36 in) a fine-scale alternate-pair twining equivalent to textiles recovered from the Seip mound (average yarn diameter = 0.7 mm, average fabric count = 17.9), based on the fact that a 46 × 46 centimeter bag that she made at a scale five times larger took her about 300 hours to twine (Church 1984:11). Likewise, E. White determined by experimental replication that the fine oblique interlacing (10 elements per cm) she discovered on the surfaces of Hopewell copper artifacts would require 30 minutes per square centimeter to produce, or 200 hours for a 20 × 20 centimeter (8 × 8 in) fabric, sufficient in size to wrap a copper celt (1987:90).

These two replication projects produced production time figures quite a bit higher than what would be expected from my data and calculations. Additional experimental work, plus data from skilled craftspeople such as New Zealand Maoris, who still regularly create large, fine twined fabrics, would be useful to refine these figures. Meanwhile, my calculated figures should perhaps be taken as minima.

In Table 11 are listed rough calculations of production times for an average Wickliffe plain-twined, alternate-pair-twined, weft-faced, and interlinked-warp textile of a size comparable to the Tennessee garment, using mean values of fabric attributes from Table 8. The alternate-pair-twined garment from Tennessee, calculated to take 144 hours of work not counting edge finishes, was made from a fabric slightly finer than the average of all Wickliffe impressed textiles but slightly coarser than the average Wickliffe alternate-pair-twined textile. The decorated textile would represent a considerable investment in time, not only because of its patterning but also because

Table 11. Estimates of production times for typical Wickliffe textiles (in hours)

Step	Plain twining	Alternate-pair twining	Weft-faced	Interlinked warps
Fiber processing	5	6	10	4
Yarn production	46	69	71	64
Fabric construction	82	98	72	331
Total (hours)	133	173	153	399

Note: Estimates are based on mean attributes for each structure category from Table 8. Fabric dimensions are taken as 60 × 120 centimeters (24 × 47 in). Edge-finishing time, which could be considerable, is not included.

it is comparatively small in scale. A fine plain-twined textile, the same scale as the average for plain twining plus interlinked warps, would take 290 hours.

The decision processes and additional manipulations required to produce complex edge finishes would require significantly more time. Although fringed edges produced by knotting weft yarns together or simply leaving warp ends to hang free from the last row of twining can be produced relatively quickly, the edge finishes used at Wickliffe by no means were limited to such simple forms. For instance, those illustrated in Figures 43 (bottom) and 44, as well as that reported by Kuttruff (1990) for the edge of an actual textile fragment from Wickliffe, represent a significant investment of time beyond that required to produce the body of the fabric.

What was the amount of labor time invested in the types of textile artifacts deduced to have been manufactured at Wickliffe? What might this imply in terms of total time invested in textile-making? From the information summarized in Table 11, an undecorated, medium-coarse garment-sized textile, equivalent in size to a medium-sized bag (Tables 3 and 4), might take between 100 and 200 hours to make.

For a woman to produce, say, one relatively coarse and one relatively fine garment for herself every year, plus three mantles or blankets for other members of her family, plus two large storage bags, all undecorated, would require over 1,200 hours, the equivalent of 300 days at 4 hours per day. Even if Wickliffe textile makers produced fewer items (say, half as many) or were significantly faster than my spinning and twining estimates would indicate, this still would represent a considerable time investment. Most likely, every woman would have to be a textile maker, devoting a significant proportion of her time to this craft. She also would be unlikely to waste textiles so laboriously produced.

Additional evidence with respect to the "value" of various types of textiles at Wickliffe can come from comparing their condition at the time they were used in the pottery-manufacturing process (Drooker 1989b:Table 17). Knotted and weft-faced fabrics were least worn, followed by plain twining, alternate-pair twining, and finally by complex fabrics combining two or more structures. Knotted and weft-faced fabrics in general were made of strong yarns and were very sturdy, but they also are at the low end of complexity for fabrics impressed on pottery at Wickliffe. It is the most complex fabrics, in which both more labor and more decision making have been invested, that tend to be most worn. One possible explanation is that these "higher-value" textiles, most of which probably were clothing, were used for a longer time than the simpler fabrics, which may have been discarded earlier because they were more easily replaced.

Fabrics employed to manufacture pottery may or may not still have been in use for their original purpose as well. They could have been garments, used casually when pottery-making day came around and then washed and wrapped around their owner to serve as a skirt or mantle once again. Alternatively, they might have been discarded rags, no longer employed for their original purpose, as inferred for the "bedding" found in a Kentucky rockshelter (Webb and Funkhouser 1936:116–123).

Within the southeastern region, evidently textile items often were utilized for quite some time after they began to show signs of deterioration. The garment from Tennessee (Figure 20) was marred by a large hole near center bottom, possibly marking the sitting position of the wearer. Examples of textile artifacts that had been repaired, sometimes repeatedly, have come from a number of southeastern sites (e.g., Kuttruff 1987a; Webb and Funkhouser 1936:122). Thus, it seems strange that no repairs at all were found on Wickliffe impressed textiles. Perhaps this reflects a relative affluence: people there did not need to "make do" but could toss worn-out fabrics into the rag pile and take time to make a replacement.

What about decorated textiles? Were they the product of specialists, or were they turned out routinely by most craftspeople? Many Wickliffe fabric makers obviously took care to turn out a well-made product. Although there certainly were numerous examples of unskillful or careless construction, these were not in the majority. Even the coarsest fabrics had a reasonably high probability of being constructed of well-spun yarn put together in regular, straight-line grids. Finer and more complex fabrics would take somewhat more spinning and construction skill and a greater investment in time, but none of them would have been beyond the reach of an average craftworker who had mastered the basics. Although design shapes in the various fabrics incorporating transposed, interlinked warps may have been similar to each other, the nonstandardization of other textile attributes such as yarn size argues that these fabrics were not all produced by the same hands (e.g., see Figures 27–28 and the ranges of attributes listed in Table 8).

What types of textile artifacts, present at other Mississippian sites or deduced from pictorial evidence, are not represented in Wickliffe textile impressions? Are there functional reasons, related to pottery construction or use, that such items would be rejected for making textile-impressed pottery? Is there any reason to expect that they would have been made and used at Wickliffe? Can any conclusions be drawn about the total textile complex at Wickliffe?

Evidence for one type of large textile item, probably fairly common throughout the Southeast, was missing from the Wickliffe pottery impressions: the feather mantles so frequently mentioned in early historical accounts of southeastern textiles and encountered in a number of Tennessee and Kentucky cave inhumations (Chapter 4). Because of their appendages, these garments would not have been functionally suitable for the pottery-making process, but they certainly could have been made and used at Wickliffe. Production time probably was not excessive for the type of featherwork in which feathers were attached to a fabric backing, as described among the Natchez by Le Page du Pratz: Conrad and Bohn (1988) produced a lined feather mantle on a commercially made net backing in approximately 120 hours. Like feathered garments, fabrics with other appendages, such as the bone beads woven into the narrow fabric analyzed by Kuttruff (1990), would not have been appropriate for pottery-making and indeed do not occur in "saltpan" impressions.

Also not present in Wickliffe impressed textiles were any examples of twined tapestry or complex lacelike openwork (Figure 52 below) such as have been excavated from elite mortuary contexts at Spiro and Etowah. These both are extremely time-consuming techniques, the products of which are very unlikely to have been employed in utilitarian pottery-making. No examples of the former and only one example of the latter have been found impressed on pottery from any Mississippian site. They may or may not have been part of the textile complex at the moderate-sized Wickliffe village—quite possibly not.

How do the textiles impressed on pottery reflect the total range of fabrics produced and used at Wickliffe? My opinion is that they probably reflect well the range of textile structures, yarns, and fabric scales employed within that settlement to make large-sized, utilitarian fabric items. For instance, the lack of any fabrics in "balanced interlacing" (Figures 10a, 10b, 10d) constructed of yarns (as opposed to cane or bark strips) probably indicates that this structure was not used at Wickliffe to make everyday skirts, mantles, or blankets. Its presence on pottery from other sites (Table 13 below) demonstrates that it was not functionally unsuitable for ceramic production, so there is no reason to expect that it would not be impressed on Wickliffe "saltpans" if available in fabrics of suitably large size.

The complete range of types of structurally decorated fabrics may or may not be represented in the sample analyzed. The number of structural variations encountered seemed to increase directly with the sample size, and a larger sample could well yield additional variations.

Totally lacking from the pottery-impression evidence would be information about structures and yarns used to make smaller items such as sashes or sandals. Also lacking is any substantial information about basketry production, except for the fact that twill interlacing was employed.

The relative rarity of knotted textiles, most likely used primarily in male activities associated with hunting, probably simply underlines the fact that pottery-making in the Southeast was women's work. It could also reflect the fact that knotted netting, with its prominent protuberances and large voids, is functionally less suitable for pottery-making than smoother fabrics. Certainly, the diversity and high craftsmanship of the knotted netting indicates a well-developed technology, evidence that this type of textile probably was more common at Wickliffe than is apparent from the textile-impressed pottery.

Without much firm evidence, my feeling is that the high end of the scale of Wickliffe textiles is not fully represented in the ceramic record. The "oddball" fabrics such as those illustrated in Figures 26, 28, and 29 could not possibly have been one-time inventions. Rather, the level of sophistication and expertise involved in their production would have required a substantial background of experimentation and practice. Thus, their relative rarity as impressions on pottery probably does not reflect their actual occurrence. Quite possibly most such textiles were too "expensive" to "waste" in pottery manufacture, or in some way dysfunctional for that purpose.

The comparatively infrequent occurrence of decorated textiles on pottery does not necessarily imply that such fabrics were reserved for an elite minority or were obtained only through exchange. For instance, the early historical figured skirts and the bags decorated with representational designs in a textile structure similar to that in Figure 26 do not seem to have been restricted in manufacture or use to any unique group of people. Decorated bags like those in Figures 16–17 were used for a variety of purposes, from medicine bundles to clothing storage to sewing bags (Whiteford 1977:61).

Some types of textiles were perhaps actually produced at only one or two localities and obtained elsewhere by exchange. This possibility will be explored a bit further in Chapter 7.

SOCIAL "MESSAGES" FROM WICKLIFFE FABRICS

The types of fabrics produced and used at Wickliffe and the choices involved in employing some or all of them in the pottery-making process may be culturally influenced as well as functionally or economically determined. As culturally embedded artifacts, textiles and textile-impressed pottery are capable of yielding clues about social relationships among Wickliffe residents, as well as between them and their neighbors.

What can be deduced about the purpose of decorative designs on the Wickliffe textiles studied? On what types of artifacts did they likely occur? Do design shapes/motifs correlate with designs used on other media at Wickliffe or elsewhere in the Southeast? Designs produced by combinations of textile structures within Wickliffe fabrics all would be best appreciated at close quarters. The relatively small scale of the diverted-warp structures, along with the relatively subtle texture variations that made up the geometric designs in the fabrics with transposed, interlinked warps, argue against their use for ceremonial, ritual items intended to be viewed from a great distance. For example, while the size of some motifs on Wickliffe fabrics decorated with holes formed by interlinked warp yarns may be comparable to that of the yellow circles-and-crosses on the elite burial fabric from Etowah (ca. 5–6 cm, or 2 in) the visual impact of a medium-scale textured design would be far less than that of a brightly colored one.

In spite of the fact that structural designs were used in historical times to decorate storage bags (e.g., Figure 16), I am inclined to categorize most of these Mississippian decorated items as clothing, because their fabrics all were relatively fine and supple (Figure 33). If they did function as clothing, their visual impact would be similar to the decorated items used in Yugoslavian folkdress to distinguish people belonging to different villages at intermediate and close range, rather than to those used to distinguish people's affiliations from a long distance (Wobst 1977:330–337). The one exception is the possible double-faced fabric (Figure 26); designs in contrasting colors at the scale of this textile would be quite prominent and easily seen at a distance.

No evidence of twined tapestry, used at Spiro to make highly visible ceremonial "hawk man" mantles (among other things), has been found at Wickliffe. Colored patterns like the large-scale dyed or painted designs on Spiro fringed garments would not be apparent in fabric impressions. However, from the structural evidence that is available, it seems that decorations on Wickliffe impressed textiles generally are consistent with these fabrics' use within the everyday activities of village life and perhaps during ordinary interaction with residents of nearby villages, rather than for any focal ceremonial purpose. Intermediate-scale designs, such as these are inferred to be, would have the potential of functioning within Mississippian society to distinguish clan or family affiliations. In post-Contact times, designs on Choctaw pouches were used to distinguish members of different bands (Swanton 1946:480). It is not unlikely that before southeastern peoples turned to purchased, machine-made cloth, at least some of their clothing was fashioned to convey messages about group membership.

Because of the small size of the pottery sherds, it was not possible to distinguish entire design motifs. If panregional symbols such as those associated with "Southeastern Ceremonial Complex" objects (Waring and Holder 1945; Galloway 1989) were found to be present in Wickliffe decorated textiles, their ordinary-versus-ceremonial (or horizontal-versus-vertical) function would have to be reassessed.

Were the textiles impressed on pottery at Wickliffe likely representative of elite textiles made for a special group of people, of ordinary textiles made for everyday use, or of a cross-section of both? Probably most of these fabrics were utilitarian artifacts common in everyday use. The low percentage of knotting, most likely employed as nets by male hunters and fishermen, may point to a preponderance of domestic textiles used primarily by women.

Even though some relatively fine and complex fabrics are included, there was no obvious evidence that some of these were reserved for members of a special group. However, I did find one conceivable instance of "elite" textiles.

The 10 thin sherds and the fine, plain-twined textile impressions on most of them were nagging anomalies begging to be explained. For what purpose were the thin vessels constructed? How did it happen that they were impressed with such similar fabrics? Functionally, a thin-walled vessel might have called for a fine fabric in its manufacturing process, but then why were none of the thin sherds impressed with fine alternate-pair-twined textiles?

I found a possible answer by comparing these textiles with the plain-twined textiles from Etowah elite burials (Table 3). The finest of them (smallest-diameter yarns, largest number of elements per cm) were very similar in all attributes to the Peabody Foundation plain-twined Etowah fabric, and all but one of the rest ranged between it and the six plain-twined Etowah textiles analyzed by Schreffler, at least one of which came from a burial with large amounts of high-status grave goods (1988:154–155). The Peabody Foundation fabric is adorned with prominent, bright yellow circle-and-cross symbols. This fine-scale plain-twined fabric in and of itself represents a significant but not inordinate time investment: approximately 250 hours of work to construct a garment-sized textile, exclusive of painting or dyeing.

If very fine plain-twined fabrics do indeed represent upper-class garb, could the thin pottery vessels have been made by elite women, using their own skirts or mantles in the process? It certainly is not inconceivable that elite people engaged in artisanry. At the Morgan site (16Vm9), an important Middle-Late Coles Creek (ca. A.D. 800 to at least 1100) cultural center on the Louisiana Gulf Coast, unequivocal evidence was found of pottery-making on top of a major mound (Fuller and Fuller 1987:54–56, 80–83; I. Brown 1987:159, 162). The pottery from the mound was better made and much more elaborate and diverse than that within the premound midden, some of it exhibiting striking similarities to Weeden Island ware typical of the Florida coastline. Among other evidence, the preponderance of serving vessels over cooking vessels and mammal over fish and turtle remains on the mound versus in the midden pointed to differences in status between mound inhabitants and nonmound inhabitants. This led to the suggestion that the mound dwellers might have been an artistic elite, with pottery production an esteemed occupation, possibly important in an extensive intercultural contact zone along the Gulf Coast (Fuller and Fuller 1987:83; I. Brown 1987:161–164).

From the sparse available evidence, proposals about elite costume and elite pottery-making at Wickliffe can be put forth only as speculation. However, they may well warrant additional research into correlations between pottery and textile attributes.

In contrast to the structural designs on impressed textiles, the bone beads on the "elite" "sash" analyzed by Kuttruff (1990) would have been highly visible. This textile certainly could have functioned as ceremonial garb, "readable" from a significant distance away. As Kuttruff points out, the beads also would have been "hearable"—if actually on a sash, they would have clinked against each other with every movement of the wearer. Such a sash would have been particularly effective as part of a dance costume, not necessarily confined to wear by a high-ranking person but still marking an out-of-the-ordinary event.

According to Dickens (1980), whose study was based on comparison of ceramics among Woodland period sites, diversity can be an indicator of intergroup contact. The wide range of structural variations in everyday Wickliffe fabrics, particularly from "Late" Wickliffe contexts, could well be an indicator of increased intercommunity contact and exchange. The strategic location of the village, just below the confluence of the Ohio and Mississippi rivers, certainly gave its residents easy access to outside influences, and the high frequency of exotic materials as cemetery burial offerings (T. Lewis 1934:27–28) showed that interaction with other groups did take place.

TEMPORAL CHANGE

Do the textiles impressed on pottery at Wickliffe vary significantly over time in terms of attributes and/or artifacts represented? Do any such variations correlate positively with other changes in material culture at Wickliffe? Although the sample of impressed textiles from "Early" Wickliffe contexts is small, two striking changes were noted between them and textiles from "Late" Wickliffe contexts: the complete lack of structurally decorated fabrics, and the comparatively high proportion of weft-faced fabrics (Table 10, Figure 47). As discussed above, it seems possible that the decline in use of weft-faced fabrics may be functionally related to the pottery manufacturing process, reflecting a preference for either a more supple fabric or a less highly textured one. It is impossible to tell whether the shift from relatively more weft-faced fabrics to relatively more alternate-pair-twined fabrics represents a change in the proportion of textile types actually produced at Wickliffe. However, it can be said at least that this shift to more alternate-pair twining (finer and denser, on average, than plain twining) represents a greater time investment in textiles impressed on "saltpans" (Table 11). The option exercised by Wickliffe craftswomen to invest more time in textiles eventually used for pottery-making, and perhaps in textile production as a whole, may signal an increase in relative affluence—that is, less time needed to satisfy basic subsistence needs—in "Late" Wickliffe times.

Such an implication is substantiated as well by the "Late" Wickliffe use of structurally decorated fabrics in "saltpan" construction. Furthermore, since there seems to be no functional reason to start using these relatively fine and "expensive" textiles in pottery making, their presence on fabric-impressed "saltpans" only during "Late" Wickliffe times very likely does signal a change in the Wickliffe textile complex during that period, namely, an increase in the proportion of decorated fabrics, primarily for use as clothing. This is the time period during which mounds functioned as the focus of Wickliffe village life. It is not surprising that the increased ceremonialism and hierarchical social distinctions often associated with the production and maintenance of large-scale public structures should be reflected by higher quality and more complex designs in craft production for personal adornment.

REGIONAL COMPARISONS

Wickliffe was but one village among many that were active in the Mississippian Southeast. How did its textile complex compare with those of other Mississippian settlements, large or small, nearby or distant, contemporary or noncontemporary? Do comparisons among sites suggest any trends or regional divisions? Were textiles of any significance in intersettlement interactions and regional socioeconomic systems?

These questions are addressed below, through comparison of textile attributes from as many Mississippian sites as possible. As will be seen, the scarcity of published data hinders definitive analysis, but some general trends can be discerned, pointing the way to future research.

TEXTILE EVIDENCE FROM OTHER MISSISSIPPIAN SITES

As discussed in Chapter 4, textile artifacts are relatively rare in the archaeological record of the Mississippian, and the largest collections from single sites have been recovered either from elite mortuary contexts or from rockshelters and caves not associated with villages per se. Thus, truly equivalent evidence for comparison with the Wickliffe impressed textiles must come from analyses of the presumably utilitarian fabrics impressed on pottery at other Mississippian sites.

Following are brief descriptions of these sites and their impressed textiles, followed by site-specific summaries of quantitative data for organic fabrics from Ozark-region burials and elite interments at Spiro, Etowah, and some of the pre-Mississippian Hopewell sites. Comparisons among site textile complexes will allow the consideration of regional and temporal differences. This, in turn, will form the basis for discussion of textile production, use, and significance within the Mississippian tradition as a whole.

Impressed Textiles

Although large amounts of fabric-impressed pottery have been recovered from many Mississippian sites, analysis of the impressed textiles is not carried out routinely. Figure 49 maps the locations of sites from which data on impressed textiles are available. They indicate the general distribution of textile-impressed pottery but represent only a fraction of the sites from which fabric-impressed ceramics have been recovered.

To date, no analysis of textile attributes comparable in scope to that for

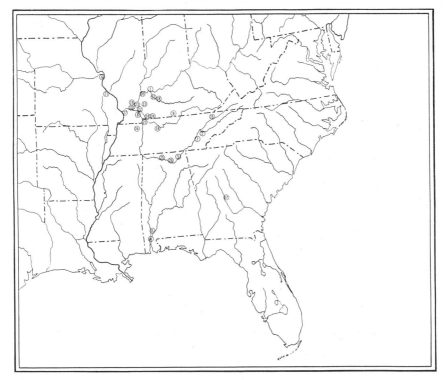

Figure 49.
Mississippian sites yielding published information about textiles impressed on pottery. See Table 12 for key.

Wickliffe has been published for any other site. In fact, only rarely have published site descriptions included any quantitative data on the nature of the impressed textiles. Table 12 summarizes the depth of published information about fabrics impressed on Mississippian pottery from various sources employed in this study. As can be seen, most information consists simply of illustrations or general descriptions of textile structures present. In a few cases, actual measurements of yarn diameters or the spacing of yarn elements within the fabric were included, but that sort of information was rare and the measurement procedures were not standardized, so it is very difficult to make comparisons among sites.

To make the most complete possible use of available material, I extracted as much attribute information as I could from published accounts, standardized the numerical data to allow intersite comparisons, and supplemented this sparse and not uniformly reliable information by analysis of small samples of fabric-impressed sherds from seven sites within the northern Mississippian region: Angel, Kimmswick, Kincaid, Obion, Slack Farm, Stone, and Tolu (designated as 1, 6, 10, 16, 20, 21, and 23 in Figure 49), plus two from the far south: Bottle Creek and Salt Creek (locations 4 and 3 in Figure 49). Published information from seven more locations—Beckum Village, Herrell, Hiwassee Island, Martin Farm, Mound Bottom, the Norris Basin, and Ocmulgee (3, 6, 7, 2, 14, 15, and 17 in Figure 49)—was quantitative enough to allow some comparison of textile attributes in addition to fabric structures alone.

Because published data for fabric-impressed sherds are not uniformly reliable and the sherd samples that I personally examined all were relatively small, intersite comparisons are only preliminary. Each one of these collections—along with totally unreported collections from many other sites—is worthy of in-depth analysis. Pertinent questions for future research involving many of them are noted in the following discussion.

The sites from which there are available quantitative data from impressed textiles are discussed in roughly geographic order from north to south. Unless otherwise mentioned, all yarns had a final **S** twist, and all twining was in the **S** direction.

The *Kimmswick* site, a salt-spring location northwest of the town of Kimmswick, Missouri, and across the Mississippi River from the major Early Mississippian "city" of Cahokia, is the type locality for Kimmswick Fabric Impressed pottery. Ceramics collected there by Bushnell in 1902 were divided between the Harvard Peabody Museum and the University of California (Bushnell 1907, 1908). Later excavations were carried out not only at the spring but in two nearby village sites (Adams 1941, 1949; Keslin 1964).

Textile impressions on pottery recovered from the Elizabeth *Herrell* site were analyzed and reported by Munger and Adams (1941). Although their qualitative comments were based on examination of a 9,500-sherd sample, published quantitative data were restricted to measurements of warp and weft diameter and distances between warps and wefts on a "representative" subset of only 30 fabrics. No statistical summary was included.

My analysis was based on the Kimmswick ceramics in the Harvard Peabody Museum collection (Drooker 1989b:255–261, 409–412). Of 107 fabrics on 104 sherds, 55 (51%) were plain twining, 51 (48%) were alternate-pair twining, and 1 was weft-faced. Of textiles with multiple structures (8.5%), 7 incorporated grouped-weft-row banded designs, while 2 consisted of plain twining plus transposed, linked warps. Alternate-pair twining with fairly close weft rows in "fluffy" yarn (comparable to Figure 35, center right) was common. As at Wickliffe, alternate-pair twining was consistently finer than plain twining.

The banded designs did include doubled twining rows but tended to have at least three closely grouped rows per band. In one example of transposed, interlinked warps the "holes" formed a geometric design (Drooker 1989b:Figure 60), while in the other (Figure 50) they occurred along a fabric edge, in two rows separated and enclosed by pairs of close-twined rows. These transposed-warp fabrics were relatively dense, with 6–7 warps per centimeter and warp diameters of from 1 to 1.25 centimeters.

Seven sherds included fabric edges. Six were either starting or terminal edges, and the seventh was a rolled-up side edge (Drooker 1989b:Figure 61). Two starting edges were similar to those from Wickliffe (Figures 41a, 42), with warp loops overlapping in the same order and two close twining rows at the edge of the fabric. Four edge finishes included additional decorative elements close to the selvage (Figure 50). In all of them, the warp loops along the edge were spaced too closely together to see exactly where they reentered the fabric. They probably were starting edges, but at least one could have been a terminal edge with cut warps bent back into an adjacent warp slot for the last few rows of twining. All included some **Z**-twist twining—probably three-element braided twining—in closely spaced rows.

One-third (35) were rim sherds. From them, it did seem that there was more than a chance relationship in fabric orientation with respect to the vessel. Four of the seven fabric edges were laid alongside or under vessel rims, parallel or near-parallel to the lip. Although data on angle of fabric relative to vessel rim were not as detailed as for Wickliffe, they were consistent with a scenario in which the starting edge of a textile tended to be laid directly under the lip of a vessel: of seven rim sherds with fabric weft rows

Table 12. Published data for textiles impressed on Mississippian pottery

I.D. No. Site[a]	Location	Type of Data Presented[b]					Sample Size[c]				Reference
		1	2	3	4	5	<11	11–100	101–500	>500	
1 Angel	Vanderburgh Co., IN	x	x	x	x					x	Rachlin 1955a; Kellar 1967
			x								Drooker 1989b
2 Bat Creek	Loudon Co., TN	x	x					x			Schroedl 1975
3 Beckum Village	Clarke Co., AL		x			x				x	Wimberly 1960
4 Bottle Creek	Baldwin Co., AL	x	x	x	x			x			Drooker 1991a
2 Ft. Loudon	Monroe Co., TN	x	x		x					x	Kuttruff 1980
5 Guntersville Basin	Tenn. R., AL	x	x							x	Heimlich 1952
6 Herrell	Jefferson Co., MO	x	x		x			+			Munger & Adams 1941
7 Hiwassee Island	Meigs Co., TN	x	x	x						x	Lewis & Kneberg 1946
9 Jewell	Barren Co., KY	x	x								Hanson 1970
8 Jonathan Creek	Marshall Co., KY	x								x	Webb 1952
6 Kimmswick	Jefferson Co., MO	x	x						x		Bushnell 1907, 1908
		x	x			x			x		Drooker 1989b
10 Kincaid	Massac Co., IL	x	x	x	x	x				x	Orr 1951; Wilder 1951
		x	x						x		Drooker 1989b
11 Kreilich, Cole	Ste. Genevieve Co., MO	x	x	x	x					x	Keslin 1964
12 Livermore	McLean Co., KY	x	x	x	x			x			Johnson 1962
8 Ml/8	Marshall Co., KY	x	x	x	x				x		Johnson 1962
8 Ml/14	Marshall Co., KY	x	x	x					x		Johnson 1962
2 Martin Farm	Monroe Co., TN	x	x	x		x				x	Schroedl et al. 1985
13 Morris	Hopkins Co., KY	x	x	x					x		Johnson 1962
14 Mound Bottom	Cheatham Co., TN	x	x	x		x				x	Kuttruff & Kuttruff 1986; Kuttruff 1987b
15 Norris 5	Tenn. R., N.E. TN	x	x	x	x		x				Griffin 1938; Webb 1938
15 Norris 9	Tenn. R., N.E. TN	x	x	x		x		x			Griffin 1938; Webb 1938
15 Norris 10	Tenn. R., N.E. TN		x			x		x			Griffin 1938; Webb 1938
15 Norris 11	Tenn. R., N.E. TN	x	x			x		x			Griffin 1938; Webb 1938

Site[a]	Location	1	2	3	4	5	Sample size[c]	References
15 Norris 17	Tenn. R., N.E. TN	x	x		x			Griffin 1938; Webb 1938
16 Obion	Henry Co., TN	x	x				x	Baldwin 1966; Garland 1990
17 Ocmulgee	Bibb Co., GA	x	x	x				Drooker 1989b
18 Paradise	Ohio Co., KY	x	x	x	x			Fairbanks 1956
11 Saline River	Ste. Genevieve Co., MO	x	x	x				Johnson 1962
3 Salt Creek	Clarke Co., AL		x	x	x			Bushnell, 1914
19 Salt Spring	Gallatin Co., IL	x					x	Drooker 1991a
20 Slack Farm	Union Co., KY	x	x	x	x			Sellers 1877; Miner 1936
21 Stone	Stewart Co., TN	x	x	x				This volume; Coe & Fischer 1959; Drooker 1990b, 1991c
22 Tinsley Hill	Lyon Co., KY	x	x	x	x			Johnson 1962
23 Tolu	Crittenden Co., KY	x	x	x	x	+		Webb & Funkhouser 1931; Johnson 1962; Drooker 1989b
2 Toqua	Monroe Co., TN	x	x	x		x	x	Polhemus 1987; Reed 1987
24 Tr/10	Trigg Co., KY	x	x	x		x		Johnson 1962
25 Wheeler Li/36	Limestone Co., AL	x	x	x	x	x		Griffin 1939
26 Wheeler Ma/4	Marshall Co., AL	x	x	x	x	x		Griffin 1939
27 Wickliffe	Ballard Co., KY	x	x		x		x	Miner 1936; Drooker 1989b, 1990a, 1990c
28 Williams	Christian Co., KY	x	x	x	x			Webb & Funkhouser, 1929; Miner 1936

[a] See Figure 49 for location of sites.
[b] Type of data presented:
1 = illustrations of representative examples;
2 = listing/description of textile structures present;
3 = statistical summary of fabric structure types;
4 = measurements of fabric attributes (e.g., yarn diameter) for representative examples; and
5 = measurements of fabric attributes for all fabrics in sample and/or statistical summary.
[c] Sample size indicates entire body of data consulted; if a significant sample of selected actual measurements is included, its size is indicated by " + ."

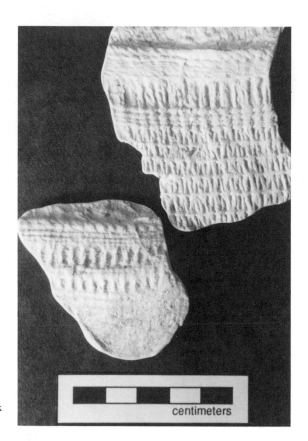

Figure 50.
Examples of Kimmswick
fabric edge structures.

parallel to the edge, three consisted of fabric starting edges placed right at the edge of the rim, and four were nonedge fabrics that seemed to extend past the edge. The rolled-over side edge also was placed directly under the lip.

Only seven of the textiles (7%) were "worn." Of three overlapped fabrics, none were lined up or oriented with respect to each other in any particular way.

The *Angel* site, located 50 kilometers (30 mi) west of the Ohio-Wabash River junction and opposite the confluence of the Green River with the Ohio, was a major fortified Mississippian town and mound site covering 40 hectares, with population perhaps as high as 3,000 (Green and Munson 1978:311–313). It served as the single paramount center within a region otherwise characterized by smaller sites, ranging in size from small villages and hamlets (¼–1 ha, or 0.6–2.5 acre) down to farmsteads and camps (< ¼ ha). The Angel phase has been radiocarbon-dated to approximately A.D. 1050–1450 (Green and Munson 1978:305–313). The complete collection from Angel is housed at the Glenn A. Black Laboratory of Archaeology, Indiana University, Bloomington. Although Rachlin analyzed some 1,300 textile-impressed sherds in great detail, a complete report of her findings never was published, and the data sheets unfortunately do not survive today (Rachlin, personal communication 1989). A statistical summary of fabric structure types was included in the site report (Kellar 1967:472), and Rachlin has given a qualitative description of them, along with ranges of yarn diameters and yarn elements per centimeter (1955a).

For the entire 10,184 fabric-impressed sherds recovered, 7,947 are listed as plain twined, including 188 with "close weft," 230 were identified as "plain plaiting" (diagramed as open "balanced" 1/1 interlacing), 1,829 are given as alternate-pair twining, 163 as "octagonal openwork" (plain twining with transposed interlinked warps), 13 as "net impressed" (knotted netting), 1 as a combination of plain twining and alternate-pair twining, and 1 as a combination of plain twining and plain interlacing. Of the plain-twined and alternate-pair-twined textiles, 272 (2.7%) were reported to have "paired weft" or "triple weft," that is, grouped-weft-row banding.

The sherds and "positive molds" of sherds from Angel and Tolu (below) that I examined are in the collection of the University of Michigan Museum of Anthropology. I studied them because, of all Mississippian sites, these two had been reported in the literature to have the greatest structural variety in their impressed textiles. The "positive molds" clearly were made to exhibit this variety: the ones from Tolu sherds served as illustrations in Webb and Funkhouser's report on that site (1931:Figures 54–58), and those from Angel included examples of all complex structures reported by Rachlin (1955a).

Of the 25 "type" casts from Angel that I analyzed (Drooker 1989b:254–255, 408), three textiles were knotted, two of thin yarns (0.5–0.6 mm), and one of 2-millimeter-diameter yarn with a close mesh. Six were of alternate-pair twining, one of which included a paired weft-row band design. The rest were plain twined, including five weft-row band designs containing consistent numbers of twining rows (two, three, or four) in the weft-row groups, one plain-twined textile with transposed, interlinked warps, and one plain-twined fabric with diagonally diverted warps, similar to those from Wickliffe (Figures 9f, 25, top). In addition to the diagonal lines formed by diverted warps, the Angel textile also incorporated paired-weft-row bands. With a fabric count of 13, the Angel fabric with transposed interlinked warps was of a scale between that of the two finest examples in Figure 27. Another interlinked-warp textile, on a sherd displayed at the Angel site museum, appeared to be finer. Since none of these "type" casts included any interlacing, I am inclined to be somewhat skeptical about the "plain plaiting" category in Kellar's report. If identification for most of the sample was directly from sherds rather than from casts, it would be relatively easy to mistake fine alternate-pair twining (as in Figure 23, top) for plain interlacing.

Most of the "type" cast textiles were relatively fine, ranging up to maximum fabric counts of 16.8 for a plain-twined fabric and 18 for an alternate-pair-twined fabric. The coarsest example had 4-millimeter-diameter warps and a fabric count of 3.0. Rachlin gave a yarn diameter range of from 0.25 to 2 millimeters for all twined textiles and noted higher fabric counts for alternate-pair twining than for plain twining (1955a:6).

The *Slack Farm* site, just opposite the confluence of the Wabash and Ohio rivers, is famous (or infamous) as an important Late Mississippian settlement location that recently was systematically pillaged by looters (Fagan 1988). Archaeological investigations were carried out to recover as much data as possible. A preliminary analysis of a 5% random sample of recovered artifacts has been carried out at the University of Kentucky, where the collection is curated, and a two-year in-depth research project began in mid-1991 (Munson and Pollack 1990).

This 14-hectare (35-acre) village and cemetery has been assigned to the Caborn-Welborn phase (ca. A.D. 1400–1700) based on its location, size, features, and ceramic types and the presence of European trade goods. A pre-Mississippian Woodland component also exists at the site, but "no significant Angel phase component" (Munson and Pollack 1990:9). Caborn-Welborn settlements, many of which were located downriver from the Angel site, are characterized by large villages, rather than by a single paramount center at the top of the settlement size range (Green and Munson 1978:319). Total population is estimated to have been similar to that of the Angel phase but distributed differently among settlements (Munson and Pollack 1990:15). Pottery includes some types present during the Angel phase, plus distinctive decorated jars and effigy vessels (Green and Munson 1978:300–301; R. Lewis 1990b:409). The presence of large storage pits and the absence of fortifications at Slack Farm and at Caborn-Welborn settlements in general has led to the hypothesis that occupation, unlike that at Angel, was seasonal rather than year-round (Munson and Pollack 1990:8–9).

A very large number of fabric-impressed saltpan sherds have been recovered from Slack Farm, of which I analyzed a grab sample of 127 sherds from 16 locations (97-34, 99-69, 720-282, 861-19, 862-6, 863-18, 913-21, 921-14, 952-63, 974-13, 988-11, 999-69, 1036-2, 1036-8, 1090-53, "general provenience"), mostly looters' piles or holes.

No fabric structure other than twining was present. Of the 126 textiles from 124 sherds that could be analyzed, 104 (82.5%) were open plain twining, 21 (16.7%) were alternate-pair twining, and 1 consisted of parallel yarns. An unexpectedly large proportion of fabrics was decorated (34.9%), in three structural variations. There were 21 plain-twined and 3 alternate-pair-twined fabrics (19.0% of the total) with grouped-weft-row bands in a very consistent pattern: two rows close together but not touching, as in Figure 8. One damaged alternate-pair-twined textile may have had a pattern of three rows grouped together. Fifteen textiles (11.9%) consisted of plain twining plus interlinking, including some sherds large enough that motif shapes could be discerned. For example, Figure 51 shows a cast from two large sherds on which were impressed a fabric in this structural combination that was decorated with parallel zigzag lines, six warps (three linked pairs) wide. The third type of decoration is unknown so far from any other site: "stripes" consisting of several rows of **Z**-twisted warp twining over weft-row pairs. This kind of warp striping occurred on one alternate-pair-twined example and three plain-twined examples possibly from the same textile (Figure 51, bottom).

Yarns were relatively fine and restricted in size range (mean = 1.4 mm, with only one fabric having yarn diameters larger than 3 mm), but not highly processed. For instance, only 35% of the warp yarns could be seen to be two-ply, compared with 66% at Wickliffe. Alternate-pair-twined fabrics had finer yarns than plain-twined fabrics (averaging 1.3 vs. 1.4 mm) as well as much higher fabric counts (11.2 vs. 7.8 elements per cm). Plain-twined fabrics with interlinking had still finer yarns (mean = 0.96 mm) and higher fabric counts (mean = 11.5). For the entire sample, warp counts averaged 4.83, weft counts averaged 3.46, and fabric counts averaged 8.36, notably finer than Wickliffe (mean = 7.59). Fabrics also averaged denser than Wickliffe.

Two sherds with overlaid fabrics were found (1.6%). "Worn" textiles constituted 23.8% of the total. The sample included only three rim sherds (average diameter = 70 cm, or 28 in).

All of the Slack Farm fabrics from this sample would be appropriate for garments. This may help to explain the high proportion of decorated textiles—it may be a direct indicator of the percentage of decorated garment fabrics (as opposed to Wickliffe, where impressed fabrics most likely included both garments and coarser textiles used for other purposes). The dearth of overlaying implies generous dimensions, but data are too sparse to estimate "saltpan" diameters reliably. Analysis of a much larger textile sample, in conjunction with reanalysis of a comparable sample from Angel, is highly recommended.

Tolu, an 8-hectare (20-acre) mound and village site on the Ohio River between the Kincaid- and Angel-dominated regions, was excavated by Webb and Funkhouser (1931). It is said to have "many similarities to Obion" (see below) but possibly dates to somewhat later (Baldwin 1966:394). The diver-

Figure 51.
Examples of Slack Farm decorated textiles: *top*, plain twining plus transposed, interlinked warps in pattern of parallel zigzag lines (three parallel lines, each the width of three pairs of interlinked warps, start at top center, travel down to the right, then down to the left, and finally down to the right); *bottom*, plain twining plus "stripe" of **Z**-twisted warp twining over pairs of weft yarns.

sity of its impressed fabrics is perhaps the greatest reported in the literature. Most of the Tolu artifacts are located at the University of Kentucky, Lexington. A sample of 191 textile-impressed sherds was analyzed with regard to textile structure by Johnson (1962:14), and a few examples of textile attribute measurements are included in the original report (Webb and Funkhouser 1931:389).

The sample from Tolu that I analyzed is part of the collection of the University of Michigan Museum of Anthropology (Drooker 1989b:249–254, 406–407). It included 24 casts, many of which were photographed and published by Webb and Funkhouser (1931:Figures 54–58), plus 43 sherds from which I made my own casts. Clearly, the sample was preselected to include a variety of different structural combinations and cannot be thought of as statistically representative of all impressed textiles from that site. However, it certainly does illustrate the wide range of textile structures in use there.

Of the textiles I examined, 2 were knotted (both rather fine, with yarn diameters averaging 0.75 mm), 11 were of alternate-pair twining, and 54 were of plain twining. None were weft-faced. Three of the alternate-pair-twined textiles and four of the plain-twined textiles incorporated grouped-weft-row bands, most of which were irregular in sequence. One plain-twined fabric, very well made and regular, alternated groups of thick yarns (1.8-mm diameter) with groups of thinner yarns (0.5–0.8-mm diameter) in the warp, forming a visually prominent striped pattern. Five plain-twined fabrics with transposed, interlinked warps were included in the sample, plus one example of a design formed by extra weft twists, similar but not identical to the drawing in Figure 2f.

Alternate-pair-twined textiles were finer on average than plain-twined textiles, with a maximum fabric count of 17.5. One example was found of a dense but relatively fine alternate-pair-twined fabric constructed with "fluffy" weft yarns. The examples of fabrics with geometric "hole" designs formed by transposed, interlinked warps are similar in scale to those from Wickliffe (Figure 27).

Of 67 textiles, 17 (25%) were "worn."

The *Kincaid* site, with its 19 mounds and palisade enclosing some 70 hectares (173 acres), was the most imposing Mississippian settlement in the lower Ohio Valley area. Its location on the Ohio River, opposite the mouths of the Tennessee and Cumberland rivers, was a commanding one in terms of transportation and communication. The settlement was active ca. A.D. 900–1400, with major mound construction completed by ca. 1250–1300 (Butler 1990:269–271; Muller 1987:12; Yerkes 1988:342).

Excavated artifacts are housed at the Southern Illinois University at Carbondale. The site report made a conscientious effort to quantify information about impressed textiles, but unfortunately the statistics are inconsistent, and the textile descriptions show some unexpected aberrations (Cole 1951; Orr 1951; Wilder 1951). Unlike textiles impressed on pottery from all other Mississippian sites, drawings of Kincaid fabrics showed them as twined in the **Z** direction, and descriptions use the ambigous term "clockwise." In addition, the reported yarn sizes and fabric count data seemed anomalously large compared with those from other sites (Orr 1951:317–319; Wilder 1951).

Because such characteristics, if actual, could be important in tracing regional relationships among textile complexes, I studied a small "grab sample" from this site to double-check the published textile attributes, analyzing all of the textile-impressed sherds in one box out of a total of 12½ from the "Late Kincaid" Mx^v1-c domiciliary area. In this 54-sherd sample, all of the twining was in the **S** direction, contrary to published reports. The fabrics I saw did seem to be somewhat finer in scale with smaller-diameter yarns than those reported by Orr, but the sample was too restricted to make any definitive conclusions (Drooker 1989b:247, 249–250, 404–405).

Of the sherds I examined, 41 (76%) were plain twined, 11 (20%) were alternate-pair twined, and 2 (4%) were weft-faced. No banded designs were found, but the plain-twined textiles included one with a geometric design in transposed, interlinked warps (Drooker 1989b:Figure 57). This is entirely consistent with Orr's report of 2.1% occurrence for "octagonal work," and "rare" occurrence of double-weft-row bands. He noted that "octagonal openwork" design shapes were "frequently found as strips in association with plain twining strips on same fabric," although shapes other than strips also did occur (Orr 1951:319; Cole 1951:Plate 31F). Alternate-pair twining made up 12% (62 examples) of the 504-sherd sample on which he reported, while 80% of it (401 examples) was plain twining (Orr 1951:319). He found 1 example of a "balanced interlaced" textile with a 1/1 structure, plus 10 examples of 3/3 interlacing with flat strips, "presumed to be mats." The flat elements ranged between 3 and 15 millimeters (0.1–0.6 in) wide. Seventeen examples were described as plain twining over twig warps. Leaf impressions also were present but "rare." Wilder (1951:372) and Orr (1951:319) noted that "octagonal openwork" yarns were consistently of small diameter, 0.5–1.0 millimeter.

Part of the difficulty in measuring yarn diameters may lie with the nature of the pottery matrix. At least in the sample I examined (from Mx^v1-c, P400–P474), the matrix, while shell tempered, was very sandy and did not yield clear impressions of fabrics. It was difficult to tell yarn ply or amount of twist, and even yarn diameters were difficult to judge in some cases. Orr gave a range of 1–6 millimeters for yarn diameters in single-structure twined fabrics, with mean values for subsamples that seem to point to an average yarn diameter of about 2 millimeters. The yarns in my sample averaged 1.4 millimeters in diameter, even excluding the "octagonal work" example, on which the yarns averaged 0.65 millimeters in diameter.

Orr reported several changes in Kincaid textile impressions over time, although he did not specify the nature of the sample(s) on which his figures were based (1951:317). Interlacing with flat strips declined from 10% of impressions in Early contexts to 0% in Middle Kincaid. From Early to Late Kincaid, plain twining increased from less than 50% to more than 76%, while alternate-pair twining decreased from 19% to 5%. Leaf impressions and high percentages of smoothed "saltpan" vessels appeared during the later portion of site occupation.

Obion is a large village site with seven mounds located on the upper reaches of the Obion River, a tributary of the Mississippi, about 105 kilometers (65 mi) southeast of Wickliffe in Tennessee. The two settlements were roughly contemporaneous. Corrected radiocarbon dates from the early Obion occupation fall between A.D. 1025 and 1154 (Crane and Griffin 1970; Stuiver and Becker 1986), and the entire occupation is estimated to extend from approximately 1050 to 1300 or 1350 (Baldwin 1966: 395; Garland, personal communication 1989).

The fabric-impressed sherds that I examined were excavated by a Harvard expedition in 1913. Later excavations were carried out by the University of Tennessee. Baldwin analyzed textiles on 65 Harvard-held sherds (47 of which had impressions clear enough for me to analyze) and on 637 held by the University of Tennessee (Baldwin 1966:248–258; Garland 1990).

Of 50 different fabric fragments that I analyzed from 47 sherds, 39 (78%) were plain twined, 8 (16%) were alternate-pair twined, and 3 (6%) were weft-faced (Drooker 1989b:245–247, 402–403). Except for two examples of closely spaced twining adjacent to a selvage, no banded weft row patterns were found. There was at least one example of alternate-pair twining with fairly close weft rows in "fluffy" yarn.

Baldwin's larger sample exhibited a greater proportion of alternate-pair twining (30%) and included one example of warp "stripes" consisting of alternating pairs of thick and thin yarns (1966:249, Plate 60). This was the only example of a structurally decorated fabric in the Obion sample. Baldwin identified four sherds with a "twined pattern in which the warps are crossed" as "the only complex pattern noted among the textile marked sherds" (1966:251, Plate 61). In fact, these were pairs of textile starting edges sewn together, identical in structure, scale, and joining technique to those from Wickliffe (Figures 41b, 42). Except for a single textile, in which three rows of closely spaced **Z**-direction twining occurred at the edge of a sherd on an otherwise **S**-twined textile (possibly a fabric edge structure), all twining was in the **S** direction.

Average yarn diameter in the impressions I analyzed was 2.2 millimeters, and average fabric count was 5.9—relatively coarse. This does not accord with Baldwin's data on "cord size," which would seem to give a mean value somewhere between 1 and 2 millimeters for the 700 impressions she analyzed. Because of the very small sample size, my measurements must be taken with more than a grain of salt. In the impressions I measured, alternate-pair twining was consistently finer, in yarn size and fabric scale, than plain twining.

Two textile overlaps were identified. In each case the top fabric was frayed and torn, and no particular care was apparent in the placement of the fabrics relative to each other. Ten fabrics (20%) had torn or missing threads.

The *Stone* site, on the Cumberland River in northern Tennessee, was a short-lived settlement that may have had one mound (Coe and Fischer 1959). Limited excavations were carried out during a survey connected with construction of the Barkley Reservoir. The excavators called attention to a very complex fabric impressed on 13 of the "saltpan" sherds from the site, which they tentatively identified as Spanish lace, indicative of a post-European-contact date for the site. Later excavations, as yet unpublished, yielded two radiocarbon dates, calibrated to A.D. 1441 with a one-sigma range of 1426–1486 (UGA-2181) and A.D. 1281 with a range of 1038–1440 (UGA-2182) (Carstens 1991, personal communication 1991; Drooker 1991c:3–4), plus an additional lot of fabric-impressed sherds, now in the collection of Murray State University.

I analyzed the 229 textile-impressed Stone site sherds (233 fabrics) curated at the Frank H. McClung Museum of the University of Tennessee at Knoxville in connection with a study of the complex "lace" textile (Drooker 1990b, 1991c). It turned out to have much closer affiliations to prehistoric complex openwork textiles excavated at Spiro and Etowah than to European lace (Drooker 1991c). Besides the 13 sherds impressed with the complex openwork, 130 of the fabrics (55.8%) were plain twined, 76 (32.6%) were alternate-pair twined, 1 (0.4%) was weft-faced (an edge structure on a fabric that probably was not weft-faced), and the rest (5.6%) had unidentifiable structures. Twenty-three (9.9%), including both plain- and alternate-pair-twined fabrics, had grouped-weft-row bands, and 1 combined plain twining with both transposed crossed warps and transposed interlinked warps. In all, then, 15.9% were decorated.

Yarn diameter averaged 1.50 millimeters. While plain- and alternate-pair-twined fabrics did not differ greatly in average yarn size, the latter were

Figure 52.
Cast of Stone site complex openwork, made from two impressed sherds.

considerably finer (mean fabric count = 10.3 vs. 6.7 for plain twining) and denser (total density = 10.7 vs. 7.4). Banded textiles were relatively fine but open (mean yarn diameter = 1.2 mm, mean fabric count = 8.1, mean density = 7.4), and the transposed-warp textile was similar to them in its attributes.

The lacelike openwork textile (Figure 52) consisted of 0.8-mm yarn elements, with a fabric count of 8.1, a total density of 7.4, and complexity indices numbers 1 and 2 of 6.9 and 8.4, more complex than any textile at Wickliffe. It combined oblique interlacing, transposed elements, plain twining, and large holes formed by dropping, then picking up, yarn elements. The major design motif consisted of three concentric circles with an outer diameter of 8–10 centimeters (3–4 in) (Figure 53a). Each circle was defined

a   b

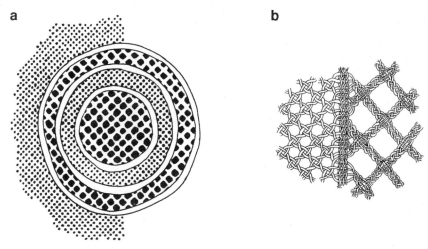

Figure 53.
Diagrams of complex openwork from the Stone site: *a*, major design motif, consisting of three
concentric circles outlined by twining; *b*, major textile structures—1/1 oblique interlacing
with transposed crossed elements (Emery describes this structure as oblique interlacing plus
oblique twining [1966:Figure 84]), close-spaced twining (shown around single elements but
also occurring around two elements at a time), and 1/1 oblique interlacing (braiding) with four
elements. The first of these structures forms the background of the fabric. (Figure 53b from
Drooker 1991c:Figure 2. Copyright 1991 Southeastern Archaeology Conference; used by
permission.)

by three close-set rows of twining (usually over two elements, but sometimes over one) that enclosed, in turn, two different openwork patterns
(Figure 53b).

One very faint impression of laced-together starting edges (as in Figure
41b) was found, as well as a single terminal edge structure that consisted of
seven rows of close plain twining securing close-cut yarn ends. In all, 32%
of the fabrics were "worn." There was no particular pattern to relative angles
of overlapped textiles.

The *Mound Bottom* site was a large settlement on a tributary of the
Cumberland River, about 33 kilometers (20 mi) west of Nashville (O'Brien
1977). Its 36-hectare (89-acre) layout included a plaza surrounded by 11
platform mounds, along with habitation areas. The occupation period was
approximately A.D. 900 to 1350. Kuttruff analyzed a 510-sherd sample of
fabric-impressed pottery from Mound Bottom habitation sites (Kuttruff
1987b; Kuttruff and Kuttruff 1986), measuring several of the textile attributes included in the Wickliffe analysis. Her measurements for the most
part are reported as ranges.

Fabric structures could be identified for 345 of the textiles. Among them were plain twining (77%), alternate-pair twining (17%), weft-faced (0.5%), and combinations of two or more textile structures (4.6%), including grouped-twining-row bands and diverted warps formed by a combination of plain twining and twining around two warps at a time (Figure 9f, 25, top). Yarn diameters ranged from 1 to 4 millimeters.

In his survey of the upper Tennessee River *Norris Basin*, Webb (1938) excavated five sites with fabric-impressed "saltpans": Irvine Village (site No. 5), Harris Farm Mounds (No. 9), Ausmus Farm Mounds (No. 10), Walter's Farm Village (No. 11), and Lea Farm Village and Mounds (No. 17). All but the Walter's Farm site, a fair-sized village, contained both mounds and habitations, and all included late Mississippian (Dallas) components (Lewis and Kneberg 1946:10). Griffin analyzed the ceramics, including the impressed textiles. He listed actual measurements of warp spacing and weft spacing (given as "width of 5 warp/weft"), where they could be discerned, for all "saltpan" sherds, specifying whether the fabrics were plain twined or alternate-pair twined (1938:318–319, 336, 341, 354, 358). However, samples were small—from 5 to 61 textiles per site with measured attributes. For the purpose of intersite comparison the information from these five sites therefore has been grouped together as a single data set, totaling 210 fabrics with identifiable fabric structures, 90 with measured warp spacing, 109 with measured weft spacing, and 85 with both. Altogether, 76% were plain twined, and 24% were alternate-pair twined, with weft-faced textiles considered "rare." No structurally decorated textiles were reported.

The *Hiwassee Island* mound and village site, at the confluence of the Tennessee and Hiwassee rivers in eastern Tennessee, with a settlement area estimated at 7–8 acres (3 ha), contained both early Mississippian ("Hiwassee Island") and late Mississippian ("Dallas") components. Analysis was carried out on 2,590 Mississippian fabric-impressed sherds. Plain-twined (1,421), alternate-pair-twined (1,076), weft-faced (30), and balanced interlaced (63) textiles were identified, and drawings of grouped-weft-row bands as well as of a pattern possibly formed by extra weft twists (or possibly just by worn and missing warp elements) were included in the report (Lewis and Kneberg 1946:107–109). Interlaced fabrics, including both plain weave (9 examples) and twill weave (54), were present only in Dallas contexts. Otherwise, textile assemblages for early and later Mississippian apparently were similar, but no separate breakdown was given for fabric types from the two time periods. Yarn diameters were reported as coarse ("averaging 4 mm in diameter"), medium ("about 2 mm in diameter"), or fine ("1 mm in diameter").

The *Martin Farm* site, on the Little Tennessee River in eastern Tennessee, included pre-Mississippian and Early Mississippian components. Its "Mississippian I" (A.D. 900–1000) and "Mississippian II" (1000–1200, equivalent to the "Hiwassee Island" component at the Hiwassee Island site) included one mound plus habitation structures (Schroedl et al. 1985:iii). The fabric-impressed pottery incorporated quartz-tempered, sand-tempered, limestone-tempered, and shell-tempered wares. Cord-marked pottery was another significant type. Although some limestone tempering was associated with Early Mississippian contexts, most Mississippian fabric-marked pottery was shell tempered, and the numbers reported below are from that type alone.

Unlike most other Mississippian sites from which data are available, significant proportions of yarns with final **Z** twist were reported here, although the percentage of **Z**-twisting declined considerably from that of earlier Woodland components (Schroedl et al. 1985:163–165, 184–195). For example, two-ply cords on Woodland limestone-tempered cord-marked ceramics contained up to 70% **Z**-twisting, while "nearly an equal percentage of shell tempered sherds had **S**-twisted cordage impressions" (Schroedl et al. 1985:187). On fabric-impressed shell-tempered "saltpan" ware, only 12 warp sets and 13 weft sets from 538 textile impressions were identified as **Z**-twisted (2%). Yarn diameter in the entire shell-tempered sample ranged from 0.5 to 7.0 millimeters, with an average of 2 millimeters (calculated from data in Schroedl et al. 1985:Table 32). Three examples of twill interlacing were found, but the vast majority of the textiles were reported to be plain twined. Following Lewis and Kneberg's method of organization for Hiwassee Island data, fabrics were grouped as "coarse open simple twined," "fine open simple twined," "coarse closed simple twined," and "fine closed simple twined." From photographic examples the 56 "coarse closed simple twined" textiles apparently are equivalent to the Wickliffe weft-faced category, and some of the "fine closed simple twined" may be as well. However, at least one and possibly two photographs of sherds in the latter category appear to be alternate-pair twining, and a description of nine possibly weft-faced textiles containing a diagonally aligned pattern of twists also may well be alternate-pair twining (Schroedl et al. 1985:193, Figures 91h, 91i). No structurally decorated fabrics were illustrated or described.

No analysis of impressed fabrics came from the nearby *Bat Creek* site. However, the photographs of fabric-impressed sherds included one of a join exactly like those from Wickliffe (Figure 41b), except that it occurred between two coarse alternate-pair-twined fabrics rather than plain-twined ones (Schroedl 1975:Figure 58; Chapman 1985:Figure 7.1f).

The early Mississippian *Ocmulgee* site, on Georgia's Macon Plateau, included seven mounds (Fairbanks 1956:43, 47, 49, 55, 80–84). It is described as probably closely related to Hiwassee Island and to Irvine Village and Lea Farm Village and Mounds in the Norris Basin but perhaps predating them somewhat, and definitely predating Etowah. Based on a 183-sherd sample, fabrics impressed on pottery there are reported to consist almost entirely of plain twining, but with rare instances of alternate-pair twining and weft-faced fabrics, plus some cane basketry in 3/3 twill. Yarn diameters are given as 1 to 2 millimeters, with "warp spaced 1 to 3 millimeters." Both **S**- and **Z**-twisted cord were found, but "twining is always right hand twist" (Fairbanks 1956:47).

A small amount of attribute information is available from three sites in southern Alabama, far distant from all of the other sites for which "saltpan" textile attribute data have been published. From the *Beckum Village* site, 1,337 sherds of fabric-impressed pottery, representing 22% of all ceramics, were recovered. This site is at a large salt spring close to the Tombigbee River, about 60 kilometers (40 mi) north of Mobile, Alabama. Measured fabric attributes were not reported for this site alone, but for all "Langston Fabric Marked" pottery from a survey of 18 village and mound sites in southern Alabama (Wimberly 1960). However, since the 1,337 sherds from Beckum Village represented 97.4% of all such sherds included in the study, the attributes of impressed textiles described for this ceramic type are taken as typical of Beckum Village. The fabric complex as reported includes the only impressions of looped netting and plain interlacing with flat elements that have been reported from any site. Plain twining, "rare" fine weft-faced textiles, and knotted netting also were found. Alternate-pair twining was not reported, but a very fine, almost weft-faced, fabric type that was noted seems more characteristic of this structure than of plain twining. A yarn diameter range of 1 to 5 millimeters was noted; warp spacing commonly was 1–2 millimeters apart, but ranged up to 20, while weft row spacing ranged from 0.3 to 5.0 (Wimberly 1960:163–165, 186–187). In light of the unusual structures reported and the uncertainty of some of the descriptions, re-analysis of these impressed textiles would be decidedly worthwhile.

A small number of fabric-impressed sherds collected from another Clarke County saline site, *Salt Creek*, represent a far more restricted range of textiles (Drooker 1991a). Only interlaced twill matting and a medium-coarse weft-faced structure were found on nine sherds. The two weft-faced sherds had two-ply wefts averaging 2.75 millimeters in diameter, with 1.0–1.3 warp elements and 5.5–7.3 weft elements per centimeter. Five Salt Creek Cane Impressed sherds were impressed with 4/1 broken twill. Elements were consistently large, 5–6 millimeters wide, with 1.85 to 2.50 elements per centimeter, giving extremely dense fabrics (23.2 mean total density). Two sherds of Salt Creek Cane Impressed incorporated both 4/1 broken twill and a straight twill forming straight lines, as in typical mat borders (Figure 21). These fabrics were finer (3.6 mm average element width, 2.4–2.8 elements per cm) and less dense than those lacking straight twill structures.

The major mound site of *Bottle Creek*, in the Mobile-Tensaw river delta 50–60 kilometers (31–37 mi) south of the two saline sites, is considered to be related to Salt Creek by virtue of the presence of Salt Creek Cane Impressed ware (I. Brown, personal communication 1991). Bottle Creek is approximately contemporaneous with the very large and complex Moundville site in west-central Alabama (Figure 1), which flourished ca. A.D. 1200–1500 (N. Holmes 1963:26; Peebles 1978). A limited excavation in the 1930s by the Alabama Museum of Natural History yielded a small sample of matting- and fabric-impressed sherds, plus a piece of daub from house construction (Drooker 1991b). The single weft-faced impressed textile had 4.5-millimeter weft yarn spaced at two elements per centimeter. The 19 twill matting impressions that could be analyzed (from a total of 21) all incorporated 4/1 broken twill, and 2 may incorporate straight twill as well. Their scale encompassed the same range as the Salt Creek matting: element width 3.0–6.5 millimeters (mean 4.6) and warp/weft count 1.6–3.1 elements per centimeter (mean 2.4), but there was no clear difference between sherds with only 4/1 twill impressions and those also containing straight twill. On all rim sherds, fabric impressions extended all the way to the vessel lip. One-third of the twill matting impressions were "worn." The daub impression was very different from the matting: 1/1 interlacing of 3 millimeter wefts on 7-millimeter warps, less dense than the matting (total density of 15 vs. 22 for the twill average), with elements that were sharply cut and totally unworn.

For the remainder of the sites listed in Table 12, information about impressed textiles was limited to lists of fabric structures present (which may or may not have been comprehensive or accurate) and/or photographs or drawings of typical textiles. Their major usefulness is as proof of the presence of a particular type of fabric. Table 13 summarizes this information, which will be discussed comparatively below, in the section "Geographic and Temporal Variation in Mississippian Textile Attributes."

As can be seen from these brief descriptions, the quality and quantity of available numerical data are ragged indeed. Many of the samples, including most of those that I analyzed myself, were so small and selective that they cannot be considered to be statistically representative of the textile-impressed pottery at the site from which they came. Moreover, the non-standardized terminology and measurement methods employed in the orginal reports hamper direct comparison between sites.

Thus, rather than employing this information as if it were statistically representative of specific sites, it is most usefully considered only as generally indicative of the range of variation in textiles impressed on pottery at Mississippian sites. In addition, it must be kept in mind that even if samples of fabric-impressed sherds from given sites adequately represent the actual populations of textiles impressed on pottery—which many of these samples probably do not—dissimilar groups of textiles from separate locations may or may not reflect different textile-making traditions. Rather, they may merely indicate different criteria in choosing textiles for use in pottery production.

Organic Textiles

To provide additional perspective on textile production and use within the Mississippian, comparative data on organic textiles from pre-Mississippian elite Hopewell burials, nonelite Mississippian Ozark-region burials, and elite interments from the major Mississippian ceremonial centers of Spiro and Etowah also were considered. They, too, of course, represent specially selected samples from the entire body of Mississippian fiberwork.

Most of these sites already have been mentioned in connection with textile artifacts. To supplement that information, very brief site descriptions and summaries of fabric attributes are given below. There is almost no overlap between sites with moderate to large collections of fabric-impressed pottery (e.g., Figure 49) and sites that have yielded fabric collections of any size (e.g., Figure 12).

A fairly large number of *Hopewell* period (ca. 100 B.C.–A.D. 300) fabric fragments have been analyzed, and their attributes are summarized here as exemplary of pre-Mississippian high-status textiles. Hopewell peoples, whose culture centered on the southern Ohio region but also extended to Illinois, were notable for their elaborate mortuary practices (Brose and Greber 1979). Although their yarns were not as highly processed as those found at elite Mississippian sites such as Etowah (Yerkes 1991:543), fabrics from Hopewell burials were remarkable for their fineness. For example, the mean diameter of yarns in 29 alternate-pair-twined textiles from the Seip, Harness, and Hopewell mound groups in Ohio was 0.92 millimeters, they averaged 9.6 warps per centimeter, and the mean fabric count was 20.4 elements per square centimeter, almost double that of alternate-pair-twined textiles at Wickliffe (raw data from Church 1984). Warp elements per centimeter ranged up to 15 for twined textiles (Hinkle 1984:328–330; Peabody Foundation No. 61414). Yarns as fine as 0.2 millimeters occurred (E. White 1987:77). Similarly fine oblique interlacing (10 elements per cm) was ubiquitous on the surfaces of copper artifacts from the Hopewell mound group (E. White 1987:60–69).

Also notable were large-scale, strikingly colored painted, stenciled, or stamped designs on fine alternate-pair-twined cloth adhering to copper

Table 13. Textile structures impressed on Mississippian pottery at various sites

I.D. No. Site	Twining					Interlacing[d]			Unknown	Netting	
	Plain	Alternate-pair	Banded[a]	Diverted warps[b]	Transposed warps[c]	Plain	Twill	"Lace"	Weft-faced[e]	Knot	Loop
1 Angel	x	x	x	x	x	x			x	x	
2 Bat Creek	x	x	x		x	x	x,	+		x	x
3 Beckum Village	x					+			x	x	x
4 Bottle Creek							+		x		
2 Ft. Loudon	x	x				x	x			x	
5 Guntersville Basin	x	x				x					
6 Herrell	x	x	x								
7 Hiwassee Island	x	x	x			x	x			x	
9 Jewell	x	x									
6 Kimmswick	x	x	x		x				x		
10 Kincaid	x	x	x		x	x	+		x		
12 Livermore	x	x									
8 MI/8	x										
8 MI/14	x	x							x		
2 Martin Farm	x	(x)					x			x	
13 Morris	x	x							x		
14 Mound Bottom	x	x	x	x					x		
15 Norris 5	x	x							x		
15 Norris 9	x	x							x		
15 Norris 10	x	x							x		

15 Norris 11	x					x
15 Norris 17	x					
16 Obion	x					x
17 Ocmulgee	x				+	x
18 Paradise	x					
11 Saline River	x			+		x
3 Salt Creek					+	x
19 Salt Spring	x	x				x
20 Slack Farm	x	x		x		
21 Stone	x	x		x, +		☆
22 Tinsley Hill	x	x				
23 Tolu	x	x	+	x		x
2 Toqua	x	x		x		x
24 Tr/10	x	x				x
25 Wheeler Li/36	x	x		x	+	
26 Wheeler Ma/4	x			x	+	x
27 Wickliffe	x	x	x	x, +	+	x
28 Williams	x	x	x			

Note: The information is from published sources listed in Table 12 and from personal inspection. For diagrams of these structures, see Figures 9 and 10.

[a] Banded = grouped weft rows, in either plain or alternate-pair twining.

[b] Diverted warps = plain twining with diverted warps, not transposed. Here x = caused by combination of plain twining and twining around two warps at a time; + = caused by extra weft twists.

[c] Transposed warps = plain twining with transposed warps. x = interlinked; + = crossed, not interlinked.

[d] Here x = spun yarns or element type unknown; + = flat strips, probably of bark or cane (basketry, not cloth); and ☆ = combination of oblique interlacing and transposed crossed warps similar in appearance to European bobbin lace.

[e] In weft-faced, the warps are not visible; the structure is either plain twining or plain interlacing.

"breastplates" in Hopewell burials such as at the Seip mound group, and attached decoration in the form of copper cutouts and beaded patterns (Shetrone and Greenman 1931:451–454; Hinkle 1984:33, 42). Five small fragments of weft-faced twined tapestry were excavated at the Hopewell mound group (E. White 1987:70). Other cloth structures reported present in Hopewellian burials include spaced plain twining, some of it with grouped-weft-row bands; weft-faced twining, some of it countered; double oblique twining; weft-faced interlacing; and looping (Hinkle 1984:19–115; E. White 1987:58–77). Twill interlacing with flat elements was used for matting.

Aside from rare countered twining on some weft-faced fabrics, wherever twining twist direction was noted, it was **S**. For example, **S**-twining occurred in 134 of the 135 twined fabrics from seven Ohio mound groups studied by Hinkle, and countered twining in only 1 (1984:326–330). Both **S**- and **Z**-twisted yarns have been found, although the **S** direction was far more common (Hinkle 1984:328–330; E. White 1987:85). Some yarns incorporated fur or feathers (Hinkle 1984:328–330; E. White 1987:85). Among fabric structures, decorative combinations of plain twining plus manipulated warps are notably absent.

The two largest collections of actual (organic) Mississippian textiles and artifacts come from elite mortuary contexts at opposite sides of the larger Mississippian culture area, Spiro, Oklahoma, and Etowah, Georgia (Figure 1).

Etowah is an imposing 21-hectare (52-acre) site on the Etowah River that had residences, numerous mounds, and two large plazas enclosed by a bastioned palisade and moat (Larson 1989:135–136). It dates to ca. A.D. 950–1450 (Larson 1971:61), with some later components (Jeffrey Brain, personal communication 1990; M. Smith 1987:48, 90, 91). One of the three largest mounds, Mound C, was excavated by a Smithsonian expedition in 1884, an R. S. Peabody Foundation expedition in 1925, and the Georgia Historical Commission in the 1950s, yielding over 300 burials, numerous high-status grave goods in exotic materials, including many that have been assigned to the Southeastern Ceremonial Complex, and a fair number of yarns and fabrics. Virtually all of the Etowah textiles are fragments, not definitively recognizable as specific artifacts, although most probably were garments or burial wrappings. Some costumes included "small mica discs and crosses . . . fastened to garments like sequins," and headdresses and other accoutrements provided evidence that certain people did array themselves like the "hawk man" figures portrayed in Mississippian art (Larson 1989:140).

Only two Etowah fabrics were published prior to this decade, and then only in the form of pictures: a plain-twined textile with circle-and-cross designs in bright yellow on a dark background, and an example of complex openwork that is similar in some respects to the Stone site impressed fabric (Figures 52 and 53) (Moorehead 1932:Figures 34, 64; Byers 1964). Additional examples of the complex openwork have been described but not completely analyzed or diagramed by Sibley and Jakes (1986, 1989), who also identified complex wrapped yarns incorporating feathers. Schreffler analyzed yarns and 12 textiles from two groups of Etowah graves, finding braiding (3), oblique interlacing (3), and **S**-twisted spaced plain twining (6). Diameters of 59 individual yarn fragments from Etowah Mound C outer burials averaged 0.8 millimeters (from Schreffler 1988:149–150). Of 41 two-ply yarns, 5% had a final **Z** twist. Although no examples consisting entirely of alternate-pair twining have been published, there is at least one extant Etowah textile fragment in this structure, part of the collection of the R. S. Peabody Foundation, Andover, Massachusetts (No. 61414). Attributes of this and seven other twined mortuary fabrics from Etowah were included in Table 3. No edge structures have been reported.

Several fragments plus a large, as yet unfolded, bundle of the complex openwork have survived from Etowah. They are similar in structure but simpler in design than the impressed textile from Stone (Drooker 1991c), containing bands of large holes formed by sections of braiding outlined by weft-faced twining, contrasted against background areas of oblique interlacing combined with transposed crossed elements (Figure 53b, left). These pieces are the only known examples of textiles with structural designs that have come from Etowah. Yarns are predominantly nettle (*Urticaceae boehmeria* or *U. urtica*) mixed with a second, hemplike fiber (possibly *Cannabis sativa* L. or *Apocynum cannabinum* L.), but some also incorporate "fibers with a cotton-like appearance" (Sibley et al. 1989:195–197, 209). Cotton is not known to have grown in the prehistoric Southeast, but it could have been an item of exchange.

The *Spiro* site, a 32-hectare (79-acre) civic-ceremonial center at a strategic location on the Arkansas River dating to ca. A.D. 1200–1350, capped a three-level hierarchy of settlements in the surrounding region (J. Brown 1976a:124; J. Brown et al. 1978:178, 189). In contrast with Etowah, the huge mortuary mound at Spiro yielded a very large group of textiles and textile artifacts, many of which were dug by nonarchaeologists but some of which were excavated under controlled conditions by the University of Oklahoma (J. Brown 1976b; Burnett 1945; Willoughby 1952). The center of a far-flung exchange network, Spiro hoarded exotic raw materials and "expensive" decorated artifacts of the Southeastern Ceremonial Complex, the most famous of which probably are its engraved shell cups and gorgets (J. Brown 1984; Phillips and Brown 1978).

Attributes of Spiro garments (mantles or skirts) in alternate-pair twining,

1/1 oblique interlacing, and countered twined tapestry with colored decoration have been discussed in Chapter 4 and are partially summarized in Table 3. One fine balanced plain-interlaced fabric of cotton is considered to be an exchange item from the Southwest, where cotton was cultivated and woven on looms (King and Gardner 1981:137; Kent 1947, 1983). Spiro burial fabrics of unknown function included the only instances yet reported of a nonimpressed textile containing plain twining plus paired transposed, interlinked warps (Burnett 1945:46, Plate 91; J. Brown 1976b:327, 338, 340, Figure 67). The largest of the extant fragments measures 17.5 × 8.5 centimeters (6.9 × 3.3 in). Its terminal-edge selvage, 0.6 centimeter (0.2 in) wide, consists of eight rows of three-strand braided twining (Figure 9c) used to secure warps that were doubled back into the adjoining warp ends. The body of the fabric is comparatively fine, with about 15 warp ends and 5 weft rows per centimeter. One fine weft-faced twined fabric had 13 warps per centimeter and 6.3 weft rows per centimeter (J. Brown 1976b:326). Additional fabric structures included plain twining, knotting, wrapping, twining with grouped-weft-row bands, and complex openwork in a combination of oblique interlacing, transposed crossed warps, and twining with a design of holes and crosses-in-holes, similar in structure but different in design from the lacelike Stone and Etowah fabrics (J. Brown 1976b:323–342; Burnett 1945:Plates 88, 91; Drooker 1991c; King and Gardner 1981; Willoughby 1952). A few edge finishes were described by Kuttruff (1988a:97, 107–108): narrow bands of warp twining occurred along side edges of large weft-twined textiles, and terminal-edge treatments included fringes probably held in place by twining, braided fringes, and overcasting. Baerreis (1947) analyzed Spiro cane basketry, which included complex geometric designs in bicolored broken and straight-twill interlacing.

Kuttruff made extensive measurements and analyses of 71 textiles from Spiro as well as of 48 textiles from Mississippian burials at eight *Ozark rockshelters,* all in the general region of the three Ozark sites included in Figure 12. The sites and their dates are discussed individually by Kuttruff (1988a:72–77). Ozark fabrics used by her are curated at the University of Arkansas Museum, while the Spiro textiles in her study came, in addition, from the Smithsonian Institution and the University of Oklahoma.

Kuttruff's structural subcategories did not coincide with mine, so a complete statistical breakdown of textile structures comparable to those given above for impressed fabrics cannot be provided. However, it can be said that Spiro had twice the proportion of alternate-pair-twined fabrics as the Ozark sites (13% vs. 6%), as well as far more "compact" (weft-faced, not necessarily plain) twining (38% vs. 2%), but no weft-faced interlacing, compared with 10% for Ozark burials (Kuttruff 1988a:92–111). Whereas Ozark twined textiles were fairly equally divided between **Z**- and **S**-twisted twining (56.5% vs. 43.5%), the Spiro sample had 60% **S**, 17% **Z**, and 19% countered twining (from Kuttruff 1988a:96).

The sole example of structural decoration reported from an Ozark rockshelter is a plain-twined fabric that included two rows of interlinked warps twisted in groups of three, between which was a row of transposed, crossed warps like those in Figure 9h (Pu-150 from Putnam Farm shelter, Scholtz 1975:122–126). Its weft yarns are approximately 1 millimeter in diameter, with 7 warp elements and 3 weft elements per centimeter. In addition to bag edge finishes, a number of terminal edge structures on flat fabrics from Mississippian contexts have been described and illustrated by Scholtz (1975:122–126). A terminal edge finish on a fine plain-twined inner wrapping for an infant burial consisted of three close rows of twining, after which the warps were cut off at a length of 1 millimeter (item No. M3-23 from Montgomery Shelter 3). Another plain-twined fabric (Pu161-c from Putnam Farm shelter) had a terminal edge consisting of warps bent back 180 degrees and included with the adjacent warp in three closely spaced rows of twining (Figure 15e). An alternate-pair-twined fabric of hard bast fibers associated with a child's burial had an edge similar to a bag edge, with twisted groups of warp loops secured by a braid, as in Figure 15c (M4-136, from Montgomery Shelter 4). In contrast with Spiro, no fringed edges were found at Ozark sites (Kuttruff 1988a:107–108).

Data on yarn diameter and warp elements per centimeter for twined fabrics from Spiro (high-status) and Ozark (low-status) burials were extracted from Kuttruff's measurements, for comparison with impressed twined textiles. Forty-eight Spiro twined fabrics averaged 5.2 warp elements per centimeter (maximum = 15), while 23 Ozark twined fabrics averaged 1.5 warp elements per centimeter (maximum = 12) (from Kuttruff 1988:241–246). Spun yarn diameters for all textiles analyzed by Kuttruff averaged 1.7 millimeters for Spiro and 3.0 millimeters for the Ozarks (from Kuttruff 1988a:125, 127). When unspun yarns were included, the averages were 2.0 and 3.6 millimeters. For all one- or two-ply yarns, final twist was 23% **S** and 77% **Z** for Spiro, and 33% **S** and 67% **Z** for Ozark sites (from Kuttruff 1988a:124).

From other Mississippian sites, generally no more than a few textile fragments have been recovered. A fairly large collection of structurally decorated cane matting came from Mounds Plantation, Caddo Parish, Louisiana (Webb and McKinney 1975). Some fragments of twill-interlaced matting also came from Hiwassee Island (Lewis and Kneberg 1946:107–108). At Cherry Valley, Crittenden County, Arkansas, charred pieces of coarse plain and alternate-pair twining were recovered from a mound interment (Perino

1967:24, 29). Other Mississippian mound sites that have yielded textile fragments (but with little or no published data) include Davenport, Iowa (Holmes 1884:411–412); Peoria County, Illinois (Simpson 1936); Pickwick Basin Site Lu°63, Lauderdale County, Alabama (Haag 1942:Plate 185); Dallas Focus sites near Hiwassee Island (Lewis and Kneberg 1941:17); Hollywood, Richmond County, Georgia (Thomas 1894:321, 324); and Lake Jackson, Florida (B. Jones 1982:12–15, 39). A charred alternate-pair-twined textile from the Late Mississippian Loy site in eastern Tennessee has **S**-plied two-ply yarn averaging 1.5 millimeters in diameter, with 7.5 warp elements and 6.6 weft elements per centimeter (personal inspection, courtesy of Richard Polhemus).

A large number of fabric fragments were recovered from graves at the protohistoric Milner Village site, Alabama (M. Smith et al. 1989), but they have yet to be analyzed. From a slide of a small sample of them, their structures appear to include oblique interlacing and braiding, with fabric count ranging between 12 and 24 elements per square centimeter and two-ply, **S**-twisted yarn diameters ranging between 0.5 and 1.0 millimeter. Other extant protohistoric textiles include oblique interlacing from an intrusive grave at Angel, interpreted as a shroud (Black 1967:252–254), and a kiltlike garment from Woods Island, Alabama, in an "over and under basketry type of weaving" (perhaps interlacing) stitched to a "pounded fibrous material" (Morrell 1965). The Trudeau site, associated with eighteenth-century Tunica Indians, yielded 1/1 interlaced cloth of mulberry-bark-fiber yarns as well as twill-interlaced cane basketry (Brain 1979:253).

Table 14 summarizes textile structures reported from Hopewell, Mississippian, and protohistoric mortuary contexts, in a format parallel to that used for impressed fabrics in Table 13. Also included are data from Tennessee and Kentucky rock-shelter burials reported by Holmes (1896) and described in Chapter 4.

As discussed above, measured textile attributes for samples of any significant size were available only from Spiro, Etowah, and Ozark sites and, for temporal comparison, Hopewell sites. In the following pages, these data will be compared with measured attributes from fabrics impressed on "saltpan" pottery. However, it must be emphasized that—just as with published data from impressed fabrics—the available information is far from complete. In no case were attribute data obtained from all of the fabrics recovered from a site or group of sites: textile samples were selected from certain groups of burials within a site (e.g., Kuttruff 1988a; Schreffler 1988) or on the basis of examples present within collections of a particular museum (e.g., Church 1984; E. White 1987). Nonstandard terminology and incomplete reporting of attributes also hamper comparisons among data from these studies.

Table 14. Structures of textiles from mortuary contexts

Period and site	Twining — Plain	Twining — Alternate-pair	Twining — Banded[a]	Twining — Diverted warps	Twining — Transposed warps[b]	Tapestry	Interlacing[c] — Plain	Interlacing — Twill	Interlacing — "Lace"	Unknown — Weft-faced[d]	Netting — Knot	Netting — Loop	Featherwork
Hopewell sites, OH	x	x	x			x	x	+		x		x	x
Uncertain time period													
Kentucky and Tennessee rock-shelters	x	x						+				x	x
Mississippian													
Hiwassee Island, TN								+					
Etowah, GA	x	x	x				x	+	? *				x
Mounds Plantation, LA								+					
Cherry Valley, AR	x	x					+	+					
Ozark rock-shelters	x	x	x		|, +					x	x		x
Spiro, OK	x	x	x		x	x	x	+	*	x	x		x
Protohistoric/Historic													
Angel, IN							x &/or x						
Milner Village, AL							x						
Trudeau, LA							x	+					

[a]Banded = grouped weft rows, in either plain or alternate-pair twining.

[b]Transposed warps = plain twining with transposed warps. x = interlinked warp pairs; + = crossed, not interlinked; | = three warps twisted together.

[c]Interlacing excludes narrow braids. x = spun yarns or element type unknown; + = flat strips (basketry, not cloth); * = combination of oblique interlacing and transposed crossed warps similar in appearance to European bobbin lace.

[d]In weft-faced, the warps are not visible; the structure is either plain twining or plain interlacing.

With these caveats in mind, along with similar ones for the impressed textile data, it will be possible to make cautious use of the information summarized above. Like most previously published descriptions of southeastern fabrics, these site-specific textile attribute data are of only passing interest in and of themselves. However, additional useful cultural information can be elicited by comparing fabrics manufactured and used by peoples of different time periods, different geographic regions, different settlement types, and/or different social status.

GEOGRAPHIC AND TEMPORAL VARIATION IN MISSISSIPPIAN TEXTILE ATTRIBUTES

Although textiles from Mississippian sites do have many characteristics in common, they also show some consistent variations over time and among regions. Some of these intersite and intercomponent differences may relate to social, economic, and/or technological contrasts, while some may have utility as markers of different "ethnic" groups. More data must be collected and analyzed before such hypotheses can be tested definitively, but the small-scale, preliminary comparisons discussed below can be useful to point the way toward further research.

To date, the only published studies involving such comparisons have been aimed at examining possible hierarchical relationships as revealed by differences in mortuary textiles. While Kuttruff did succeed in demonstrating statistically significant differences between textile attributes from high-status burials at Spiro and low-status burials at Ozark Bluff rock-shelters (1988a), Church (1983, 1984) and Hinkle (1984) were unable to find significant differences in fabrics from Hopewell interments in different Ohio mound groups, at least in part because of restricted sample size.

Given the larger data base available with impressed textiles, many other comparisons are possible, all of which could add considerably to our understanding not only of textile production and use during the Mississippian but also of interactions among Mississippian people in general. Along similar lines to the Spiro-Ozarks comparison, it could prove instructive to make detailed statistical comparisons between impressed fabrics from different living areas within a site, from sites of different sizes within a settlement hierarchy, from widely separated sites of similar size, or from sites of different functions, such as a salt-processing location versus a nearby settlement. Large-scale comparisons between northern and southern sites within the Middle Mississippi area (Figure 1) or between Middle Mississippi and contemporary Fort Ancient, Caddoan, or Appalachian regional data are of obvious potential interest. Comparisons of textile data from earlier and later components at a given site or between earlier and later phases within a region can provide insights into development of both technology and style. Comparisons between ceremonial garment fabrics, such as have been preserved in elite mortuary contexts, and everyday garment fabrics, such as apparently were pressed into pottery at many Mississippian sites, can give indications about allocation of time and resources, as well as about symbolic functions of clothing within different social spheres. When larger samples of textile attribute data are available from more sites, statistically rigorous comparisons of these sorts can be achieved (cf. Croes 1977; Croes and Blinman 1980). Meanwhile, some interesting similarities and differences can be seen, even from the current limited record.

Geographic Variation

In looking at geographic variation in textiles, three classes of information proved useful: yarn and twining twist direction, yarn and fabric scale, and fabric structure type. Clear regional differences are connected with the first and last of these.

Direction of yarn twist and twining twist often have been advanced as markers of "ethnic" group boundaries. For the Mississippian Southeast, significant variations do exist. **S**-twisted twining in combination with yarns having final twist in the **S** direction seems to be the overwhelming rule for Middle Mississippi sites (Figure 1), certainly for all of those that I have examined personally. However, proportions of yarns with final **Z** twist may be somewhat higher in the southeastern portion of this region. For example, whereas the percentage at Wickliffe was 0.3%, at Martin Farm 2% of yarns in fabrics impressed on shell-tempered "saltpans" were **Z**-twisted, and at Etowah a small sample of two-ply yarns had 5% **Z**-twisted. **Z**-twisting also occurred at Ocmulgee but in unknown proportions (Fairbanks 1956:47). Data from additional eastern sites are needed.

In Fort Ancient and Caddoan peripheral areas, percentages of **Z**-twisted yarns are much higher. **Z**-plying was typical of eight out of nine eastern Fort Ancient components examined by Maslowski, occurring in 81%– 100% of yarns (1984:55). A small sample of ca. A.D. 1000–1650 impressed cordage from the eastern Kentucky Paintsville Reservoir area was heavily weighted toward a final **Z** twist (Adovasio 1982:836). Single-ply yarns from Spiro and Caddoan Mississippian Ozarks sites were twisted equally in either direction, and 82% and 63%, respectively, of plied yarns from these two localities were **Z**-plied (Kuttruff 1988a:123).

Although textile attribute measurements from most sites are very limited, an attempt was made to compare available data among sites. In the absence of more detailed information, ranges of yarn diameter and fabric scale can give some idea of the refinement and functional diversity of fabrics produced and used at different locations. Figures 54 and 55 summarize this information in graphic form. The first figure compares yarn diameters from textiles and textile impressions at various sites, while the second compares warp counts (yarn elements/cm). The latter measurement was chosen as an indicator of textile scale rather than fabric count because it was available for more data sets. On the graphs, sites are organized roughly from west and north (top) to east and south (bottom).

From Figures 54 and 55, it is apparent that although evidence of the finest yarns and finest fabrics comes from elite mortuary contexts at Etowah, Spiro, and pre-Mississippian Hopewell sites, still, many of the presumably utilitarian fabrics from pottery impressions at sites such as Angel, Stone, Wickliffe, and Kimmswick approach the upper range of delicacy exhibited in the burial textiles. Average warp counts from Kimmswick, Stone, and Slack Farm were only slightly lower than the average for twined textiles from Spiro, and Wickliffe was not far behind. The sample of spun and unspun Spiro yarns recorded by Kuttruff actually has a larger mean diameter than yarns from impressed textiles at Kimmswick, Martin Farm, Slack Farm, Stone, or Wickliffe. Etowah mortuary fabrics averaged slightly finer than those from Spiro, but the currently available sample size is too small to draw any definite conclusions. Twined textiles from Ozark burial sites averaged considerably coarser (thicker yarns, lower warp counts) than impressed fabrics from any of the Mississippian village sites from which a numerical average was available, and also coarser than the few textiles from cave and rock-shelter burials in Kentucky and Tennessee for which attribute data are available (Chapter 4, Table 3). Making allowance for status differences, it is possible that, in general, yarns and textiles from Caddoan Mississippian sites are coarser than those from sites farther east.

In comparisons limited to textiles pressed into "saltpans," no clear-cut contrasts emerge among sites or regions. For example, Kincaid, the largest site from which yarn diameter and warp count data are available, is represented by somewhat coarser yarns and fabrics than some of the less-imposing sites. Relatively fine yarns and fabrics come from the salt-processing locality of Kimmswick. Wickliffe data are in between. Martin Farm yarns and fabrics are coarser than any other site (except Ozark rock-shelters), but whether this is a regional difference or a temporal one cannot be known for certain until more quantitative data are available for other eastern Tennessee sites.

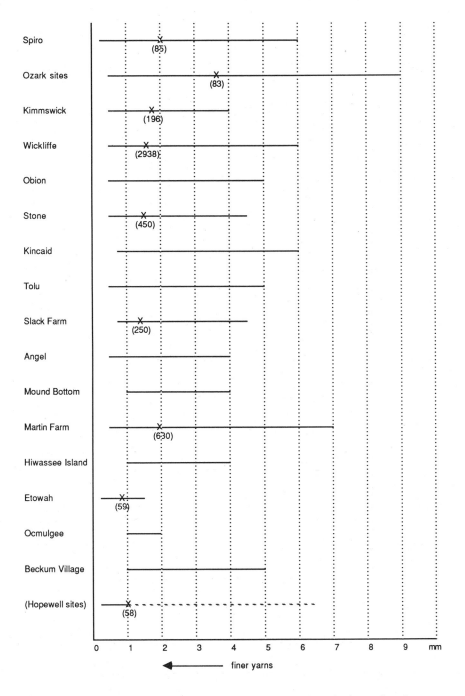

(----- = reported range. X = measured average; sample number in parentheses)

Figure 54.
Comparison of yarn sizes for selected sites. Included for comparison to Mississippian twined textiles and impressed textiles are data from pre-Mississippian Hopewell sites. All examples except those from Etowah represent average yarn diameter per textile; Etowah examples were individual yarns. Hopewell data are from alternate-pair-twined fabrics. See text for references and discussion of data.

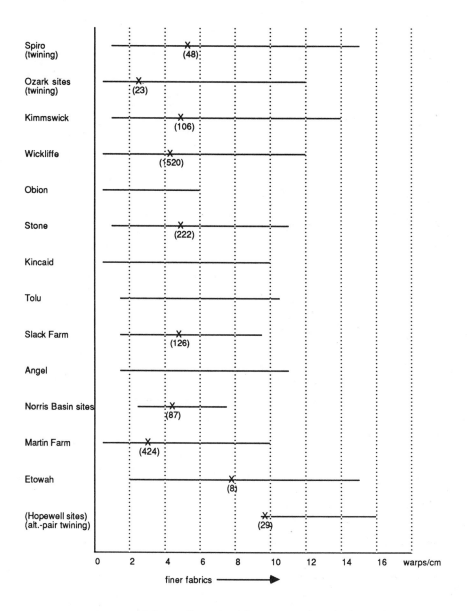

(---- = reported range. X = measured average; sample number in parentheses.)

Figure 55.
Comparison of fabric scale (warp elements per cm) for selected sites. Included for comparison
to Mississippian twined textiles and impressed textiles are data from pre-Mississippian
Hopewell sites. Hopewell examples included in average are alternate-pair-twined fabrics. See
text for references and discussion of data.

Table 15. Frequencies of occurrence of textile structures at selected Mississippian sites, given as percentages

Textile structure	Wickliffe (1,574)	Kincaid (474)	Angel (10,184)	Obion (466)	Stone (220)	Mound Bottom (345)	Hiwassee Island (2,590)	Martin Farm (538)	Norris Basin sites (210)
Plain twining	53	82	75	51	51	77	55	89[a]	76
Alternate-pair twining	29	13	16	30	32	17	42	present[a]	24
Knotting	0.6	0.1	0.1	—	—	—	—	—	—
Weft-faced[b]	6.9	3.1	1.8	17	0.5	0.5	1.2	10	"rare"
Plain interlacing (not basketry)	—	0.1	2.3[c]	—	—	—	0.3	—	—
Twill interlacing (not basketry)	—	—	—	—	—	—	2.1	0.6	—
Plain twining + transposed, interlinked warps	0.9	2.1	1.6	—	0.5	—	—	—	—
Other combinations of more than one structure	4.6	—[d]	2.7	—	15	4.6	—[d]	—	—

Note: The size of each sample (i.e., the identifiable textile structures) appears in parentheses beneath the name of each site. See Table 12 for the sources of data.

[a]Alternate-pair twining is not reported in the write-up but appears to be present in the photographs.

[b]Fabrics identified as weft-faced may not be exactly equivalent. At Kincaid, they are described as plain twining with "very small or no interweft spaces"; at Angel, as "plain twining, close weft"; at Obion, they include "simple twined, close" and "plaited," close; at Mound Bottom, "possibly compact 2-strand twining"; at Hiwassee Island, "simple twined close fabrics"; and at Martin Farm, they are described as "coarse closed simple twined."

[c]Plain interlacing is reported as "plain plaiting." See discussion in text.

[d]Grouped-weft-row "stripes" are present at Kincaid and Hiwassee Island, but the proportion is unknown.

Currently available data are far more numerous for fabric structures present than for measured textile attributes such as yarn diameter and warp count. From the textile structure data, some broad indications of regional differences in textile complexes do begin to emerge.

Textile structures known to be present on fabric-impressed pottery from 28 Mississippian sites were summarized in Table 13. Comparable information for fabrics from mortuary contexts was presented in Table 14. For some of the sites with textile-impressed pottery, large enough samples (at least 200 sherds) were available to allow comparison of relative proportions of fabric structure types present. These data are summarized in Table 15.

Impressions of spaced plain twining were absent from only two sites with very small sherd samples, Salt Creek and Bottle Creek (Table 13). This fabric type clearly was the most-available or most-preferred textile used in "salt-pan" manufacture, constituting from 51% to 89% of impressed textiles at the sites listed in Table 15. Its importance throughout the prehistoric Southeast is underlined by the relatively large number of burials from which examples of it have been recovered (Table 14).

Alternate-pair twining occurred at almost all "saltpan" sites, in proportions from 13% to 42% of the total. Although it also was found at many mortuary sites, it represented only 6% of the fabric sample from Ozark burials and 13% at Spiro. It is possible that this structure existed but was overlooked at the few "saltpan" sites where it was not reported, as seems to be the case at Martin Farm. One site where the apparent absence of alternate-pair twining should be reconfirmed is Beckum Village, where 1,337 sherds were analyzed. This location, far distant from most of the others listed, is the only one from which impressions of looping were reported, and its textile complex may well differ significantly from others farther north. The other two southern Alabama sites were even more aberrant in having only weft-faced fabrics (no spaced plain or alternate-pair twining), plus high percentages of impressed matting. Dense, relatively fine alternate-pair fabrics made of "fluffy" yarns were noticed at Wickliffe, Kimmswick, Obion, Stone, and Tolu and were hypothesized to be used for winter garments. Do such textiles occur at sites farther south? If not, their preferred use at northern sites may well be climate-related.

Weft-faced textiles are present at two-thirds of the sites listed in Table 13. Their frequency of occurrence varies significantly, from "rare" to 17% at sites in Table 15. As this is not a topologically differentiated category and varying criteria were used by different researchers when sorting their textiles, intersite comparisons should be made with caution. However, these heavy, dense textiles do seem to have been a common Mississippian fabric type, so their very low frequency of occurrence on pottery at such well-documented localities as the Norris Basin, Mound Bottom, Stone, Tolu, and Slack Farm is notable. Corroborating their infrequent occurrence elsewhere, Johnson (1962:13) found only "four or five examples" of completely weft-faced textiles in her sample of 1,157 Kimmswick Fabric Impressed sherds from eight sites in Kentucky (Table 12). They are not particularly numerous among organic textiles from any of the sites discussed above, but small samples make it difficult to make comparisons with the impressed fabrics. Of the sites listed in Table 15, Obion apparently has the largest proportion of weft-faced fabrics, with Martin Farm second in rank, followed by Wickliffe, Kincaid, and Angel. These proportions cover a wide range: 17%, 10%, 6.9%, 3.1%, and 1.8%.

Knotted netting, probably functionally less suitable for "saltpan" manufacture than other fabric structures, was found impressed on pottery at one-third of the sites. Its highest frequency of occurrence at sites listed in Table

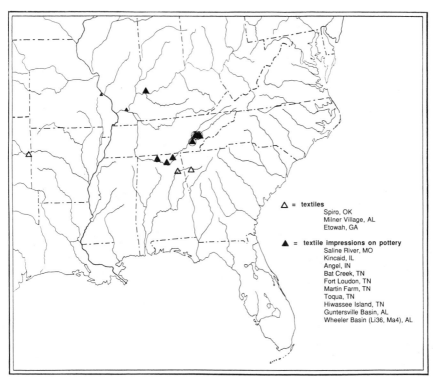

△ = textiles
  Spiro, OK
  Milner Village, AL
  Etowah, GA

▲ = textile impressions on pottery
  Saline River, MO
  Kincaid, IL
  Angel, IN
  Bat Creek, TN
  Fort Loudon, TN
  Martin Farm, TN
  Toqua, TN
  Hiwassee Island, TN
  Guntersville Basin, AL
  Wheeler Basin (Li36, Ma4), AL

Figure 56.
Locations of textiles in "balanced interlacing." Site areas where twill interlacing occurs—at Bat Creek, Fort Loudon, Hiwassee Island, and Martin Farm—are circled. Only single examples have been reported from Saline River and Kincaid. See Table 12 for sources of data on fabric impressions.

15 was only 0.6%. Impressed looped netting was reported only from Beckum Village. Knotting and looping also were not common among textiles from Mississippian burials (Table 14).

"Balanced interlaced" textiles (as distinct from weft-faced plain weave or basketry utilizing interlaced flat elements) were impressed on pottery at 12 sites, as well as surviving in fabric form at Spiro, Etowah, Milner Village, and at least two other protohistoric sites (Figure 56). Occurrences of impressed examples were concentrated in and around eastern Tennessee, particularly along the middle reaches of the Tennessee River. This region also is the only area from which interlaced twill textiles have been reported. Only single examples of interlacing were reported from Saline River, Missouri (Bushnell 1914:Plate 56), and Kincaid (Orr 1951:319). The 230 examples from Angel classified as "plain plaiting" may or may not have been correctly identified, as discussed above, but a protohistoric intrusive burial there did yield oblique interlacing. In all instances where selvages of interlaced fabrics are photographed or described, they are indicative of oblique interlacing rather than two-element interlacing. (A generalized drawing of a two-element plain weave fabric is shown in the Hiwassee Island report, but it is included only as one of the "diagrams of weaving techniques" [Lewis and Kneberg 1946:Plate 49].) At no site do balanced interlaced textiles constitute as much as 3% of the impressed fabrics.

Interlaced matting may show regional variation in the twill structures used, but samples examined so far are too small to be definitive. Only straight twill has been reported from the most northerly sites. Wickliffe's only example is 3/3 straight twill, and all 10 of the examples from Kincaid are reported as 3/3 straight twill (Orr 1951:319). Ocmulgee impressed matting is reported as 3/3 twill (Fairbanks 1956:84). At Hiwassee Island, 3/3 or 2/2 straight twill is implied by the drawing of a reconstructed mat (Lewis and Kneberg 1946:Plate 102); at that site, cane matting fragments are reported from structures and burials, but not impressed on pottery, and their structures are described only as "twilled plaited" (Lewis and Kneberg 1946:107). However, the nearby Bat Creek site has yielded at least one example in broken twill (Schroedl 1975:Figure 58). Two sherds from site Ma°4 in the Wheeler Basin of northern Alabama were impressed with 2/2 and 3/3 twill matting (Griffin 1939:151). Impressed matting from southern Alabama sites all has a base structure of 4/1 broken twill, sometimes combined with bands of straight twill floats like those on the undated mat from Tennessee (Figure 21). A variety of more complex motifs (e.g., undulating lines, birds' heads), worked in long floats contrasted against a background of 4/1 broken twill, occurred on matting associated with elite burials at the Mounds Plantation and Spiro sites. Complex motifs, along with even more structural variations than at Spiro or Mounds Plantation, have been found on matting and baskets from Ozark rock-shelters (Scholtz 1975:87–107), some of which are of Mississippian age. Such motifs may well be a feature of sites primarily south and west of the Middle Mississippi region, but more information is needed. In general, matting seems to be much more common in mortuary contexts than in pottery impressions (Tables 13 and 14); in pottery impressions it occurs with high frequency only in southern Alabama.

Decorative combinations of structures in pliable textiles occur relatively infrequently as impressions on "saltpans." Many of those noted at Wickliffe are small-scale and subtle, easy to miss in a once-over-lightly analysis of a large sample of fabric-impressed sherds. The two most commonly reported types of structural decorations, however, are easy to spot, even directly from sherds: grouped-twining-row bands (Figures 8, 24) and geometric designs

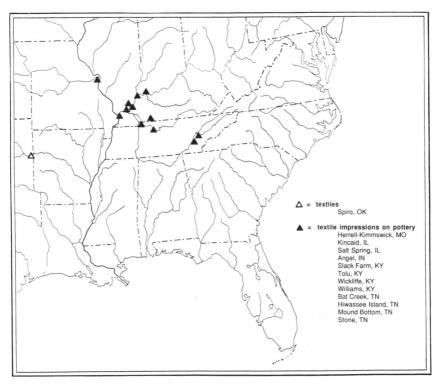

Figure 57.
Locations of textiles with grouped-weft-row bands. See Table 12 for sources of data on fabric impressions.

formed by the combination of plain twining and interlinked warps (Figures 27–28, 50–51).

Banded designs on textiles occur at Spiro and Ozarks sites and have been impressed on "saltpans" at saline sites and large and small settlements (Figure 57). They have been more frequently reported from northern Mississippian sites than from those to the southeast, but they do occur at Hiwassee Island and Bat Creek. At Angel and Wickliffe, these grouped-weft-row fabrics constitute less than 3% of all impressed textiles, but at Stone, 10% of all fabrics were banded. The percentage also was relatively high (6.5%) in the small sample from Kimmswick and reached extreme proportions in the 127-fabric sample from Slack Farm, where banded textiles made up 19.8% of the total.

There is some indication that different types of "stripe" sequences may have had greater or lesser popularity at different sites. For example, most regularly repeating sequences at Wickliffe involved the grouping of two twining rows, while Kimmswick banded patterns more often were based on a sequence of three or more grouped rows. At Angel, 271 double rows but only 1 triple row were recorded (Kellar 1967:472). Likewise, at Slack Farm 24 double rows but only 1 possible triple row occurred.

Designs formed in plain twining by transposed interlinked warps apparently are restricted entirely to the northern Middle Mississippi region, with impressed examples coming from Kimmswick, Wickliffe, Kincaid, Tolu, Angel, Slack Farm, Stone, and Gray Farm (unpublished collection, McClung Museum) and textile fragments from Spiro (Figure 58). It is perhaps of significance that percentages of occurrence of this textile type in pottery impressions at roughly contemporaneous Mississippian sites seem to be positively correlated to site size: 0.9%, 1.6%, and 2.1% from Wickliffe, Angel, and Kincaid, respectively.

Although fabric scale in "octagonal openwork" textiles covered a fairly broad range, the basic structure was always the same: **S**-twisted plain twining and **Z**-twisted interlinked warps (Figure 9i). The holes formed by the linked warps were used to delineate both horizontal lines and geometric shapes. Of the textile-impressed sherds that I have analyzed, only a joined pair from Slack Farm was large enough to clearly indicate geometric shapes (Figure 51). Even those did not reveal complete motifs. Several from Wickliffe, Slack Farm, and Angel could have been portions of circles. Although it is impossible at this time to compare design motifs among sites, one characteristic does at least hint at a regional stylistic preference: decorative borders formed by horizontal rows of interlinked warps along fabric starting or terminal edges were found only at Kimmswick (Figure 50) and Spiro (J. Brown 1976b:Figure 67). The examples of "octagonal openwork" recovered from Spiro are finer than any I have so far found impressed on pottery: 14 warp and 10 weft elements per centimeter (Kuttruff 1988a:246), compared with 11 warps and 8 wefts per centimeter of the finest-scale Wickliffe example.

Other types of structurally decorated textiles only rarely have been published. All of the examples on fabric-impressed pottery come from the northern Mississippian region. Warpwise "stripes" delineated by differences in yarn diameter or by sections of warp twining are known from Wickliffe, Obion, Tolu, and Slack Farm. Plain twining with "diagonal line" diverted warps (Figure 25, top) occurs at Angel, Wickliffe, and Mound Bottom, while diverted-warp designs formed in plain twining solely by extra weft twists (Figure 2f) come from Tolu and an unnamed Ohio Valley site (Webb and Funkhouser 1931:Figure 58b; Holmes 1896:44). Wickliffe has designs combining plain twining with oblique interlacing as well as with warp inter-

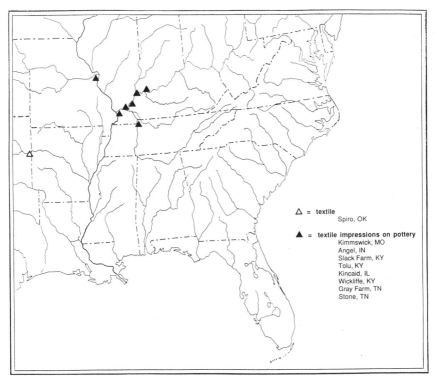

Figure 58.
Locations of textiles with plain twining plus transposed interlinked warps. See Table 12 for sources of data on fabric impressions.

linking and extra weft twists, plus a double-faced fabric with the potential to produce bicolored designs (Figure 26). A fabric from the Putnam Farm, Arkansas, site included a design that combined sections of transposed warps crossed in pairs with sections of yarn elements interlinked in groups of three rather than the two that are typical of all other Mississippian examples (Scholtz 1975:123).

Fabrics with visually prominent structural designs have survived primarily as actual textile fragments. Although twined tapestry was produced at pre-Mississippian Hopewell sites, the only known Mississippian examples are from Spiro, including the strikingly patterned fragments of "hawk man" mantles. Spiro and Etowah elite burials included examples of very complex openwork based on oblique interlacing, similar in yarns and fabric structures to the example impressed on pottery at the Stone site in north-central Tennessee (Figure 52). The Stone and Spiro examples share virtually all the same fabric structures and are similar in yarn size (0.79 and 0.75 mm, respectively) and fabric count (12.0 and 14.7 elements per sq cm), while Etowah examples are finer (0.3–0.7 mm yarns; fabric count of 23.3) and contain some different structural combinations (Drooker 1991c:Tables 2–3). Designs on each fabric are different. From Spiro there are circle and circle-and-cross motifs, from Stone, concentric circle motifs, and from Etowah, fragments that most likely represent large-scale linear motifs (Drooker 1991c:Figures 3–4). Bold colored patterns in yellow on red or brown have come from both Spiro and Etowah, but from none of the rock-shelter burials. Featherwork has been found in both mound and rock-shelter burials across the Southeast (Table 14).

A variety of starting, terminal, and side-edge finishes were used by Mississippian textile makers (Table 16). Some types of structures, such as the starting edge diagramed in Figure 41a or the bag-rim finish depicted in Figure 15c, may be typical of the entire Mississippian (and probably not exclusive to it), while others, such as close rows of three-strand twining, may be restricted to a particular region. Edge finishes have the potential to serve as sensitive markers among southeastern "ethnic" groups, but as yet not enough data have been amassed to allow a definitive comparison. At present, edges produced within the eastern Middle Mississippi region (Figure 1) and the far south are virtually unknown. The diversity found at Wickliffe probably is a function of a relatively large sample size. When more large collections of textile impressions have been analyzed in detail, statistical comparisons of edge structures can be undertaken.

To summarize apparent regional trends, then, **S**-twisted twining and yarns with a final **S** twist are typical of Mississippian areas east of the Mississippi River, and overwhelmingly present from the Cumberland River north. Yarns and fabrics from the Caddoan Mississippian region may be coarser than those from farther east. In terms of textile structures, there seems to be a possible division between fabric types from sites more to the north and west versus those more to the south and east. "Balanced interlacing" is more commonly found at southeastern than northwestern Middle Mississippi sites, and only in the east does twill interlacing occur (Figure 56). The combination of plain twining with interlinked warps is diagnostic of the northern Middle Mississippi region. In general, structurally decorated textiles are far more common in the north (Figures 57–58), and structural diversity seems to be higher there as well. The finest and most complex fabrics and the most visually prominent decorative designs have come from the elite mortuary contexts at Spiro and Etowah, setting them apart from both nonelite burial fabrics and utilitarian village textiles. However, Spiro fabrics seem to be far more diverse and complex than those from Etowah. Although this may well be due to small sample size for Etowah, it may

Table 16. Edge finishes present at Mississippian sites

Site	Side edges				Starting edges					Terminal edges			
	Knotting (9a, 20)	Warp twining (41d, 44)	Twisted weft groups (44)	"Casing" (15d)	Over-lapped warp loops (41a)	Structural decoration bordering edge (50)	Joined starting edges (overcast) (41b, 42)	Close 3-strand twining[a] (9c, 50)	Twined fringe (43)	Close twining over cut ends	Close twining over bent ends (41c, 43)	Braid (15b)	Twisted warp groups plus band (15c)
Kimmswick					x	x		x			x		
Wickliffe	x	x	x		x		x	x	x		x		
Obion					x		x	x?					
Stone					x		x						
Bat Creek							x						
Tennessee rock-shelters	x			x					x				x
Ozark rock-shelters										x	x	x	x
Spiro	x	x						x	x	x	x	x	x

Note: The numbers in parentheses show figure numbers that illustrate the various edge finishes.

[a] Close three-strand twining occurs as both starting and terminal edges.

perhaps reflect regional differences. (Alternatively, as discussed below, the distinction may be time related). The overwhelming predominance of cane matting in impressions from two out of three sites in southern Alabama seems to put them in a class by themselves, but samples are far too small to be conclusive.

Wickliffe fabrics definitely cluster with those from the more northerly sites. Moreover, the diversity of structures present within the 5%–6% of Wickliffe textiles that include combinations of two or more structures is on a par with the diversity at Tolu and Angel, the sites from which the greatest numbers of different structures preserved as textile impressions have been reported. In turn, impressed fabrics from these three sites approach the diversity and the fineness, but not the complexity, of the justifiably famous fabrics excavated from elite burials at Spiro.

Temporal Change

Some of the tentatively identified regional differences in yarn and fabric structure may be tied to changes over time. At four sites—Martin Farm, Kincaid, Wickliffe, and Hiwassee Island—differences between early and late components of the textile complex have been identified. Do the trends noted at these locations extend to other sites in a consistent pattern?

Yarns with a final **S** twist are typical, even diagnostic, of all Middle Mississippi sites from which impressed textiles have been examined to date. Wickliffe, with 99.7% of its yarns having a final **S** twist, appears to be typical of Mississippian sites after A.D. 1000. However, this trait may or may not have been prevalent within the region prior to that time. At Martin Farm in eastern Tennessee, high percentages of yarns with final **Z** twist (up to 70%) impressed on pre-Mississippian ceramics gave way to even higher percentages of yarns with final **S** twist (98%) on later shell-tempered fabric-impressed pottery (Schroedl et al. 1985:163–165, 184–195). To determine whether this apparent evolution was widespread or merely local, more data are needed from very early sites within the Middle Mississippi region. For example, fabric-impressed vessels are known from Emergent Mississippian sites like Pettit in southwestern Illinois (B. Butler and M. Hargrave, personal communication 1988), and analysis of their textiles would be helpful.

At Kincaid, interlaced matting or basketry made of flat strips of bark or cane was impressed only on early Mississippian "saltpans" but was absent from later components. There is no firm evidence that this trend is present at other sites, but data are sparse. The lone Wickliffe example was from a disturbed context. The Bat Creek site, where matting impressions occur with unknown frequency, is considered to be Early-Middle Mississippian ("late Hiwassee Island") (Schroedl 1975:vii). In contrast, in southern Alabama, where matting may have predominated in "saltpan" production, the Bottle Creek site dates to Middle-Late Mississippian.

At Kincaid, impressions of alternate-pair twining were reported to decline over time in proportion to plain twining. This is in direct contrast to Wickliffe, where the opposite relationship held true. Multicomponent data currently are available for no other sites, and data from early versus later Mississippian sites show no consistent trends.

Except in the far south, frequent usage of weft-faced textiles in pottery-making may be typical of earlier rather than later Mississippian components (i.e., before ca. A.D. 1200). The proportion of weft-faced fabrics impressed on pottery at Wickliffe apparently decreased significantly over time, from 15% for "Early" Wickliffe to 7% for "Late" Wickliffe (Table 10). The two other sites where weft-faced fabrics occur with high frequency are Obion and Martin Farm (Table 15). At Martin Farm, the most recent components (Mississippian I and II) date to ca. 900–1000 and 1000–1200, respectively. At Obion (ca. 1050–1350), Baldwin categorized "textile marked salt pans" as early at the site because of their predominant clay tempering (Baldwin 1966:306). Both the high frequency of weft-faced textiles and the virtual lack of structurally decorated textiles on Obion pottery are more congruent with the "Early" Wickliffe than the "Late" Wickliffe fabric assemblage. The relatively late Slack Farm site exhibited no weft-faced fabrics within a 127-sherd sample, while the Stone site, with radiocarbon dates spanning the thirteenth to fifteenth centuries, yielded only one, probably an edge finish.

Structurally decorated textiles seem to peak in usage over a wide area during Middle Mississippian times, ca. A.D. 1200–1450. Numerous variations occur at Spiro (ca. 1200–1350). At Wickliffe, such fabrics were impressed only on pottery from "Late" Wickliffe (ca. 1200–1350). Leaving aside textile fragments from interments at Ozark sites, Spiro, and Etowah, structurally decorated fabrics are reported predominantly from sites within the "vacant quarter," where most mound-and-village settlements became inactive after ca. 1450, and from a few eastern sites containing components roughly equivalent in date to "Late" Wickliffe, such as Hiwassee Island and Bat Creek (Figures 57–58). Structurally decorated fabrics do apparently persist within the northern Mississippian region into the fifteenth century and beyond, but in a geographically restricted area. In fact, based on relatively small samples, percentages of structurally decorated fabrics are highest at the two sites that may be the most recent of those that were considered within this northern region: Stone (16.5%) and Slack Farm (34.9%). However, the range of yarn sizes and fabric counts in the complex textiles there, as well as the number of different structural combinations, are less than for earlier sites such as Wickliffe, Tolu, and Angel. I have found no instances of impressed structurally decorated textiles from contexts limited to Early Mississippian (e.g., Martin Farm), nor any attributed to Late Mississippian components south of the Cumberland River. To more clearly define the initial development of structurally decorated fabrics, additional data for the Early Mississippian should be sought from sites with significant time depth, such as Kincaid.

At Hiwassee Island, textiles in "balanced interlacing" were not found in early components, only in Dallas-phase (Late Mississippian) contexts. However, at some other eastern Tennessee sites, including Martin Farm and Bat Creek, interlaced textiles did occur in earlier contexts. Their production persisted into the protohistoric (Table 14). Again, more data are needed to trace the development and use of interlaced textiles in the Southeast.

Thus, for textiles impressed on pottery, weft-faced fabrics may be more typical of the Early Mississippian (to ca. A.D. 1200), and structurally decorated textiles may be more typical of Middle Mississippian (ca. 1200–1450). Regional differences also must be taken into account, however: use of weft-faced fabrics persisted or occurred later in the far south, while use of structurally decorated textiles persisted later in the north.

In considering a still longer time span, Mississippian fabrics do seem to be more structurally diverse than earlier ones. Hopewell mortuary textiles, while notably fine and decorated by sophisticated colored designs, included no examples of twined fabrics with decorative patterns achieved by warp manipulation. Although structurally decorated textiles have come from a few elite mortuary contexts in eastern North America dating to two millennia or more before the present (M. E. King 1968; Heckenberger et al. 1990), Middle Mississippian "saltpans" provide the first evidence of their common use in everyday life.

TEXTILE PRODUCTION AND USE IN THE MISSISSIPPIAN

Even from this limited comparative material, it is possible to begin to discuss the Mississippian textile complex in the same terms as the Wickliffe textile complex: the functions of its textiles, the technology that produced them, and their socioeconomic significance. Perhaps the most important aspect of such a discussion is the new questions and speculations that arise. If large samples of fabric impressions on pottery from many additional Mississippian sites were to be analyzed systematically and in detail and then reported in consistent terms, we could reliably reconstruct many more aspects of fabric production and use during this period.

Functions of Mississippian Textiles

At Wickliffe, it seems apparent that textiles impressed on "saltpans" were not originally produced for the purpose of pottery manufacture. Their diversity of both fabric structure and fabric scale, together with the significant amount of time and skill invested in their production, indicate that they were designed to serve many purposes. Probably these included garments made of fine plain twining, of medium to fine alternate-pair twining, and of structurally decorated twining, and perhaps some heavier garments of medium-coarse weft-faced cloth; blankets of coarse weft-faced construction; mats of interlaced bark or cane strips; large bags of coarse to medium-scale plain and alternate-pair twining; and hunting and fishing nets fashioned by knotting. Vegetable rather than animal fibers seem to be typical of all yarns. Impressed textiles were selected for large size, and there may have been a trend over time away from the use of less supple and more highly textured textile structures such as weft-faced and knotted fabrics, but otherwise the impressions probably provide a fair representation of large, utilitarian textiles in use at Wickliffe during the early centuries of this millennium. Not represented in the pottery record are smaller items such as sashes, ceremonial items with large-scale designs in complex structures, or functionally unsuitable items such as feathered mantles and relatively rigid mats made from thick, wide elements.

How, then, do Wickliffe textiles compare functionally with those from other Mississippian sites? What insights derived from a detailed study of Wickliffe fabrics can be applied to the interpretation of textile impressions and fragments from elsewhere, most of which have been analyzed in much less detail?

At no site is there evidence for textiles being produced specifically to be used in pottery manufacture, but, as at Wickliffe, fabrics do seem to be selected for certain properties, including large size, moderate texture, and, in most cases, suppleness. At a few sites, attributes of impressed textiles imply that textiles may have been chosen to serve rather specific functions in the pottery-making process.

Wherever impressed textile size has been estimated, it is found to be large (e.g., Rachlin 1955a:7). In the small sherd samples that I examined from various Mississippian sites, only Kimmswick sherds exhibited a relatively high proportion of textile edges (7 out of 104 sherds, or 6.7%), perhaps indicative of textile widths that were smaller, on average, than vessel diameters. However, the high frequency of fabric edges there is much more likely due to the high proportion of rim sherds in the sample (33%), combined with the proclivity of Kimmswick potters to place a fabric starting edge immediately underneath the vessel lip.

Nowhere do Mississippian fabrics impressed on pottery approach the functional standardization of the fine oblique interlaced textiles used in Hopewellian copper manufacture (E. White 1987). Just as at Wickliffe, fabrics used in "saltpan" manufacture at most other Mississippian sites are relatively diverse, although few sites have yet revealed diversity on a par with that at Wickliffe. At all but one site listed in Table 13, at least two different textile structures were present, and where measured attributes are known (Figures 54–55), they are by no means standardized. For example, the number of warps per centimeter within impressed textiles covers a range of at least 5, up to as much as 13, at sites for which information is available. Even at the Mound Bottom site, where impressed textiles were considered to be relatively simple (Kuttruff 1987b; Kuttruff and Kuttruff 1986), standardization could not be demonstrated. For instance, yarn diameters there ranged from 1 to 4 millimeters, and a number of different fabric structures were present. However, two particular instances of less diverse impressed fabric complexes are notable enough to warrant further discussion, even though both are based on small sherd samples. If real, their restricted range of attributes might possibly be tied to pottery-making functions.

The most restricted and idiosyncratic range of fabrics was found on sherd samples from Bottle Creek and Salt Creek, Alabama, which were impressed only with cane matting and coarse weft-faced textiles. These heavy, sturdy, comparatively stiff fabrics might serve a different function in "saltpan" production than cloths used at sites farther north—perhaps lifting heavy vessels was more important than moderating the drying process. At some northerly sites weft-faced and matting impressions seem to be more common in earlier components, possibly indicating a change in pottery-making practices. In fact, the fade-out of interlaced basketry impressions from earlier to later components at Kincaid occurred concurrently with a shift away from heavier, thicker vessels (Orr 1951:319–320). A similar correlation between heavy vessels and sturdy fabrics could be occurring at the Alabama sites, but to test this hypothesis will require more data.

At Slack Farm, "standardization" of a different sort shows up in the small sample of textile impressions. All fabrics analyzed were within the range assigned to garment fabrics at Wickliffe. Weft-faced fabrics and coarse textiles similar in scale to those illustrated at the bottom right of Figures 22 and 23 were totally lacking. On average, yarns were notably thinner, and fabric counts and densities were higher than the Wickliffe textiles as a group. Yarns generally were not highly processed (single-ply, not tightly twisted) but did appear soft. Such textiles would be excellent for retarding the drying process on heavy molded vessels and could have been chosen for that purpose.

Plausible as functional explanations like these may seem, still other hypotheses can be advanced to account for sites like Bottle Creek, where fabric impressions on pottery exhibit relatively little structural diversity or complexity (Tables 13 and 15). First and foremost, the textile complexes at these settlements could actually have been less diverse, perhaps correlated to settlement size, site function, geographic location, or time period. Alternatively, a few specific types of textiles could have been chosen for use in the pottery manufacturing process, but the motivation could have been other than functional. For instance, such choices could be contingent on economic motivations such as unwillingness to "waste" laboriously produced structurally decorated textiles, or on social motivations such as the reservation of certain fabric types for use by a restricted number of special individuals, thus making them unavailable to the potters, or on a particular fashion in clothing like an upswing in the use of skins. Later in this chapter, some of these possibilities will be considered further.

Where particular types of impressed textiles (e.g., coarse weft-faced fabrics, or plain twining with transposed interlinked warps) were made, they undoubtedly served much the same functions as postulated for the Wickliffe textiles. At virtually all sites, plain twining was the "staple" fabric structure, produced in a broad range of yarn types, fabric counts, and densities—that is, to serve many different specific purposes. Without exception, wherever measurements were made, alternate-pair-twined textiles averaged finer in scale than plain-twined textiles, very likely an indication of their predominant use as garments.

At all sites where the information is available, structurally decorated textiles, particularly the examples of plain twining plus transposed interlinked warps, were finer on average than single-structure fabrics. In all of the "octagonal openwork" examples of plain twining plus transposed interlinked warps, yarn and fabric structure (**S**-twisted yarns, **S**-twisted twining, **Z**-twisted interlinking) is totally consistent. However, other attributes were not standardized: if two or more examples are available from a given site, they always vary in yarn size and fabric count. As at Wickliffe, attributes of structurally decorated textiles from all sites are consistent with their use as garments.

The only utilitarian fabric structure not present on Wickliffe "saltpans" that has been found elsewhere is "balanced interlacing," including both 1/1 and twill structures. I myself have examined only a few examples of impressed interlaced textiles, so I can make no assessments of their function based on measured attributes such as yarn characteristics or fabric density. The few examples reported from Etowah consistently have 5 yarn elements per centimeter (Schreffler 1988:155). The largest textile fragments in this structure (up to 24 × 135 cm, or 9½ × 53 in) come from Spiro and are interpreted as skirts or mantles. All are of animal hair mixed with feather and plant fibers, with 3 to 9 yarn elements per centimeter, fairly high densities, and selvages indicating that their construction technique was oblique interlacing rather than weaving with two sets of elements (M. E. King, personal communication 1991; Kuttruff 1988a:211–223, 232–246, 254–266; Willoughby 1952:114–118, Plates 141, 148). At least some of these Spiro textiles were decorated with large-scale colored designs, probably signifying their ceremonial function. A small sample of interlaced fragments from burials at the protohistoric Milner Village, Alabama, site (Smith et al. 1989), which I examined from a slide, seem to be of similar scale (6 to 12 elements per cm) and construction and could also have been fashioned from animal hair. They were completely opaque (high density). Most likely, the balanced interlaced fabrics impressed on "saltpans" originally served as garments or blankets, although a few bags in this structure also are known from post-Contact examples (Bushnell 1906, 1909, 1914; Burnham 1976:363).

Also not present at Wickliffe—indeed, almost entirely absent from the record of pottery impressions—are the extremely complex textiles with visually prominent designs that have been recovered from elite interments at Spiro and Etowah. Unlike the vast majority of "saltpan" textiles, these examples of twined tapestry and lacelike openwork undoubtedly functioned as ceremonial garments. With the very high labor investment in them, it is surprising indeed to find evidence of even one such openwork example (from the Stone site) used in the manufacture of pottery.

Feathered yarns and fabrics, as well as textiles with attached decoration such as beads, are known from burials but not from pottery impressions. They are by no means restricted to elite mortuary contexts or to ceremonial centers (Table 14) but would have been functionally unsuitable for use in ceramic production.

Mississippian Yarn and Fabric Production Technology

By detailed analysis of yarns and fabrics, along with historical information on yarn and fabric production methods, it was possible to postulate some specific techniques as most likely to have been used at Wickliffe. Is it probable that the same techniques were used throughout the Mississippian Southeast, or might spinning and textile production technology have varied there, geographically or temporally?

As discussed in Chapter 6, the final **S** twist of Wickliffe yarns, together with the small diameters of a significant percentage of them, did not seem compatible with the technique of thigh spinning. (Thigh spinning by a right-handed person normally produces **Z**-plied yarn, and modern practitioners assert that production of small-diameter yarns is difficult if not impossible by means of this technique.) It seems likely that some sort of weighted tool, if not "the spindle" as we know it, was used at Wickliffe to produce yarns. Kuttruff (1988a:158–159) notes that the short, slippery fur fibers spun into yarns at Spiro would be most easily spun by use of a spindle.

In general, yarns with a final **S** twist are characteristic of the Mississippian, in dramatic contrast to those of the non-Mississippian Southeast, in which significant proportions of final **Z**-twisting occurred. Is it possible to tie this attribute to a specific technology such as spindle spinning? Direct evidence, in the form of complete spindles with or without associated yarn, is lacking from the archaeological record, but indirect evidence, such as a correlation between small yarn diameter and **S**-plying, would at least be suggestive. Because there seem to be so few examples of **Z**-plied yarns from centrally located Mississippian sites, it is necessary to turn to the periphery—in both geographic and temporal terms—for comparative data on **S**- and **Z**-plied yarns.

E. White found that in the carbonized Hopewell cordage and fabrics she studied, **Z**-plied two-ply cordage averaged 6.4 millimeters in diameter, while **S**-plied two-ply yarns averaged only 1.2 millimeters (1987:85). Of the 158 examples she analyzed, 87% were **S**-plied.

At the Woodland–Early Mississippian Martin Farm site in eastern Tennessee, both **S**- and **Z**-plying were present in fabrics impressed on ceramics. In random samples from shell-tempered pottery, 66 **S**-plied two-ply cords averaged 1.7 millimeters in diameter, 71 **Z**-plied cords averaged 2.3 millimeters in diameter, and 62 braided cords averaged 4.5 millimeters in diameter (Schroedl et al. 1985:184–187).

Data from the Caddoan Mississippian region, on the western periphery of Mississippian influence, are more equivocal. Using Kuttruff's measurements of yarns from Spiro and Ozark sites (1988: 254–261), 93 examples of **Z**-plied yarns averaged 2.3 millimeters in diameter, and 31 examples of **S**-plied yarns averaged 2.2 millimeters.

From the meager available data, there does seem to be a positive correlation between smaller yarn size and **S** ply, a direction not usually associated with thigh spinning. The positive correlation between **S**-plying and the Mississippian is strong and firmly established. Although it is not possible at present to assess whether Mississippian yarns in general are finer than those from earlier time periods or other regions of the country, almost all of the Mississippian sites from which yarn diameter measurements are available include at least some proportion of yarns 1 millimeter or less in diameter (Figure 54), probably indicative of at least some spindle spinning. Although, again, the data are sparse, it is worth repeating that the earliest historical descriptions of thigh spinning in eastern North America come from Virginia and New Amsterdam, outside the area directly associated with the Mississippian tradition (John Smith, quoted in Swanton 1946:448; Charles Wooley, quoted in Browning 1974:95), while the few mentions of spindles (e.g., Barcia Carballidoy Zuniga, quoted in Swanton 1922:149; Adair 1968:422) come from within it. It does seem possible that some sort of tool analogous to a spindle was employed in yarn production throughout the Mississippian Southeast.

At Wickliffe, it seems likely that many if not most textiles were constructed on free-hanging warps, attached at their top (starting) edge to a fixed cord or stick. To date, no evidence from other Mississippian sites conflicts with such a fabric-construction technology. It is suitable for the production of both twined and oblique-interlaced fabrics and perhaps even essential for some structurally decorated fabrics that employ diverted warps. For instance, because of potential tension problems, combinations of structures in geometric patterns that take up warps differentially, such as plain twining plus transposed interlinked warps, are far more likely to have been made on free-hanging warps than on warps fixed at both ends.

To my knowledge, the use of plain twining plus interlinked warps in large textiles has been found nowhere in the world outside of the northern Mississippian "heartland." For example, Fraser's exhaustive compendium of weft-twining structures (1989) mentions it from nowhere else. Its development within this region may well have been contingent upon the type of textile-production setup employed.

Oblique-interlaced textiles can be made on free-hanging warps, although some technique or tool is necessary to prevent unraveling while work is in progress. For narrow braids, control can be maintained by the craftsperson's hands alone, but for wider textiles this is not sufficient. A second cord or stick, gradually lowered as work progressed on the interlacing, would do the trick. Hairy yarns (as will result from the use of some animal fibers) or relatively rigid elements (such as cane strips) can be capable of holding their places without the need of any additional tool. It is of interest here that all of the large-sized oblique-interlaced textiles from Spiro were fashioned at least partially of animal fiber yarns (Kuttruff 1988a:232–239, 254–261).

Like simple twining, oblique interlacing *can* be done on a fixed-warp frame or backstrap arrangement, in the technique of sprang (Appendix A; Collingwood 1974). This technique is used in South America to make hammocks, and among the Hopi to make sashes (Cardale-Schrimpff 1972; Kent 1983:70–72). A complete sprang textile will have a characteristic center structure, but that evidence can be obliterated by cutting the fabric in half across the middle. No such diagnostic center structures have been discovered in textiles from the prehistoric Southeast, and sprang construction seems highly unlikely for the large oblique-twined garments from Spiro. However, although there is no positive evidence for use of this technique, neither is there conclusive evidence against it.

A textile-production setup with free-hanging warps can function adequately for the construction of oblique-interlaced fabrics and can work well for twining, in which the paired weft yarns hold their place on the warps by virtue of encircling each element tightly. However, such a configuration is not nearly as suitable for interlacing utilizing a separate weft because gravity will cause the weft yarn to slip down and out of place unless it is very rough, such as in the coarse bark-strip interlaced mats made by recent-day Menomini (Hoffman 1896:Plates 20, 22). For a description of the difficulties of producing rush mats on free-hanging warps in structures other than weft twining, see Rogers (1983:11). In weaving nonoblique interlaced textiles, it is far easier to work with a fixed-warp or weighted-warp loom than with free-hanging warps.

There is some evidence for the use of such a setup in historical times. In the eighteenth century, Adair quoted a Muskogee-speaking informant's description of what probably was a frame loom with a continuous, fixed warp, similar in concept if not in detail to the familar loom used in historical times to weave Navajo rugs (Adair 1968:422; see Chapter 6 above). The description clearly was of two-element interlacing—"weaving" in the ordinary sense—rather than of twining or oblique interlacing. Use of such a loom setup to weave balanced interlaced fabric would be far faster than to produce either twining or oblique interlacing on free-hanging warps and could be considered a technological breakthrough. Of course, this could have been a post-Contact European introduction, in spite of the protestations of Adair's informant, but it would be possible to use the archaeological record to test the hypothesis that such a loom was employed prehistorically in the Southeast, in the following way.

All evidence to date from organic textiles (Spiro, Milner Village, Angel, and pre-Mississippian Hopewell sites) points to the exclusive use of single-element interlacing rather than two-element interlacing to make large fabrics in the Southeast: only selvages with yarns turning back into the fabric at an oblique angle have been found (Kuttruff 1988a:232–239; Black 1967: Figure

237; E. White 1987:61–64). As we have seen, impressions on pottery of interlaced textiles seem to be relatively common at sites in and around eastern Tennessee and exist at other sites as well (Figure 56). However, no information on their selvage structure has been reported in the literature. If analysis of interlaced fabric impressions does turn up some examples of selvages with perpendicular intersections of warp and weft elements, a good case might be made for the utilization of some sort of fixed-warp "loom" prior to European contact. And if such selvages were confined to the more southerly regions of the Mississippian Southeast rather than coming from the northern region, where the interlinked-warp and diverted-warp textiles, which likely required free-hanging warps, were made, a division in fabric-production technology might be postulated.

The complex openwork fabrics from Stone, Spiro, and Etowah, often described as resembling European bobbin lace, have a base structure of oblique interlacing plus transposed crossed elements and undoubtedly were developed by expert craftspeople familiar with the technology required to produce large-sized oblique interlacing. European bobbin lace makers, who produced only relatively narrow fabric widths, worked on a horizontal surface, utilizing pins and weighted bobbins to control the position of their threads. Southeastern craftspeople, making textiles a meter or more in width, would have had to devise some method to keep their yarns in order as they worked. Utilizing completely free-hanging elements would have been virtually impossible. One clue as to technique may lie in the small bundle of yarns with attached stem sections from Whitney Shelter, Arkansas, interpreted by Scholtz as a group of weighted warp threads (1975:146).

The twined tapestry textiles from Spiro are in countered weft-faced twining, a structure in which twining rows alternate twist direction (**S, Z, S, Z**). In my experience, countered twining tends to occur naturally when a weaver's warp is not attached to a stationary frame, so that she can easily turn her work in progress upside-down at the end of a twining row in order always to work either left-to-right or right-to-left. If she continues to twist her twining in the same direction with her work in the new position, countering will result. In the prehistoric Southeast, countered twining often was used to make slippers and sandals, which would have been fashioned without the use of any support (J. Miller 1988). The structure of the Spiro twined tapestry mantles thus might indicate that they were not made on warps attached to a fixed pole or cord. Countered twining certainly also can be done on warps fixed to a stationary support or supports, but in that case it requires a conscious decision to change twining twist direction at the end of each row. (The justifiably famous twined tapestry Chilkat blankets from the

Northwest Coast, made on warps hanging from a fixed support, did not utilize countered twining [C. Samuel 1982].)

Warps with looped terminal ends, as found on some bags (Figures 15a, 15c), probably were made by passing a continuous yarn element back and forth between two cords or sticks. After the initial row of twining was made in the middle of the warp, it could be suspended in the same way as free-hanging, separate warp elements (Kuttruff 1987a; Douglas et al. 1968), allowing spiral or circular twining from that point onward.

Specialization and Labor Investment in Mississippian Textile Production

From the evidence of fabrics impressed on pottery, it was not necessary to postulate the existence of specialist craftspeople at Wickliffe. Although some of the textiles produced there were quite fine and reasonably intricate, the amount of time or skill required to produce them would not be inordinate for a craftsperson of average capabilities working part-time, incidental to other tasks (Chapter 6). Everyday fabrics at Wickliffe, as at all Mississippian settlements, could well have been products expected of every adult female. However, this is not necessarily true for a few types of very complex textiles, associated primarily with the ceremonial centers of Spiro and Etowah.

The twined tapestry mantles from Spiro would be extremely time consuming to produce. Because they are weft-faced, although not particularly fine, they require much more yarn than balanced interlaced textiles or non-weft-faced twined fabrics. Some of the yarns used in elite textiles at Spiro combined vegetable and animal fibers together with down from birds, a type that is much more intricate and difficult to produce than single-material yarns spun from long, nonsmooth fibers such as bast (King and Gardner 1981). The yarn for tapestries also required the extra step of dyeing in various colors, including time for gathering and processing dye plants and obtaining mordants (if used) on top of that for the actual dyeing. And the weaving process is extremely slow. A modern tapestry weaver working in weft-faced plain weave, a significantly faster technique than weft-faced twining, may require months to complete a pictorial tapestry on the scale of the Spiro mantles. As an example of the economic value of such a product, the Royal Tapestry Factory of Madrid, Spain, currently charges from $500 to over $5,000 per square meter for its products; a weaver there may require up to three months to produce one square meter of fabric (Foster 1990:34). Dyeing processes for the ceremonial garments from Spiro and mortuary fabrics from Etowah that were adorned with visually prominent yellow motifs on darker backgrounds might well have been complex enough that they, too, would have been made by craftspeople with specialized skills.

The openwork textiles that combined twining, oblique interlacing, and crossed elements in a complex, lacy structure (Figure 52) are remarkable not so much in terms of their colors or their yarns—which do have relatively fine average diameters, and may even contain exotic cotton fibers—but rather in terms of their intricate structure and designs. Master weavers polled by Kuttruff in connection with the validation of her Textile Production Complexity Index rated the Spiro textile in this technique as the most complex one they were shown, although by the TPCI it would be rated as less complex than the twined tapestry (Kuttruff 1988a:83–84, 202–209). Speaking as a weaver, I would say that this is because such a fabric would require both mental and physical dexterity to produce (and also perhaps because modern weavers may tend to take colored yarns for granted). Although only a few structures are involved, the way they are put together into designs in the Mississippian openwork fabrics would require a significant amount of preplanning and many decision points during the production process. This is not a process that can be carried out automatically, and it is not one that can be mastered quickly by a novice. In Europe, young girls, facile of eye and hand, were taught bobbin lace-making techniques in schools or poorhouse classes and followed designs pricked out on paper rather than working from mental images. During the time that lace was the rage in European royal and upper-class costume, its production was a reasonably lucrative occupation for lower-class girls and women working as either part-time or full-time practitioners and made rich men of the merchants who controlled its dissemination (Levey 1983).

This is the level of intricacy that might possibly require specialist artisans for its production, as might the twined tapestry fabrics with their colored dyes and complex yarns. Both types of fabrics, used for elite, special-purpose items, are good candidates for production by skilled experts during the Mississippian. However, even though it seems unlikely that all women made them, their apparent rarity argues strongly against any full-time craftspeople being dedicated to their production.

Based on impressed textiles alone, without any knowledge of elite or special-purpose fabrics that were not preserved on pottery, the quality and diversity of Wickliffe utilitarian textiles provides strong evidence for their importance in the Wickliffe economy. Probably significant amounts of every Wickliffe woman's time were expended in the production of fabrics. The same very likely was true for other Mississippian settlements, particularly those in the northerly region, where structurally decorated textiles were fairly common.

It does seem that more time may have been invested in everyday textiles within the northern Mississippian "heartland" starting in the period associated with major mound building, perhaps A.D. 1200–1400. At least, this is when and where structurally decorated fabrics were available in such abundance that they regularly found their way into the pottery manufacturing process. After that time, at Caborn-Welborn sites, the average time invested in ordinary textiles could have been even greater—at least, those impressed on pottery at Slack Farm would have required more time to construct, on average, than those impressed on pottery at Wickliffe. (This observation needs to be corroborated by analysis of more and larger samples of Caborn-Welborn impressed textiles.) Farther south, twined and interlaced garments, whether decorated or not, continued to be made in great numbers well into the sixteenth century, as evidenced by Spanish chroniclers. In certain areas such as southern Louisiana, textile-making was an important part of women's work up into the eighteenth century (du Ru 1934:39; Le Page du Pratz 1763:2:230–232).

What implications might this apparently large expenditure of time have with regard to the Mississippian subsistence economy in general? First, as observed for Wickliffe, time devoted to textiles beyond that absolutely necessary for survival implies a relative affluence. At the very least, basic food, shelter, and clothing requirements would have had to be met before time could be invested in the structural decoration of ordinary village fabrics. Beyond that rather simple relationship there are several theoretical avenues worth exploring in future, pertinent to both the evolution and the demise of typical Mississippian lifeways.

One area of interest is the connection between year-round, long-term, large-sized nucleated communities and the regular production of cloth from plant fibers. For any people living outside the tropics, adequate clothing is basic to survival. Gramly (1977; cf. Starna and Relethford 1986) has pointed out that six to eight deerskins were required for the garments worn by every Iroquois adult, and calculated that an average of 4.5 deer could be harvested annually from 1 square mile (2.6 sq km) on a sustained-yield basis. Large uninhabited areas had to be maintained as hunting territories, and task groups had to travel to them regularly to provide for clothing needs. The customary use of plant fibers rather than hides for some of these items might make possible denser and longer-term settlement patterns than would be compatible with total reliance on skins and furs for clothing. Certainly, textile production and population density were positively correlated in Old

World agricultural civilizations. The most obvious North American example comes from the Southwest, where occupants of densely populated towns actually cultivated cotton for clothing (Kent 1947, 1983:27–29, 198–199). Within the Southeast, comparisons between population density, hunting patterns, and impressed textile data from Emergent Mississippian versus later Mississippian components could provide insights into the relative importance of big-game hunting for nonfood needs and the impact of this on settlement patterns.

Both increased sedentism and nucleation, and "devolution"—change in the other direction—could leave clues in the textile complex of a site. For example, Hall has proposed what he calls the Schmoo Effect—"a frontier effect bringing about the devolution or breaking down of social organization in the face of abundance and diminished need for interdependence"—to account for the decline of Cahokia as a major regional center, asserting that "any combination of increased availability or use of beans, bison, or better-adapted corn could easily have spelled disaster for the Mississippian adaptation in Illinois" (1991:26). If Hall's theory is correct, the Caborn-Welborn adaptation should be a likely place to find the Schmoo Effect at work. Could the lack of evidence for coarse, heavy fabrics at Slack Farm be tied to a late prehistoric influx of bison into the Ohio River Valley, or at least into within striking range of the settlement's hunters or trading range of the settlement's entrepreneurs (Tankersley 1986, 1989)? If bison robes were available, it might not have been necessary to produce dense, thick textiles for garments or blankets. However, if communities had more than ample subsistence resources, textile makers still might have plenty of time to devote to producing fine, decorated warm-weather garments. Further study clearly is warranted.

At this time, connections between the amount of time and effort invested in textile production and larger Mississippian socioeconomic trends can be only speculation. Still, it is important to emphasize that studies of southeastern subsistence patterns that analyze sources of food, firewood, and/or housing materials but ignore sources of clothing cannot claim to be complete. The same holds true for studies of regional interaction that ignore the potential importance of fabrics as items of exchange.

Mississippian Textiles as Items of Value and Exchange

There is some evidence from historical accounts that at the time of European contact, textiles intended for clothing may have been produced in quantity and stockpiled. At the very least, many of the caciques encountered by de Soto could command great numbers of "shawls" to give as presents to the invading foreigners. For example (a few instances among many), the Gentleman of Elvas reported that, on meeting de Soto, the cacica of Cofitachequi (South Carolina) "presented much clothing of the country, from the shawls and skins that came in the other boats" that accompanied her, and "The cacique of Casqui [Arkansas] many times sent large presents of fish, shawls, and skins." Within abandoned villages of Cofitachequi, decimated by disease two years previous to their coming, the Spaniards found "barbacoas [in which] were large quantities of clothing, shawls of thread, made from the bark of trees, and others of feathers, white, gray, vermilion, and yellow, rich and proper for winter" (Hodge and Lewis 1907:173, 210, 174).

The large volumes of fabrics available also are evident in many of the descriptions of the spoils of battle. For example, at a captured town of Pacaha (Arkansas), "Many shawls . . . were found in the town. Numbers [of Spaniards] who had been a long time badly covered, there clothed themselves. Of the shawls they made mantles and cassocks; some made gowns and lined them with cat-skins." Again, in capturing the cacique of Pacaha, "many men and women were taken, and much clothing. Many clothes, which the Indians had in cane hurdles and on rafts to carry over [the river], floated down stream" (Hodge and Lewis 1907:209, 211). This copious supply of textiles also is evident in the large numbers of shawls demanded and obtained by the tattered remnants of the de Soto expedition to serve as sails on the boats they built to carry them down the Mississippi River and back to New Spain (Bourne 1904:1:187–191).

The value attached to textiles by Native Americans is illustrated by the fact that while the Spaniards were butchering the inhabitants of Nilco (Arkansas), their local allies "went to the houses for plunder, filling the canoes with clothing" (Hodge and Lewis 1907:232). The Indians' interest may have been in the clothing per se, or it may have been in humiliating the enemy by removing goods accumulated for use by their chiefs or by their honored dead. It is known that textiles were important mortuary goods; those taken by the Spaniards from abandoned villages in South Carolina (see quotation above) probably served that purpose (J. Brown 1976b:332). Paul du Ru, a priest accompanying a French expedition up the lower Mississippi River in 1700, may have witnessed the production of mortuary textiles. While visiting an Ouma village, he passed a rainy day in a cabin "filled with women who spin bark and work at the looms. Some of them are wives of the great chief who has been dead for some months" (du Ru 1934:29).

The Gentleman of Elvas mentioned that Indians of Cayas (Arkansas), whose territory included saline sources, made salt to "carry it into other parts, to exchange for skins and shawls" (Hodge and Lewis 1907:218). The exact nature of these "shawls" is unknown (except that any used for sails must have been relatively dense), as are the precise workings of the exchange network. J. Brown (1983; see also Brown et al. 1990) has ascertained that exchange of "low value goods" in and out of Spiro was carried out within a radius of about 450 kilometers (280 mi), while high-value goods such as embossed copper plates were exchanged over far greater distances—all the way between Spiro and Florida. Goods or materials of low value in their place of origin could assume high value in distant locations (Brown 1983:139; Cobb 1989:84). It is possible that, on a par with the highly valued copper and shell artifacts of the Southeastern Ceremonial Complex, intricate, "expensive" textiles with prominent symbolic designs might perhaps have been reserved for exchange between high-ranking members of the elite, while less complex fabrics such as "octagonal openwork" might have had wider social currency but a more restricted geographic range.

The complex, lacelike openwork textiles, with their circle and circle-and-cross motifs, are good potential candidates for exchange within an elite network (Drooker 1991c). The consistency of yarn characteristics, fabric structures, and fabric scale among the extant examples from widely separated locations in Oklahoma, the lower Tennessee–Cumberland River area, and (to a lesser extent) Georgia argues for a common standard of production, although not necessarily a single location of production.

When more data are available on design peculiarities of fabrics from specific Mississippian sites, it may be possible to actually trace exchange relationships. For example, the type of decorated edge typical of Kimmswick impressed textiles (Figure 50) also occurs on a fine "octagonal openwork" fabric from Spiro (J. Brown 1976b:Figure 67b), a veritable magpie of a site known to have had exchange interactions with Cahokia, near which the Kimmswick site is located. If additional examples of organic textiles in plain twining plus transposed interlinked warps come to light in nonutilitarian contexts outside the northern Mississippian region, where they were widely produced and used in everyday life (Figure 58), a case might be made for regional specialization and exchange.

Schambach has characterized Mississippian Spiro as a merchant outpost, a "small group of . . . entrepreneurs who were exchanging commodities, primarily hides, for the one category of goods that had the characteristics of money in Mississippian society[,] . . . the symbols and regalia of Mississippian religion" (1990:13; for a critique of some of Schambach's premises, but not exchange per se, see J. D. Rogers 1991). Even more transportable than the animal hides on which Schambach focuses are animal hair and textiles constructed of animal-hair yarn. Spiro is the Mississippian archaeological site from which the greatest number of textiles that incorporate animal hair have been recovered, virtually all of them from elite contexts. It is quite possible that such textiles or (more likely) their raw materials may also have been exchanged for elite "high value goods." Vegetable-fiber fabrics with structural patterning, in contrast, may have been produced elsewhere and acquired by Spiro residents through exchange.

In any event, it is apparent that throughout the Mississippian Southeast significant amounts of time and skill were invested in the production of textiles. Clearly, this craft was an integral and important segment of the Mississippian economy, including the exchange networks that acted to cement relationships among villages and among provinces, binding peoples together in intricate webs of mutual obligation (Brose 1979, 1989).

It should not be necessary to belabor the point that in the prehistoric Southeast it was women who developed and nurtured the special knowledge and skills that supported this important—perhaps essential—aspect of Mississippian society. Detailed familiarity with the textile complex of the prehistoric and early historical Southeast offers a road to increased understanding of the economic and social roles of women within southeastern society (cf. Watson and Kennedy 1991; Barber 1991:283-298).

Social "Messages" from Mississippian Fabrics

Attributes of textiles, like those of other artifacts from headdresses to painted pottery, can in many cases be indicators of social boundaries (Wobst 1977), social interactions (Dickens 1980), and/or social iconography (Galloway 1989). At Wickliffe (Chapter 6), the relatively subtle designs on impressed textiles seemed to be consistent with garments designed to function in intragroup contexts, possibly delineating family or clan affiliations. The complexity, fineness, and high craftsmanship of many of the fabrics impressed on pottery there seemed to indicate a relative affluence for the settlement as a whole. The diversity of structural decoration in Wickliffe textiles argued for inspiration from regular intergroup contact. However, little could be learned about elite textiles or belief-system symbolism from the fragmentary Wickliffe fabric impressions or the single organic decorated fabric that came from the site. What can be added to this picture by comparing Wickliffe impressed textiles with impressions and textiles from other Mississippian localities?

Certainly, the mention of textile products in the same breath as the intricately decorated copper and shell artifacts exchanged within the Southeastern Ceremonial Complex immediately conjures up the question of their symbolic associations. Much mental energy has been expended in attempting to unravel the symbolic significance of these and other highly valued Mississippian artifacts (e.g., Waring and Holder 1945; Galloway 1989). How do fabrics fit into the picture?

Both J. Brown (1985) and Knight (1986) have presented tripartite models of Mississippian "cult complexes" and associated symbolism. In that of Brown, the "ancestor cult " of the elite is objectified in ancestor figurines, the "falcon cult" of chiefs and warriors is objectified by litters, the chunkey game, and falcon impersonators, while the "fertility cult" of the common people is symbolized by serpents and females with agricultural implements. Knight's model differs somewhat in emphasis, incorporating a "communal cult type" centering on earth/fertility and purification, a "chiefly cult type" emphasizing hierarchical authority, and a "priestly cult type" supervising ancestor veneration and mortuary ritual and serving to mediate between the other two types. Knight recognizes three Mississippian "iconic families" roughly associated with each of his three cult types: a "warfare/cosmogony complex" objectified in high-value, portable, nonfunctional objects representing weapons and composite beings; the platform mound, objectifying the earth and community endeavors; and temple statuary, consisting of male and female figurines with deathlike features. Fabrics can be associated with most of these conceptual foci—ancestors, falcons, fertility, the chiefly power base, and communal mound building.

Textile stockpiles, as discussed above, may well have been at least partially intended for elite mortuary goods. If so, their numbers, sumptuousness, and safekeeping in a prominent place within a settlement would have been indications of the value in which the honored dead for whom they were intended were held by their direct descendents and by the community at large. Such "conspicuous consumption" of textiles certainly could have functioned as one aspect of an ancestor cult, as it has done and continues to do in many other cultures around the world (Schneider 1987; Weiner and Schneider 1989). Southeastern "ancestor cult" figurines themselves seem always to have been simply dressed, or not dressed at all.

Obviously, the fragments of multicolored "hawk man" mantles from Spiro match the symbolism of "hawk men" depicted on copper and shell artifacts (Strong 1989), undoubtedly functioning as costumes for portrayers of falcons and/or supernatural beings (King and Gardner 1981). The various bird-man depictions functioned as symbols of earthly power, sometimes as composites of Upper, Lower, and Underworld beings, and most strongly as icons of fierce, successful warriors embodying the qualities of raptors such as hawks (Strong 1989:220–221; J. Brown 1984:254–259, 1985:108–123, 1989:201, 203). Where twined-tapestry yarn fibers have been identified, they consist of mixed fibers, all containing at least some animal fur or hair (Kuttruff 1988a:224–231, 254–261). In fact, a number of the Spiro textiles, including the garments with colored designs, combine animal hair, vegetable · fiber, and bird down (King and Gardner 1981:128)—quite possibly a reflection and reinforcement of the composite-being concept. Specific fibers might well have endowed their garments with particular powers—for instance, turkey down as a war symbol (King and Gardner 1981:132, citing Howard 1968:47). Animal-fiber yarns—found in a high percentage of elite Spiro interments but virtually absent in nonelite Ozark burials (Kuttruff 1988a:158), and typical of all surviving Spiro twined and interlaced garments with large-scale colored designs—certainly could have been power symbols of the elite and also could have had symbolic links to hunting and war. The extant Spiro nontapestry garments all are red, the traditional color of war and disorder (Hudson 1976:235).

In contrast, the lacelike textiles from Etowah, Spiro, and Stone contain no obvious symbolism of war or hunting. The surviving textile fragments were made of finely processed vegetable-fiber yarns, perhaps incorporating some exotic cotton fibers, with only one fragment from Etowah containing any animal hair (Kuttruff 1988a:208; Sibley et al. 1989:196, 209; Drooker 1991c). Although the Spiro example is blackened from oxidation or burning (J. Brown 1976b:341) and the Etowah examples studied by Sibley et al. are described as either dark brown or light green in color (1989:193), the Etowah fabric at the Peabody Foundation, tinged green from contact with copper, can be seen to have been originally colored pure white, the traditional color of peace and order (E. White 1987:66–69). Motifs incorporated into these fabrics—circles, concentric circles, and circles-and-crosses—do not appear to be warlike in nature. Rather, they may be associated with the "balanced opposition"—integral to southeastern belief systems (Hudson 1976:156, 148, 317) and, incidentally, to agriculture—between the dualities of the Upper World, sun, and sacred fire, and the Lower World, water, serpents, and fertility (Drooker 1991c). The fertility connotation is reinforced by examples of Mississippian effigy pots that portray pregnant females adorned with circle-and-cross symbolism (e.g., Figure 19)—perhaps in some cases actually representing openwork shawls rather than tattoos or body paint.

Whether or not the complex openwork textiles had a symbolic connection with sun, earth, water, and fertility, their color, motifs, and "expensiveness" would have made them suitable for wear by elite members of society from chiefly or priestly lineages engaged in nonhostile ceremonies, and for ceremonial exchange between high-ranking personages from separate polities. Smith and Hally (1990:1–3) have argued that presentation of gifts such as shawls, skins, and food was a standard part of Mississippian greeting ritual at the chiefly level, noting that exchange of clothing could in some instances actually represent adoption of fictive kinship relationships by the parties involved.

Mississippian textiles from nonelite contexts tend to be constructed from plant rather than animal fibers, and the utilitarian fabrics impressed on pottery generally appear to have yarn fiber characteristics typical of vegetable fibers. If, as discussed above, animal hair and mixed-fiber yarns generally are associated with the elite and with men's concerns, their probable absence from Mississippian utilitarian, domestic textiles used by women certainly is consistent with current concepts of the Mississippian worldview.

The fact that many of these everyday fabrics were decorated is of great interest. The textiles impressed on Mississippian "saltpans" give us perhaps the earliest examples of decorated fabrics, other than colored warp stripes, from "common" contexts. Although complex textiles 2,000 or more years old have been recovered from many presumably elite mortuary contexts of eastern North America, the Mississippian record yields the first evidence of decorated fabrics in regular daily use. At Wickliffe, they seemed to become more prevalent during the mound-building period, indicative of intensifying social complexity and increased communal activities. For the Mississippian in general, the types of structural decoration that can be recorded by impressions on pottery seem to have clustered in the northerly settlements, starting during Middle Mississippian times. Most of the sites where such structural decoration has been recorded to date (e.g., Angel, Slack Farm, Tolu, Kincaid, Wickliffe) were not associated with the high-value exchange items of the Southeastern Ceremonial Complex (Brown 1983:147; Brown et al. 1990:261; Goodman 1984), although the presence of other exotic goods indicates that the people at these settlements did engage in exchange.

The time expended on ordinary textiles there after the Early Mississippian could be suggestive not only of relative affluence but also of a desire to indicate and differentiate group affiliation during increasingly common intergroup contact, for communal celebrations and ceremonies, mound building, or low-level exchange. The higher frequency of occurrence of textiles decorated with "octagonal openwork" designs at larger versus smaller sites within the lower Ohio River region during Middle Mississippian times (Table 15) may be a reflection of greater outside contact and/or greater intragroup differentiation at a larger site like Kincaid compared with a smaller site like Wickliffe. Everyday decorated textiles such as these typically incorporate subtle rather than bold decorative patterns. Such designs, visible only at comparatively close quarters, have the potential to symbolize lower-level or horizontal social relationships, such as clan or family affiliations. A comparative study of impressed textiles from different locations within a site or geographic area—for instance, the hamlets "servicing" a larger settlement such as Angel, or separate domestic areas directly associated with a major mound group like Kincaid, or contemporaneous large villages at the top of the Caborn-Welborn settlement hierarchy, or separate locations around a salt spring periodically visited by groups from different villages—might help to articulate such horizontal distinctions.

In contrast, many of the textiles recovered from elite interments at Spiro and Etowah not only represent a far greater investment of time and specialized skill than the ordinary fabrics found impressed into pottery or recovered from nonelite burials but also incorporate relatively large-scale designs, visible from a great distance—that is, indicative of symbolic "messages" conveyed across a much wider social gulf (Wobst 1977). It is unfortunate that as yet no major Mississippian sites have yielded both elite ceremonial garments and textile impressions or other evidence of garments in everyday use. (Lake Jackson, Florida, is one of the few large sites where both textiles and impressions of textiles have been recovered, but they are small in size and few in number [B. Jones 1982].) It is quite probable that the increased ceremonialism and extravagant iconography of the Southeastern Ceremonial Complex between A.D. 1350 and 1500 that Brose associates with agricultural shortages and "politically and economically disintegrating social units" (1989:34) would be reflected in the textile complex, perhaps in a heightened contrast between elaborate ceremonial garments versus simpler everyday garments. In contrast with the continued production of decorated everyday textiles in less stratified Caborn-Welborn society, the scarcity of structurally decorated textiles impressed on pottery at sites farther south during the Late Mississippian period could indicate more rigid and highly separated social stratification, more standardized production for stockpiling, or less time for textile production because of the press of subsistence activities. Or it could simply indicate a different taste in fashion, such as a preference for colored designs, rather than structural ones, on everyday fabrics.

As more and more evidence from textiles impressed on Mississippian pottery is analyzed, it should prove possible to answer some of the questions raised above, extending our understanding of the social interactions and technical capabilities of the peoples who populated southeastern North America just before the arrival of Europeans. Even from the limited data currently available, it is clear that these Mississippians had a sophisticated tradition of textile production, expressed not only in their elite, ceremonial garments but also in the ordinary, everyday fabrics produced and used in every household.

APPENDIX A.
DEFINITIONS OF TEXTILE TERMS

For over two decades, the most comprehensive and definitive classification of fabrics on the basis of structure (as opposed to production technique or technology) has been that compiled by Emery (1966). However, its greatest emphasis is on interlaced textiles, and comparable detail on twined structures is lacking. The recent treatment of weft twining by Fraser (1989) provides a far more detailed classification system, building on both Emery's system and one developed by Balfet (1957) for application to basketry. However, even Fraser's work does not include some of the structural combinations encountered at Wickliffe.

Textile terminology herein follows that of Emery unless otherwise indicated. Fraser's terminology has been included wherever it adds precision to twining terms. Diagrams of textile structures are presented in Figures 9 and 10, within the text.

Alternate-pair twining: Twining around two warp ends at a time, with alternate pairs of ends selected in alternate rows (also referred to in the literature as diagonal, twill, split-pair, or zigzag twining, and sometimes as twined openwork).

"Balanced interlacing": Interlacing in which yarn elements crossing each other are equally visible (not weft-faced or warp-faced). Generally, the term "balanced" is used to describe fabrics woven from two sets of elements (e.g., "balanced plain weave," "balanced twill") in which warp and

weft are not only equally spaced but also approximately equal in diameter and flexibility. Oblique interlacing automatically has the qualities of a "balanced" fabric, so if an interlaced textile is known to have been constructed from one set of elements there is no need to specify that it is "balanced." In this book, "'balanced interlacing'" is used as a general descriptive term in referring to interlaced fabrics of unknown construction technique. Balanced plain weave sometimes is called "checker weave" in the archaeological literature.

Banded: Used herein to designate "striped" designs formed by variable spacing of weft twining rows in a consistent pattern.

Basketry: Used herein to indicate nonpliable textiles, often but not always constructed of nonspun elements such as grass or wood or cane splints. Typical products are baskets and matting. (The term is used by some researchers [e.g., Adovasio] to include most nonclothing items, such as bags, and sometimes even as a general term for perishable artifacts.)

Bast: The fibrous outer layer of the stems of certain plants, including flax and hemp.

Bobbin lace: In the European tradition, openwork fabric structures formed by the interlacing and interlinking of individual weighted elements in intricate patterns. The set of elements is secured at one end to a hard pillow, and the pattern construction usually is guided by pins stuck into this pillow. Also known as "pillow lace."

Braid: A narrow cord made of oblique interlacing. Emery discusses broader definitions (1966:68).

Broken twill: Twill in which intersections of elements are staggered, so that no unbroken diagonal lines occur in the pattern of interlacing.

Cloth: Pliable, fibrous fabric made by any process—weaving, knitting, netting, looping, even felting—and of practically any fiber.

Complex yarn: Yarn formed of dissimilar parts (Kuttruff 1988:188).

Cordage: A general term used in the archaeological literature to denote rope, string, and yarn. It includes spun, twisted, and braided structures.

Countered twining: Twining in which rows of **S**-twist and **Z**-twist twining alternate.

Diverted warps: Warp elements the position of which changes from their normal longitudinal, parallel course. They can be "supplementary" or nonsupplementary, single or multiple, and twisted, crossed, or uncrossed between twining rows. They can occur in combination with twining or interlacing. (See also "transposed warps.")

Element: A component part of the structure of an interworked (e.g., interlaced, twined) fabric. Refers to yarn, thread, strand, cord, sinew, thong, or whatever unit of material is interworked to form a textile. Components of a "set of elements" are functionally undifferentiated and trend in the same direction.

Fabric: Generic term for all fibrous constructions.

Fabric count: Elements per square centimeter of a fabric (sum of warp threads per cm, weft threads per cm, and any supplementary threads). A partial indicator of fabric scale.

Fabric scale: Generalized term indicating fabric fineness (thin yarns, high fabric count) or coarseness (thick yarns, low fabric count).

Fiber: Structural components of any animal or plant tissue used in the construction of fabrics. As opposed to filaments, fibers are of naturally limited length.

Float: In interlacing, any portion of a warp or weft element that extends unbound over two or more elements of the opposite set.

Fringe: Edge finish consisting of hanging yarn elements (after Kuttruff 1988:187).

Interlacing: Technique and fabric formed by it in which each interworked element simply passes under and over elements that cross its path. Can be constructed from a single set of elements (see "oblique interlacing") or from two or more sets.

Knot: A tie or fastening achieved by a tightened interworking of the parts of one or more elements (usually characterized by some protuberance). Knotted fabrics may be constructed from single elements (see "knotted looping") or single sets of elements (e.g., macramé knotting).

Knotted looping: Single-element looped structure in which the loops are secured by knots. "Knotted netting" is an open knotted looping structure, in which knots are spaced at significant intervals.

Linking: Single-element fabric construction formed by successive rows of elements spiraling around the previous row.

Looping: Single-element fabric construction formed as in linking, but with the element crossing over itself as it moves on to form the next loop.

Oblique interlacing: Interlacing formed with one set of elements. The course of the elements is oblique to the fabric edges, and at least one edge consists of free (separate) element ends, except in the special case of sprang fabrics (see below).

Oblique twining: Twining formed with one set of elements. The course of the elements is oblique to the fabric edges, and at least one edge consists of free (separate) element ends (unless it is a sprang fabric [see below]).

Octagonal openwork: See "transposed warps."

Openwork: A fabric consisting largely of deliberately fashioned holes.

Overcasting: Accessory stitch with a spiral structure. Also called "whipping."

Plain interlacing: Interlacing in which each element passes alternately over and under elements that cross its path, one element at a time. Abbreviated as 1/1 interlacing.

Plain twining: Used herein to refer to twining with two elements around one element at a time, with a half-twist between each passive element (i.e., each twining element appears alternately on the top fabric surface). Sometimes also called "simple twining." Unless there is evidence to the contrary, this structure is assumed herein to be weft twining.

Plain weave: Plain interlacing with two sets of elements (warp and weft).

Plied yarn: Yarn (thread, cord) formed by twisting together two or more single (unplied) yarns. A "two-ply" yarn is made up of two singles, a "three-ply" of three singles, and so forth. A "re-plied yarn" is formed by twisting together two or more plied yarns. The term "plied" often is restricted to yarns constructed of spun fibers (Emery 1966:10); in this book, it also is used to describe yarns made by twisting together any two or more elements, spun or unspun.

Selvage: Edge of a textile closed by loops formed by a change in direction of movement of the elements making up the fabric (after Kuttruff 1988:187).

Spaced twining: Twining with spaces between twining rows. Also called "open twining" in the literature.

Spinning: The process of twisting together and drawing out massed short fibers into a continuous strand.

Sprang: Fabric formed by manipulating a single set of elements fixed at both ends. May be interlinked, interlaced, or intertwined. The structure is formed simultaneously at both ends, working toward the middle, and must be fixed at this center point by some technique (such as interlacing a separate weft element across the fabric) (Collingwood 1974:31–32). It is structurally distinguishable from nonsprang interlinking, oblique interlacing, or oblique twining by its central "join" and its four continuous edges. However, sprang fabrics sometimes are cut along their centerpoint and finished like nonsprang fabrics along the resulting edge, in which case the construction technique cannot be determined.

Spun yarn: Yarn formed from fibers of limited length that have been arranged more or less parallel, drawn out into a continuous strand, and twisted together.

Straight twill: Twill with a uniform interlacing structure in which the intersections of floats form straight, unbroken diagonal lines. Also called "plain," "regular," "simple," "biased," or "diagonal" twill (Emery 1966:92).

Supplementary element(s): Element or set of elements added to a fabric as it is constructed but not necessary to hold the fabric together.

Tapestry weave: Mosaiclike patterning formed by separate, usually different-colored, wefts interworking back and forth within separate areas. Usually refers to weft-faced interlacing, but other types, including weft-faced twined tapestry, also are known.

Textile: Cloth constructed by means of interworked elements. (Emery defines "textile" more restrictively, as an interlaced fabric [1966:xvi].)

Textile complexity: Interrelated parts and processes making up a textile. Considered to be representative of the number of decisions made during construction of the textile and to reflect production steps and total labor input (Kuttruff 1988:11, 32.) Yarn structure(s), yarn size, fabric count, textile structure(s), and textile design(s) all contribute to the complexity of a given fabric.

Textile designs: Combinations of color differences, structural variations, and/or added elements (such as beads) that form visible patterns in a fabric. Usually considered to be decorative rather than utilitarian.

Textile scale: See "fabric scale."

Transposed warps: Diverted warps interchanged in a reciprocal relationship (i.e., warps diverted in one direction always cross others oppositely diverted). The resultant fabric structure is identical on both sides. "Transposed interlinked warps" are twisted around each other, singly or in groups, before returning to their original position. Transposed interlinked warps combined with plain twining have been called "octagonal openwork" in the archaeological literature, because of the shape of the holes formed between the interlinked warps. In Mississippian textiles, these holes usually form designs on a background of plain twining. Fraser, considering the interlinking as the dominant structure, has designated plain twining combined with interlinking of alternate pairs of warps as "2-strand twining on interlinked warps" (1989:138). In parallel fashion, he designates plain twining combined with interlinking between the same two warps as "2-strand twining on full-twisted warp pairs" and plain twining combined with transposed crossed warp pairs (always crossing the same two warps) as "2-strand twining on twisted warp pairs" (Fraser 1989:135–136).

Twill: Interlacing over and under more than one element at a time, characterized by a diagonal alignment of floats. Twill structures are designated by the sequence and length of their floats; thus, in a 2/2 twill, each element travels over two and under two elements of the other set. "Twill weave" and "oblique twill interlacing" indicate, respectively, twills constructed from two or one set of elements.

Twining: The process or result of enclosing one or more elements in the twisting of two or more others.

Twining direction: See "twist direction."

Twist: The process or result of combining two or more elements by turning them about each other.

Twist angle: The angle between the vertical axis of a yarn (or twined elements) and the slant of the twist. Tightly twisted yarns have greater angles of twist than loosely twisted yarns. From 0 to 10 degrees is considered a loose twist, 10–25 degrees a medium twist, and 25–45 degrees a tight twist.

Twist direction: Designated "**S**" or "**Z**" depending on the trend of the spiraling twisted elements. If an **S**-twist yarn is held vertical, its slant is downward to the right (\), like the central portion of the letter *S*. If a **Z**-twist yarn is held vertical, its elements slant downward to the left (/), like the central portion of the letter *Z*. "Zero-twist" designates yarns with no twist at all. "**S**" and "**Z**" are used to refer to the direction of spinning, plying, and twining. In all cases, the twisted elements must be held vertical to make the assessment; if they are horizontal, a **Z** slant will appear to be **S**, and vice versa. "Clockwise twist" and "counterclockwise twist" are ambiguous terms used throughout the earlier literature to refer—usually—to **S**- and **Z**-twist directions respectively (the spiraling element is envisioned as moving along an axis toward the viewer [Fraser 1989:41]), or sometimes in exactly the opposite relationship.

Warp: Essentially parallel elements that run longitudinally on a loom, weaving frame, or fabric, crossed at more or less right angles and interworked by transverse elements.

Warp count: The number of warp elements per centimeter.

Warp-faced: Fabric in which weft elements are completely covered by warp elements. Twining in which one set of elements is covered by the other sometimes is referred to as "compact" or "close" twining.

Warp twining: Twined fabric (or technique) constructed of two sets of elements, in which the twining elements are warps. Warp-twined fabrics are consistently warp-faced and narrow in the weft direction.

Weaving: "Warp-weft interlacing of two-or-more-sets-of-elements" (Emery 1966:61), limited by some researchers to fabric produced on a loom with heddles (devices to lift warp threads automatically).

Weft: The transverse elements in a fabric (generally but not necessarily parallel to each other and to the starting and terminal edges of the fabric), which cross and interwork with the warp elements at more or less right angles.

Weft count: The number of weft elements per centimeter.

Weft-faced: Fabric in which warp elements are completely covered by weft elements. Structure can be interlacing or twining. Twining in which one set of elements is covered by the other sometimes is referred to as "compact" or "close" twining.

Weft twining: Twined fabric (or technique) constructed of two sets of elements, in which the twining elements are wefts. Weft-twined fabrics can be weft-faced or not, and can be wide or narrow in the weft direction.

Wrapped twining: Full-turn twining in which one twining element (often rigid) remains always on the same side of the fabric. (Fraser rejects this term as too easy to confuse with "wrapping" [1989: 112].)

Wrapping: Two-element structure with progressive encircling of warp elements by weft.

Yarn: Any assemblage of fibers or filaments put together into a continuous strand (after Kuttruff 1988:188). ("Threads" generally are considered to be more highly processed than yarns, e.g., finer and more tightly twisted.)

Yarn structure: Yarn construction characteristics, including presence or absence of spinning and/or plying, number of components plied together, and direction(s) and tightness of twist in each.

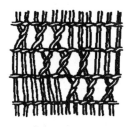

APPENDIX B.
GENERAL METHODOLOGY FOR MAKING CASTS AND TAKING MEASUREMENTS

The first step in studying an impressed textile is to make a cast ("positive mold") of it. Many previous researchers used latex for this purpose, sometimes stretching the resultant cast to larger size in order to examine it better (e.g., Rachlin 1954b, 1955b, 1955c). Most others who reported their methods said that they used modeling clay, or sometimes plaster. Modeling clay may lack the fine detail of latex, and plaster may be difficult to remove from the sherds. However, because these two media are opaque rather than translucent like most latex products, they are easier to analyze.

In looking for commercially available materials, I soon found that latex casts require repeated layers of application and many days to dry. Because of schedule constraints this method was impossible for me to consider. I settled on a modeling clay product called "Sculpey" (as well as other trade names), which gives a good, fine-grained impression, can be reused repeatedly—it is softened by kneading—and can be hardened by oven baking.

Scrupulously clean sherds are not ideal for this process because the clay often tends to stick to them, particularly so in deep crevices or holes such as can occur with a knotted fabric. If a slight film of dirt remains, that is fine, although wads of dirt that can obscure the image of the fabric must be removed. On clean sherds, talcum powder can be used to facilitate removal of the clay cast. Care must be taken to push clay into all interstices; working from the center outward seems to give good results. Care also must be taken to support the sherd fully while pressure is exerted on the clay. In spite of the sturdiness of most "saltpan" sherds, they are not immune to breakage.

In examining sherds, I made a positive mold (sometimes two or three) from each one and recorded attribute data with both the sherd and the clay impression in front of me, but working primarily from the cast. Casts of representative textiles and of distinctive components such as textile edges and structural designs were hardened and retained. For close inspection of the casts, a 6× comparator with a reticle scale graduated to 0.1 millimeter was employed.

A good light source, adjustable in height to allow side-lighting of the casts, was essential. Rotating a cast under side-lighting causes different yarn elements to become prominent, depending on their orientation. In order to be sure that no subtle structural attribute was missed, I did this for all sherds, paying particular attention when structures were complex or yarns were fine. A light-colored cast makes this process easier, because shadows and highlights contrast better.

Recorded measurements were averages, since no fabric had precisely uniform yarns or yarn spacing. Because of the large numbers of sherds to be dealt with and the particularly high variability in yarn size, I used an informal rather than a formal system of averaging this attribute, taking at least three measurements of yarn diameter within a given fabric and then selecting the median. If more than one person is recording attributes from a textile complex, it will be necessary to define more formal procedures so that all recorded measurements are consistent.

All yarn diameter measurements were made perpendicular to the long axis of the yarn. Particular care must be exercised in this regard when measuring weft yarn diameters in a twined fabric, since a measurement perpendicular to the twining row will give an excessively large diameter.

When measuring yarn elements per centimeter, as wide as possible a section (1–10 cm) was measured, then the standard number was calculated. (For instance, if there were 7 warp yarns per 3 centimeters, the number of yarns per centimeter would be calculated as 7/3, or 2.3.) Measurement was from the left side of the leftmost yarn to the left side of the rightmost yarn. Because the alternate-pair twining structure has the potential to create very dense fabrics, it sometimes was difficult to make an actual count of warp yarns for this textile structure. When this happened, the number of weft twining twists per centimeter was multiplied by 2 to calculate the number of warp ends.

The number of weft twining rows per centimeter was measured in a similar fashion to the warp ends per centimeter. If rows occurred in a banded sequence (some grouped together, some farther apart), the number of rows per centimeter was an average either over the entire sherd or, if the banded sequence was regular, over one or two repeats of the sequence.

At first I tried to measure the angle of final yarn twist directly, using a magnifier with an angle scale, but found this to be too detailed to be useful on yarns where twist was not completely consistent. So instead, I used the categories listed by Emery (1966:12)—no twist, 1–10 degrees, 10–25 degrees, 25–45 degrees, and over 45 degrees—setting up a diagram (Figure 11, bottom) to aid in the measurement. By placing the cast of a sherd on top of the diagram with yarns vertical (and if necessary laying a ruler parallel to the angle of yarn twist), it not only was easy to determine the category of final twist but also provided a reminder of yarn twist direction in the very few cases where this was **Z** rather than **S**.

Employment of a ruler or other straightedge as marker also proved useful when measuring the orientation of a fabric with regard to the rim of a "saltpan" vessel. The straightedge was laid parallel to the weft row impressions, and a protractor was laid parallel to the rim; their intersection was used to determine the fabric orientation in degrees from the horizontal, counterclockwise from 0 degrees at left to 180 degrees at right. This measurement was taken from the sherd, not from the cast of the fabric structure.

In measuring vessel diameters, the accepted standard procedure of comparing rim sherd arcs with a set of circles of regularly increasing diameters was followed. However, small sherd size, irregular rims, and uncertainty as to vessel shape made the reliability of the results problematic. Therefore, a two-step procedure was adopted. First, the outside diameter was measured with the rim held horizontal; this would represent the maximum possible diameter of a relatively shallow vessel. Second, the inside diameter was measured with the rim held at an angle to the horizontal, oriented so that the edge of the rim conformed as closely as possible to a flat surface; this would represent the minimum diameter of a relatively steep-sided vessel. Finally, the two measurements were averaged to obtain the mean diameter.

With every textile, the standard group of attributes discussed in Chapter 4 was measured, and any special characteristics of the fabric were described and/or sketched. All measurements, comments, and sketches were entered on data forms along with provenience information for each sherd, then into the computer. From those measurements, additional data variables were computed. For calculations, statistical reduction of data, and generation of tables and graphs, the SYSTAT and SYGRAPH computer programs were used (Wilkinson 1987, 1988).

Below is a checklist of variables noted, measured, or calculated in this analysis, with computational formulas included where appropriate. Each one is discussed at more length in Chapter 4. For computer coding, see Drooker 1989b:321–325.

Nonmetric fabric characteristics:
  Fabric structure(s) present (number and types)
  Structural designs present
  Structure of finished edge(s) and/or joins, if present
  Condition of fabric (worn/undamaged)
  Presence and nature of overlapped and/or joined fabrics
Measured yarn attributes:
  Warp and weft yarn diameters, in mm
  Warp ply and weft ply (numbers of yarn elements twisted together)
  Warp and weft yarn twist direction (see Figure 11)
  Warp and weft yarn twist angle, expressed as index number (see Figure 11)
Measured fabric attributes:
  Twining twist direction (see Figure 11)
  Numbers of warp and weft elements per centimeter ("warp count" and "weft count")
  Weft row diameter (for twining rows)
  Number of weft rows per centimeter (for twining rows)
Calculated yarn and fabric attributes or indices:
  Average yarn diameter: (warp diameter + weft diameter) / 2
  Weft count for twined fabrics: (number of weft rows per cm) × 2
  Fabric count: warp count + weft count
  Fabric count index: If fabric count = 0 to 4.9, index = 1, if count = 5.0 to 9.9, index = 2, if count = 10.0 to 14.9, index = 3, etc.
  Warp density: (warp count [per cm]) × (warp yarn diameter [mm])
  Weft density, interlaced fabric: (weft count [per cm]) × (weft yarn diameter [mm])
  Weft density, twined fabric: (row count) × (row diameter), or approximate by (row count) × (weft diameter)
  Fabric density: warp density + weft density
  Modified Textile Production Complexity Indices (see discussion in text)
    No. 1: Number of structures present + fabric count index
    No. 2: Index No. 1 + (warp ply + weft ply) / 2
    No. 3: Index No. 2 + warp yarn twist index number
Information from rim sherds:
  Orientation of fabric relative to rim (angle of twined rows or interlaced weft to the rim, measured in degrees, counterclockwise from 0° at left horizontal to 180° at right)
  Estimated vessel diameter, inside and outside
Calculated rim sherd information
  Average rim diameter: (inside diameter + outside diameter) / 2

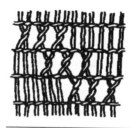

REFERENCES

Adair, James
    1968 *The History of the American Indians.* Series in American Studies, Joseph J. Kwiat, editor-in-chief. Johnson Reprint, New York. Originally published 1775.
Adams, Robert M.
    1941 Archaeological Investigations in Jefferson County, Missouri, 1939–1940. *Transactions of the Academy of Science of St. Louis* 30(5):151–221.
    1949 Archaeological Investigations in Jefferson County, Missouri. *Missouri Archaeologist* 11(3–4):5–71.
Adovasio, James M.
    1982 Basketry and Netting Impressions. In *The Prehistory of the Paintsville Reservoir, Johnson and Morgan Counties, Kentucky,* edited by James M. Adovasio, pp. 826–840. University of Pittsburgh Department of Anthropology Ethnology Monograph No. 6, Pittsburgh.
Adovasio, James M., and Rhonda L. Andrews
    1980 Basketry, Cordage, and Bark Impressions from the Northern Thorn Mound (46 Mg 78), Monongahela County, West Virginia. *West Virginia Archaeologist* 30:33–72.
Adovasio, James M., and Ronald C. Carlisle
    1982 External Affinities of the Paintsville Reservoir Perishable Industry. In *The Prehistory of the Paintsville Reservoir, Johnson and Morgan Counties, Kentucky,* edited by James M. Adovasio, pp. 840–845. University of Pittsburgh Department of Anthropology Ethnology Monograph No. 6, Pittsburgh.
Andrews, Rhonda L., James M. Adovasio, and Deborah G. Harding
    1988 Textile and Related Perishable Remains from the Windover Site (8BR246).

Paper presented at the fifty-third annual meeting of the Society for American Archaeology, Phoenix.

Baerreis, David A.
1947 *Spiro Focus Basketry.* The Museum of the University of Oklahoma Information Service Circular No. 2, Norman.

Baldwin, Elizabeth Ellen
1966 *The Obion Site, an Early Mississippian Center in Western Tennessee.* Unpublished Ph.D. dissertation, Anthropology Department, Harvard University.

Balfet, Helene
1957 Basketry: A Proposed Classification. Translated by M. A. Baumhoff. *Annual Report of the University of California Archaeological Survey* 37(47):1–21.

Barber, E. J. W.
1991 *Prehistoric Textiles: The Development of Cloth in the Neolithic and Bronze Ages, with Special Reference to the Aegean.* Princeton University Press, Princeton, New Jersey.

Black, Glenn A.
1967 *Angel Site, an Archaeological, Historical, and Ethnological Study.* Indiana Historical Society, Indianapolis.

Bourne, Edward G.
1904 *Narratives of the Career of Hernando De Soto.* A. S. Barnes, New York.

Brain, Jeffrey P.
1979 *Tunica Treasure.* Harvard University Peabody Museum of Archaeology and Ethnology, Cambridge, Massachusetts, and the Peabody Museum of Salem, Salem, Massachusetts.

Braun, David, and Stephen Plog
1982 Evolution of "Tribal" Social Networks: Theory and Prehistoric North American Evidence. *American Antiquity* 47:504–525.

Brose, David S.
1979 A Speculative Model of the Role of Exchange in the Prehistory of the Eastern Woodlands. In *Hopewell Archaeology: The Chillicothe Conference,* edited by David S. Brose and N'omi Greber, pp. 3–8. Kent State University Press, Kent, Ohio.
1989 From the Southeastern Ceremonial Complex to the Southern Cult: "You Can't Tell the Players without a Program." In *The Southeastern Ceremonial Complex: Artifacts and Analysis,* edited by Patricia Galloway, pp. 27–37. University of Nebraska Press, Lincoln.

Brose, David S., and N'omi Greber
1979 *Hopewell Archaeology: The Chillicothe Conference.* Kent State University Press, Kent, Ohio.

Brose, David S., James A. Brown, and David W. Penney
1985 *Ancient Art of the American Woodland Indians.* Harry N. Abrams, New York.

Brown, Catherine
1982 On the Gender of the Winged Being on Mississippian Period Copper Plates. *Tennessee Anthropologist* 7(1):1–8.

Brown, Ian W.

1980 *Salt and the Eastern North American Indian: An Archaeological Study.* Harvard University Peabody Museum Lower Mississippi Survey Bulletin No. 6, Cambridge, Massachusetts.

1987 Afterward: The Morgan Site in Regional Perspective. In *Excavations at Morgan: A Coles Creek Mound Complex in Coastal Louisiana,* edited by Richard S. Fuller and Diane S. Fuller, pp. 155–164. Harvard University Peabody Museum Lower Mississippi Survey Bulletin No. 11, Cambridge, Massachusetts.

Brown, James A.

1971 The Dimensions of Status in the Burials at Spiro. In *Approaches to the Social Dimensions of Mortuary Practices,* edited by James A. Brown, pp. 92–112. Society for American Archaeology Memoir No. 25, Washington, D.C.

1975 Spiro Art and Its Mortuary Contexts. In *Death and the Afterlife in Pre-Columbian America,* edited by Elizabeth P. Benson, pp. 1–32. Dunbarton Oaks Research Library and Collections, Washington, D.C.

1976a The Southern Cult Reconsidered. *Midcontinental Journal of Archaeology* 1(2):115–135.

1976b *Spiro Studies.* Vol. 4. University of Oklahoma Research Institute, Norman.

1983 Spiro Exchange Connections Revealed by Sources of Imported Raw Material. *Oklahoma Archaeological Survey Studies in Oklahoma's Past* 11:129–162.

1984 Arkansas Valley Caddoan: The Spiro Phase. In *Prehistory of Oklahoma,* edited by R. E. Bell, pp. 241–263. Academic Press, New York.

1985 The Mississippian Period. In *Ancient Art of the American Woodland Indians,* edited by David S. Brose, James A. Brown, and David W. Penney, pp. 93–146. Harry N. Abrams, New York.

1989 On Style Divisions of the Southeastern Ceremonial Complex: A Revisionist Perspective. In *The Southeastern Ceremonial Complex: Artifacts and Analysis,* edited by Patricia Galloway, pp. 183–204. University of Nebraska Press, Lincoln.

Brown, James A., Richard A. Kerber, and Howard D. Winters

1990 Trade and Evolution of Exchange Relations at the Beginning of the Mississippian Period. In *The Mississippian Emergence,* edited by Bruce D. Smith, pp. 251–280. Smithsonian Institution Press, Washington, D.C.

Brown, James A., Robert E. Bell, and Don G. Wyckoff

1978 Caddoan Settlement Patterns in the Arkansas River Drainage. In *Mississippian Settlement Patterns,* edited by Bruce D. Smith, pp. 169–200. Academic Press, New York.

Browning, Kathryn

1974 Indian Textiles as Reconstructed from Impressions Left on Long Island. *Archaeology of Eastern North America* 2(1):94–98.

Burnett, E. K.

1945 The Spiro Mound Collection in the Museum. *Contributions from the Museum of the American Indian, Heye Foundation* 14:9–47.

Burnham, Dorothy

1976 Braided "Arrow" Sashes of Quebec. In *Ethnographic Textiles of the Western*

Hemisphere, Irene Emery Roundtable on Museum Textiles, 1976 Proceedings, edited by Irene Emery and Patricia Fiske, pp. 356–365. Textile Museum, Washington, D.C.

Bushnell, David I., Jr.

1906 The Use of Buffalo Hair by the North American Indians. *Man* 6:177–180.

1907 Primitive Salt-Making in the Mississippi Valley, I. *Man* 7:17–21.

1908 Primitive Salt-Making in the Mississippi Valley, II. *Man* 8:65–70.

1909 The Various Uses of Buffalo Hair by the North American Indians. *American Anthropologist* 11(3):401–425.

1914 Archaeological Investigations in Ste. Genevieve County, Missouri. *Proceedings of the U.S. National Museum* 46:641–668.

Butler, Brian M.

1987 Review of *Mississippian Towns of the Western Kentucky Border,* edited by R. Barry Lewis. *Southeastern Archaeology* 6(1):74–75.

1991 Kincaid Revisited: The Mississippian Sequence in the Lower Ohio Valley. In *Cahokia and Its Neighbors,* edited by R. Barry Lewis and Thomas Emerson, pp. 264–273. University of Illinois Press, Champaign.

Byers, Douglas

1964 Two Textile Fragments and Some Copper Objects from Etowah, Georgia. *Congreso Internacional de Americanistas Actas y Memorias* 35(1):591–598.

Caldwell, J. R.

1964 Interaction Spheres in Prehistory. In *Hopewellian Studies,* edited by Joseph R. Caldwell and Robert L. Hall, pp. 133–143. Illinois State Museum Scientific Papers No. 12, Springfield.

Cardale-Schrimpff, Marianne

1972 *Techniques of Handweaving and Allied Arts in Colombia.* Unpublished doctoral dissertation, St. Hughs, England.

Carstens, Kenneth

1991 Is the Stone Site Protohistoric: A Unique Clay Pot from 40Sw23. Paper presented at the eighth annual Kentucky Heritage Council Archaeological Conference, Bowling Green, Kentucky.

Carter, B. F.

1933 The Weaving Technic of Winnebago Bags. *Wisconsin Archaeologist* 12(2):33–48.

Chapman, Jefferson

1985 *Tellico Archaeology: 12,000 Years of Native American History.* Tennessee Valley Authority. Distributed by University of Tennessee Press, Knoxville.

Chapman, Jefferson, and Gary D. Crites

1987 Evidence for Early Maize *(Zea mays)* from the Icehouse Bottom Site, Tennessee. *American Antiquity* 52(2):352–354.

Chapman, Jefferson, and James M. Adovasio

1977 Textile and Basketry Impressions from Icehouse Bottom, Tennessee. *American Antiquity* 42(4):620–625.

Chase, Mary A.

1982 Flax Processing. *Weaver's Journal* 7(2):5–9.

Church, Flora

    1983 An Analysis of Textile Fragments from Three Ohio Hopewell Mound Groups. *Ohio Archaeologist* 33(1):10–16.

    1984 Textiles as Markers of Ohio Hopewell Social Identities. *Midcontinental Journal of Archaeology* 9(1):1–25.

Clay, R. Berle

    1984 Morris Plain, and Other Western Kentucky Ceramic Smoking Guns. *Tennessee Anthropologist* 9(2):104–113.

Cleland, Charles E.

    1982 The Inland Shore Fishery of the Northern Great Lakes: Its Development and Importance in Prehistory. *American Antiquity* 47(4):761–784.

Cobb, Charles R.

    1989 An Appraisal of the Role of Mill Creek Chert Hoes in Mississippian Exchange Systems. *Southeastern Archaeology* 8(2):79–92.

Coe, Michael, and William Fischer

    1959 Barkley Reservoir—Tennessee Portion, Archaeological Excavations, 1959. Ms. on file, Frank H. McClung Museum, University of Tennessee, Knoxville.

Coe, Michael, Dean Snow, and Elizabeth Benson

    1986 *Atlas of Ancient America.* Facts on File, New York.

Cole, Fay-Cooper, et al.

    1951 *Kincaid, a Prehistoric Illinois Metropolis.* University of Chicago Press, Chicago.

Collingwood, Peter

    1974 *The Techniques of Sprang.* Watson-Guptill, New York.

Conrad, Anthony R., and Charlene M. Bohn

    1988 Feather Cape Reconstruction. In *A History of 17 Years of Excavation and Reconstruction: A Chronicle of Twelfth Century Human Values and the Built Environment,* edited by James M. Heilman, Malinda C. Lileas, and Christopher A. Turnbow, vol. 2, pp. 74–78. Dayton Museum of Natural History, Dayton, Ohio.

Crane, H. R., and J. B. Griffin

    1970 University of Michigan Radiocarbon Dates XIII. *Radiocarbon* 12(1):161–180.

Croes, Dale R.

    1977 *Basketry from the Ozette Village Archaeological Site: A Technological, Functional, and Comparative Study.* Ph.D dissertation, Washington State University, Pullman. Submitted to National Park Service, San Francisco. Copies available from Technical Information Service, U.S. Department of Commerce, Springfield, VA 22161.

Croes, Dale R., and Eric Blinman (editors)

    1980 *Hoko River: A 2500 Year Old Fishing Camp on the Northwest Coast of North America.* Washington State University Laboratory of Anthropology Reports of Investigations No. 58, Pullman.

Curry, Hilda J.

    1950a Negative Painted Pottery of Angel Mounds Site and Its Distribution in the New World. *Supplement to International Journal of American Linguistics* 16(4):33–90.

1950b Negative Painting of Angel Site and Southeastern United States. *Indiana Academy of Science Proceedings* 59:25–27.

Densmore, Florence

1929 *Chippewa Customs.* Bureau of American Ethnology Bulletin No. 86, Washington, D.C.

Dickens, Roy S., Jr.

1980 Ceramic Diversity as an Indicator of Cultural Dynamics in the Woodland Period. *Tennessee Anthropologist* 5:34–46.

Douglas, Frederick H., Kate Peck Kent, and N. Feder

1968 *An Osage Yarn Bag.* Material Culture Notes, Denver Art Museum, Denver.

Drooker, Penelope B.

1989a Another Piece of the Puzzle: Gleaning Information from Textile Impressions on Mississippian Pottery. Paper presented at the 1989 Southeastern Archaeological Conference, Tampa.

1989b *Textile Impressions on Mississippian Pottery at the Wickliffe Mounds Site (15Ba4), Ballard County, Kentucky.* Master's thesis, Harvard University Extension School. University Microfilms, Ann Arbor.

1990a Attributes of Textiles Impressed on Pottery, 1988 Excavations, Wickliffe Mounds (15Ba4), Kentucky. Ms. on file, Wickliffe Mounds Research Center, Wickliffe, Kentucky.

1990b Attributes of Textiles Impressed on Pottery at the Stone Site (38Sw23), Tennessee. Ms. on file, Frank H. McClung Museum, University of Tennessee, Knoxville.

1990c Textile Production and Use at Wickliffe Mounds (15Ba4), Kentucky. *Midcontinental Journal of Archaeology* 15(2):163–220.

1991a Cane- and Fabric-Impressed Sherds from the Salt Creek Site, Clarke County, Alabama. Ms. on file. State Museum of Natural History, University of Alabama, Tuscaloosa.

1991b Matting and Fabric Impressions from Bottle Creek (1Ba2), Alabama. *Journal of Alabama Archaeology,* in press.

1991c Mississippian Lace: A Complex Mississippian Textile Impressed on Pottery from the Stone Site, Tennessee. *Southeastern Archaeology* 10(2): 79–97.

Duffield, Lathel F.

1964 Engraved Shells from the Craig Mound at Spiro, Le Flore County, Oklahoma. Oklahoma Anthropological Society Memoir No. 1.

Du Ru, Paul

1934 *Journal of Paul du Ru (February 1 to May 8, 1700), Missionary/Priest to Louisiana.* Translated by Ruth Lapham Butler. Caxton Club, Chicago.

Emerson, Thomas E.

1982 *Mississippian Stone Images in Illinois.* Illinois Archaeological Survey Circular No. 6, Urbana.

1989 Water, Serpents, and the Underworld: An Exploration into Cahokian Symbolism. In *The Southeastern Ceremonial Complex: Artifacts and Analysis,* edited by Patricia Galloway, pp. 45–92. University of Nebraska Press, Lincoln.

Emery, Irene
1966 *The Primary Structures of Fabrics, an Illustrated Classification.* Textile Museum, Washington, D.C.

Fagan, Brian
1988 Black Day at Slack Farm. Archaeology 41(4):15–16, 73.

Fairbanks, Charles H.
1956 *Archaeology of the Funeral Mound, Ocmulgee National Monument, Georgia.* U.S. Department of the Interior National Park Service Archaeological Research Series No. 3, Washington, D.C.

Foster, Donald L.
1990 The Spanish Royal Tapestry Factory: A Museum That Works. *Handwoven* 11(2):34–35.

Fowler, Melvin L.
1975 A Pre-Columbian Urban Center on the Mississippi. *Scientific American* 233(2):92–101.

Fowler, Melvin L., and Robert L. Hall
1978 Late Prehistory of the Illinois Area. In Northeast, Handbook of North American Indians, vol. 15, edited by Bruce G. Trigger, pp. 560–568. Smithsonian Institution, Washington, D.C.

Fraser, David W.
1989 *A Guide to Weft Twining and Related Structures with Interacting Wefts.* University of Pennsylvania Press, Philadelphia.

Frison, George C., R. L. Andrews, J. M. Adovasio, R. C. Carlisle, and R. Edgar
1986 A Late Paleoindian Animal Trapping Net from Northern Wyoming. *American Antiquity* 51(2):352–361.

Fuller, Richard S., Diane S. Fuller, et al.
1987 *Excavations at Morgan, a Coles Creek Mound Complex in Coastal Louisiana.* Harvard University Peabody Museum Lower Mississippi Survey Bulletin No. 11, Cambridge, Massachusetts.

Fundabark, Emma L., and Mary D. F. Foreman (editors)
1957 *Sun Circles and Human Hands.* E. L. Fundabark, Luverne, Alabama.

Funkhouser, William D., and William S. Webb
1929 The So-called "Ash Caves" in Lee County, Kentucky. *University of Kentucky Reports in Archaeology and Anthropology* 1(2):37–112.

Galloway, Patricia (editor)
1989 *The Southeastern Ceremonial Complex: Artifacts and Analysis.* University of Nebraska Press, Lincoln.

Garland, Elizabeth B.
1990 *The Obion Site, an Early Mississippian Center in Western Tennessee.* Tennessee Department of Conservation Division of Archaeology Research Series No. 9, Nashville.

Gillispie, Charles Coulson (editor)

1959 *A Diderot Pictorial Encyclopedia of Trades and Industry: Manufacturing and the Technical Arts in Plates Selected from "L'Encyclopédie, ou Dictionnaire Raisonné des Sciences, des Arts et des Métiers" of Denis Diderot.* Dover, New York.

Goodman, Claire Garber
1984 *Copper Artifacts in Late Eastern Woodlands Prehistory.* Edited by Anne-Marie Cantwell. Center for American Archaeology, Evanston, Illinois.

Gramly, Richard Michael
1977 Deerskins and Hunting Territories: Competition for a Scarce Resource of the Northeastern Woodlands. *American Antiquity* 42:601–605.

Green, Thomas J., and Cheryl A. Munson
1978 Mississippian Settlement Patterns in Southwestern Indiana. In *Mississippian Settlement Patterns,* edited by Bruce D. Smith, pp. 293–330. Academic Press, New York.

Griffin, James B.
1938 The Ceramic Remains from Norris Basin, Tennessee. In *An Archaeological Survey of the Norris Basin in Eastern Tennessee,* by William S. Webb, pp. 253–358. Bureau of American Ethnology Bulletin No. 118, Washington, D.C.
1939 Report on Ceramics of Wheeler Basin. In *An Archaeological Survey of the Wheeler Basin on the Tennessee River in Northern Alabama,* by William S. Webb, pp. 127–165. Bureau of American Ethnology Bulletin No. 122, Washington, D.C.
1983 The Midlands. In *Ancient North Americans,* edited by J. D. Jennings, pp. 243–301. W. H. Freeman, New York.

Haag, W. G.
1942 A Description and Analysis of the Pickwick Pottery. In *An Archaeological Survey of the Pickwick Basin in the Adjacent Portions of the States of Alabama, Mississippi, and Tennessee,* by William S. Webb and David L. DeJarnette, pp. 509–526. Bureau of American Ethnology Bulletin No. 129, Washington, D.C.

Hall, Robert L.
1991 Cahokia Identity and Interaction Models of Cahokia Mississippian. In *Cahokia and the Hinterlands: Middle Mississippian Cultures of the Midwest,* edited by Thomas E. Emerson and R. Barry Lewis, pp. 3–34. University of Illinois Press, Urbana.

Hally, David J.
1984 Vessel Assemblages and Food Habits: A Comparison of Two Aboriginal Southeastern Vessel Assemblages. *Southeastern Archaeology* 3(1):46–64.
1986 The Identification of Vessel Function: A Case Study for Northwest Georgia. *American Antiquity* 51:267–295.

Hamilton, Henry W., Jean T. Hamilton, and Eleanor F. Chapman
1974 *Spiro Mound Copper.* Missouri Archaeological Society Memoir No. 11, Columbia.

Hanson, Lee H., Jr.

1970 *The Jewell Site, Bn 21, Barren County, Kentucky.* Tennessee Archaeological Society Miscellaneous Paper No. 8, Nashville.

Haskins, Valerie A.

1990 Wickliffe Mounds Cemetery Project, Assessment of Human Remains from Mound C, Wickliffe Mounds, KY (15Ba4): Feasibility Study. Report for the Wickliffe Mounds Research Center and the Kentucky Heritage Council. Ms. on file, Wickliffe Mounds Research Center, Wickliffe, Kentucky.

Heckenberger, Michael J., James B. Petersen, and Louise A. Basa

1990 Early Woodland Period Ritual Use of Personal Adornment at the Boucher Site. *Annals of the Carnegie Museum* 59(3):173–217.

Heimlich, Marion D.

1952 *Guntersville Basin Pottery.* Geological Survey of Alabama Museum Paper No. 32, Montgomery.

Hinkle, Kathleen A.

1984 *Ohio Hopewell Textiles: A Medium for the Exchange of Social and Stylistic Information.* Unpublished master's thesis, University of Arkansas, Fayetteville.

Hodge, Frederick W., and Theodore H. Lewis (editors)

1907 *Spanish Explorers in the Southern United States, 1528–1543.* Charles Scribner's Sons, New York.

Hoffman, Walter J.

1896 The Menomini Indians. *Smithsonian Institution Bureau of Ethnology Annual Report* 14 (pt. 1):11–328.

Holmes, Nicholas H., Jr.

1963 The Site on Bottle Creek. *Journal of Alabama Archaeology* 9(1):16–27.

Holmes, William H.

1884 Prehistoric Textile Fabrics of the United States, Derived from Impressions on Pottery. *Smithsonian Institution Bureau of Ethnology Annual Report* 3:393–425.

1888 A Study of the Textile Art in Its Relation to the Development of Form and Ornament. *Smithsonian Institution Bureau of Ethnology Annual Report* 6:189–252.

1891 The Thruston Tablet. *American Anthropologist* 4(2):161–165.

1896 Prehistoric Textile Art of the Eastern United States. *Smithsonian Institution Bureau of Ethnology Annual Report for 1891–1892* 13:3–46.

1903 Aboriginal Pottery of the Eastern United States. *Bureau of American Ethnology Annual Report* 20:1–237.

Howard, James H.

1968 *The Southeastern Ceremonial Complex and Its Interpretation.* Missouri Archaeological Society Memoir No. 6, Columbia.

Hudson, Charles

1976 *The Southeastern Indians.* University of Tennessee Press, Knoxville.

Iseminger, William

1983 A Cahokia Spindle Whorl. *Illinois Antiquity* 15(3):40–42.

Johnson, Brenda

    1962 A Study of Textile-Impressed Pottery in Kentucky. Ms. on file, University of Kentucky Museum of Anthropology, Lexington.

Jones, B. Calvin

    1982 Southern Cult Manifestations at the Lake Jackson Site, Leon County, Florida: Salvage Excavation of Mound 3. *Midcontinental Journal of Archaeology* 7(1):3–44.

Jones, Volney H.

    1948 Notes on the Manufacture of Cedar-Bark Mats by the Chippewa Indians. *Papers of the Michigan Academy of Science, Arts and Letters* 32:341–363.

Kellar, James H.

    1967 Material Remains. In *Angel Site, an Archaeological, Historical and Ethnological Study,* by Glenn A. Black, pp. 431–487. Indiana Historical Society, Indianapolis.

Kent, Kate P.

    1947 *The Cultivation and Weaving of Cotton in the Prehistoric Southwestern United States. American Philosophical Society Transactions,* n.s. 47(3).

    1983 *Prehistoric Textiles of the Southwest.* School of American Research, Santa Fe.

Kerner, Karen

    1963 Magical Counterspinning: An Examination of Peruvian "Witching Veils." *International Congress of Anthropological and Ethnological Sciences* 8(3):32–35.

Keslin, Richard O.

    1964 Archaeological Implications on the Role of Salt as an Element of Cultural Diffusion. *Missouri Archaeologist* 26:1–174.

King, Blanche B.

    1936 Fluorspar Ornaments in the King Collection. *Wisconsin Archaeologist* 16:25–27.

    1937a Ancient Buried City. *National Archaeological News* 1(3):13–15.

    1937b Recent Excavations at the King Mounds, Wickliffe, Kentucky. *Illinois State Academy of Science Transactions* 30:83–90.

    1939 *Under Your Feet: The Story of the American Mound Builders.* Dodd, Mead, New York.

King, Fain W.

    1936 The Archaeology of Western Kentucky. *Transactions of the Illinois State Academy of Science* 29(2):35–38.

King, Mary Elizabeth

    1968 Textile Fragments from the Riverside Site, Menominee, Michigan. *Thirty-eighth International Congress of Americanists,* vol. 1, pp. 117–123.

    1978 Analytical Methods and Prehistoric Textiles. *American Antiquity* 43(1):89–96.

King, Mary Elizabeth, and Joan S. Gardner

    1981 The Analysis of Textiles from Spiro Mound. In *The Research Potential of Anthropological Museum Collections,* edited by Mary Elizabeth King and Joan S. Gardner, pp. 123–139. New York Academy of Science.

Kneberg, Madeline

1959 Engraved Shell Gorgets and Their Associations. *Tennessee Archaeologist* 15:1–39.

Knight, Vernon James, Jr.

1986 The Institutional Organization of Mississippian Religion. *American Antiquity* 51(4):675–687.

Kuttruff, Jenna Tedrick

1980 Prehistoric Textiles Revealed by Potsherds. *Shuttle Spindle and Dyepot* 11(3):40–41, 80.

1987a A Prehistoric Twined Bag from Big Bone Cave, Tennessee: Manufacture, Repair, and Use. *Ars Textrina* 8:125–153.

1987b Textile Use and Manufacture as Evidenced in Fabric Impressed Pottery from Mound Bottom, Tennessee. Paper presented at the 1987 Southeastern Archaeological Conference, Charleston, South Carolina.

1988a *Textile Attributes and Production Complexity as Indicators of Caddoan Status Differentiation in the Arkansas Valley and Southern Ozark Regions.* Unpublished Ph.D. dissertation, Department of Textiles and Clothing, Ohio State University, Columbus.

1988b Techniques and Production Complexity of Mississippian Period Textiles from Spiro, Oklahoma. In *Textiles as Primary Sources, Proceedings of the First Symposium of the Textile Society of America,* compiled by John E. Vollmer, pp. 145–150. n.p.

1990 Charred Mississippian Textile Remains from Wickliffe Mounds, Kentucky (15BA4). Paper presented at the 1990 Southeastern Archaeological Conference, Mobile, Alabama.

Kuttruff, Jenna Tedrick, and Carl Kuttruff

1986 Mississippian Textile Evidence in Fabric Impressed Ceramics from Mound Bottom (40CH8), Tennessee. In *Native Fiber Industries from Eastern North America: Analyses of Prehistoric and Ethnographic Collections,* edited by James B. Petersen. University of Tennessee Press, Knoxville, in press.

Larson, Lewis H.

1971 Archaeological Implications of Social Stratification at the Etowah Site, Georgia. In *Approaches to the Social Dimensions of Mortuary Practices,* edited by James A. Brown, pp. 58–67. Society for American Archaeology Memoir No. 25. Washington, D.C.

1989 The Etowah Site. In *The Southeastern Ceremonial Complex: Artifacts and Analysis,* edited by Patricia Galloway, pp. 133–141. University of Nebraska Press, Lincoln.

Le Page du Pratz, Antoine Simon

1763 *The History of Louisiana. . . .* T. Becket and P. A. De Hondt, London.

Levey, Santina M.

1983 *Lace: A History.* Victoria and Albert Museum, London.

Lewis, R. Barry

    1987 The Mississippi Period in Kentucky. In *Kentucky State Archaeological Preservation Plan*. Kentucky Heritage Council, Frankfort, in press.

    1990a The Late Prehistory of the Ohio-Mississippi Rivers Confluence Region, Kentucky and Missouri. In *Towns and Temples Along the Mississippi*, edited by David H. Dye and Cheryl Anne Cox, pp. 38–58. University of Alabama Press, Tuscaloosa.

    1990b Mississippi Period. In *The Archaeology of Kentucky: Past Accomplishments and Future Directions*, vol. 1, edited by David Pollack, pp. 375–466. Kentucky Heritage Council, Lexington.

    1991 The Early Mississippi Period in the Confluence Region and Its Northern Relationships. In *Cahokia and Its Neighbors*, edited by Thomas Emerson and R. Barry Lewis, pp. 274–294. University of Illinois Press, Champaign.

Lewis, R. Barry (editor)

    1986 *Mississippian Towns of the Western Kentucky Border: The Adams, Wickliffe, and Sassafras Ridge Sites*. Kentucky Heritage Council, Frankfort.

Lewis, Thomas M. N.

    1934 Kentucky's "Ancient Buried City." *Wisconsin Archaeologist* 13(2):25–31.

Lewis, Thomas M. N., and Madeline Kneberg

    1946 *Hiwassee Island*. University of Tennessee Press, Knoxville.

Linton, Ralph

    1944 North American Cooking Pots. *American Antiquity* 9(4):369–380.

Lorant, Stefan (editor)

    1946 *The New World: The First Pictures of America, Made by John White and Jacques Le Moyne and Engraved by Theodore De Bry*. . . . Duell, Sloan, and Pearce, New York.

Loughridge, Robert H.

    1888 *Report on the Geological and Economic Features of the Jackson Purchase Region*. Kentucky Geological Survey Miscellaneous Geological Reports, vol. 10, pt. 1, Lexington.

Lyford, Carrie

    1953 *Ojibwa Crafts*. Bureau of Indian Affairs, Lawrence, Kansas.

Maslowski, Robert F.

    1984 The Significance of Cordage Attributes in the Analysis of Woodland Pottery. *Pennsylvania Archaeologist* 54(1–2):51–60.

Miller, Joan

    1988 Experimental Replication of Early Woodland Vegetal Fiber Slippers. *Southeastern Archaeology* 7(2):132–137.

Miller, Suzanne

    1982 Flax. *Weaver's Journal* 7(2):12–15.

Million, M. G.

    1975 Research Design for the Aboriginal Ceramic Industries of the Cache River Basin. In *The Cache River Archaeological Project: An Experiment in Contract Archaeology*, assembled by Michael B. Schiffer and John H. House, pp. 217–222. Arkansas Archaeological Survey Publications in Archaeology Research Series No. 8, Fayetteville.

1976 Preliminary Report on Zebree Site Ceramics. In *A Preliminary Report of the Zebree Project*, edited by Dan F. Morse and Phyllis A. Morse, pp. 44–49. Arkansas Archaeological Survey Research Report No. 8, Fayetteville.

Miner, Horace

1936 The Importance of Textiles in the Archaeology of the Eastern United States. *American Antiquity* 1(3):181–192.

Mitchell, Dr.

1820 A Letter from Dr. Mitchell, of New York, to Samuel M. Burnside, Esq., Secretary of the American Antiquarian Society, on North American Antiquities. *Archoelogia Americana* 1:318–321.

Moorehead, Warren K.

1932 Exploration of the Etowah Site in Georgia. *Etowah Papers* 1:1–106. Yale University Press, New Haven, Connecticut.

Morrell, L. Ross

1965 The Woods Island Site in Southeastern Acculturation, 1625–1800. *Florida State University Notes in Anthropology 2*.

Muller, Jon D.

1978 The Kincaid System: Mississippian Settlement in the Environs of a Large Site. In *Mississippian Settlement Patterns*, edited by Bruce D. Smith, pp. 269–292. Academic Press, New York.

1983 The Southeast. In *Ancient North Americans*, edited by Jesse D. Jennings, pp. 373–419. W. H. Freeman, New York.

1984 Mississippian Specialization and Salt. *American Antiquity* 49(3):489–507.

1987 Salt, Chert, and Shell: Mississippian Exchange and Economy. In *Specialisation, Exchange, and Complexity*, edited by E. Brumfiel and T. Earle, pp. 10–22. Cambridge University Press, Cambridge.

Muller, Jon, and Jeanette E. Stephens

1991 Mississippian Sociocultural Adaptation. In *Cahokia and Its Neighbors*, edited by R. Barry Lewis and Thomas Emerson, pp. 297–310. University of Illinois Press, Champaign.

Munger, Paul, and Robert M. Adams

1941 Fabric Impressions of Pottery from the Elizabeth Herrell Site, Missouri. *American Antiquity* 7(2):166–171.

Munson, Cheryl Ann, and David Pollack

1990 Slack Farm: A Protohistoric Caborn-Welborn Phase Settlement in Union County, Kentucky. Ms. on file, Kentucky Heritage Council, Frankfort.

Neuman, Robert W.

1983 The Buffalo in Southeastern United States Post-Pleistocene Prehistory. In *Southeastern Natives and Their Pasts*, edited by Don G. Wyckoff and Jack L. Hofman, pp. 261–280. Oklahoma Archaeological Survey Studies in Oklahoma's Past No. 11, Norman.

Newton, Dolores

1971 *Social and Historical Dimensions of Timbira Material Culture.* Unpublished Ph.D. dissertation, Department of Anthropology, Harvard University, Cambridge, Massachusetts.

1974 The Timbira Hammock as a Cultural Indicator of Social Boundaries. In *The Human Mirror,* edited by Miles Richardson, pp. 231–251. Louisiana State University Press, Baton Rouge.

Nunley, Parker

1967 A Hypothesis Concerning the Relationship between Texcoco Fabric-Marked Pottery, Tlateles, and Cinampa Agriculture. *American Antiquity* 32(4):515–522.

O'Brien, Michael J.

1977 *Intrasite Variability in a Middle Mississippian Community.* Ph.D. dissertation, University of Texas, Austin. University Microfilms, Ann Arbor.

Orchard, William C.

1920 *Sandals and Other Fabrics from Kentucky Caves.* Museum of the American Indian/Heye Foundation Miscellaneous Publication No. 4, New York.

Orr, Kenneth Gordon

1951 Change at Kincaid: A Study of Cultural Dynamics. In *Kincaid, a Prehistoric Illinois Metropolis,* by Fay-Cooper Cole et al., pp. 293–359. University of Chicago Press, Chicago.

Parker, Malcolm

1949 A Study of the Rocky Creek Pictoglyph. *Tennessee Archaeologist* 5(2):13–17.

Parkman, Francis

1892 *France and England in North America (part third): La Salle and the Discovery of the Great West.* 12th ed. Little, Brown, Boston.

Pauketat, T. R.

1987 A Functional Consideration of a Mississippian Domestic Vessel Assemblage. *Southeastern Archaeology* 6(1):1–15.

Peebles, Christopher S.

1971 Moundville and Surrounding Sites: Some Structural Considerations of Mortuary Practices. In *Approaches to the Social Dimensions of Mortuary Practices,* edited by James A. Brown, pp. 68–91. Society for American Archaeology Memoir No. 25, Washington, D.C.

1978 Determinants of Settlement Size and Location in the Moundville Phase. In *Mississippian Settlement Patterns,* edited by Bruce D. Smith, pp. 369–416. Academic Press, New York.

Perino, Gregory

1967 *The Cherry Valley Mounds, Cross County, Arkansas, and Banks Mound 3, Crittenden County, Arkansas.* Central States Archaeological Societies Memoir No. 1, n.p.

Perryman, Margaret

1966 Stone Effigy Figures from Georgia. *Tennessee Archaeologist* 22(1):40–42.

Petersen, James B., and Nathan D. Hamilton

1984 Early Woodland Ceramic and Perishable Fiber Industries from the Northeast: A Summary and Interpretation. *Annals of Carnegie Museum* 53:413–445.

Petersen, James B., N. D. Hamilton, J. M. Adovasio, and A. L. McPherron
  1984 Netting Technology and the Antiquity of Fish Exploitation in Eastern North
    America. *Midcontinental Journal of Archaeology* 9(2):199–225.
Peterson, Karen D.
  1963 Chippewa Mat-Weaving Techniques. *Bureau of American Ethnology Bulletin*
    186:211–286.
Phillips, Philip
  1970 *Archaeological Survey in the Lower Yazoo Basin, Mississippi, 1949–1955.*
    Harvard University Peabody Museum of Archaeology and Ethnology Paper
    No. 60, Cambridge, Massachusetts.
Phillips, Phillip, and James A. Brown
  1978 *Pre-Columbian Shell Engravings from the Craig Mound at Spiro, Oklahoma.*
    Peabody Museum of Archaeology and Ethnography, Cambridge, Massachu-
    setts.
Polhemus, Richard R.
  1987 *The Toqua Site: A Late Mississippian Dallas Phase Town.* University of
    Tennessee Department of Anthropology Report of Investigations No. 41,
    Knoxville, and Tennessee Valley Authority Publications in Anthropology No.
    44.
Prentice, Guy
  1986 An Analysis of the Symbolism Expressed by the Birger Figurine. *American
    Anthropologist* 51(2):239–266.
Price, James E., and Cynthia R. Price
  1990 Protohistoric/Early Historic Manifestations in Southeastern Missouri. In
    Towns and Temples along the Mississippi, edited by David H. Dye and Cheryl
    Anne Cox, pp. 59–68. University of Alabama Press, Tuscaloosa.
Rachlin, Carol K.
  1954a A Preliminary Report on the Relationship between Twined Textiles of Mod-
    ern American Indians and Prehistoric Middle Mississippi Culture. Paper pre-
    sented at the annual meeting of the American Anthropological Association,
    Detroit. Ms. on file, Archives of the Glenn A. Black Laboratory of Archae-
    ology, Bloomington, Indiana.
  1954b A Report on the Method Used in Analyzing the Fabric Impressions of the
    Textile Marked Pottery at the Angel Mounds Site, during the Summer of 1954.
    Ms. on file, Archives of the Glenn A. Black Laboratory of Archaeology, Bloom-
    ington, Indiana.
  1955a A Preliminary Report on the Fabrics from the Angel Mounds Site. Paper
    presented at the 1955 meeting of the Society of American Archaeologists,
    Bloomington, Indiana. Ms. on file, Archives of the Glenn A. Black Laboratory
    of Archaeology, Bloomington, Indiana.
  1955b A Report on the Methods Used in the Study of Textile-Marked Pottery at
    the Angel Mounds Site. *Eastern States Archaeological Federation Bulletin* 14:9.
  1955c The Rubber Mold Technic for the Study of Textile-Impressed Pottery.
    American Antiquity 20(4):394–396.
  1960 The Historic Position of the Proto-Cree Textiles in the Eastern Fabric

Complex: An Ethnological-Archaeological Correlation. *National Museum of Canada Bulletin* 167:80–89.

Reed, Ann
    1987 Ceramics. In *The Toqua Site: A Late Mississippian Dallas Phase Town*, by Richard Polhemus et al., pp. 553–687. University of Tennessee Department of Anthropology Report of Investigations No. 41, Knoxville, and Tennessee Valley Authority Publications in Anthropology No. 44.

Rogers, J. Daniel
    1991 Regional Prehistory and the Spiro Site. *Southeastern Archaeology* 10(1):63–68.

Rogers, Nora
    1980 Spaced-Weft Twining of Ancient Peru. *Interweave* 5(4):42–45.
    1983 Some Rush Mats with Warp Movement as Patterning. In *In Celebration of the Curious Mind*, edited by Nora Rogers and Martha Stanley, pp. 9–20. Interweave Press, Loveland, Colorado.

Rostlund, Erhard
    1960 The Geographic Range of the Historic Bison in the Southeast. *Annals of the Association of American Geographers* 50:395–407.

Samuel, Alena
    1985 Chilkat Spinning. *Threads* 1(1):55–59.

Samuel, Cheryl
    1982 *The Chilkat Dancing Blanket*. Pacific Search Press, Seattle.

Schambach, Frank
    1990 The Place of the Spiro Site in Southeastern Prehistory: A Reinterpretation. Paper presented at the 1990 Southeastern Archaeological Conference, Mobile, Alabama.

Schneider, Jane
    1987 The Anthropology of Cloth. *Annual Review of Anthropology* 16:409–448.

Schnell, Frank T., Vernon J. Knight, Jr., and Gail S. Schnell

Scholtz, Sandra Clements
    1975 *Prehistoric Plies: A Structural and Comparative Analysis of Cordage, Netting, Basketry, and Fabric from Ozark Bluff Shelters*. Arkansas Archaeological Survey Research Series No. 9, Fayetteville.

Schreffler, Virginia L.
    1988 *Burial Status Differentiation as Evidenced by Fabrics from Etowah Mound C, Georgia*. Unpublished Ph.D. dissertation, Department of Textiles and Clothing, Ohio State University, Columbus.

Schroedl, Gerald F.
    1975 *Archaeological Investigations at the Harrison Branch and Bat Creek Sites*. University of Tennessee Department of Anthropology Report of Investigations No. 10, Knoxville.

Schroedl, Gerald F., R. P. Stephen Davis, Jr., and C. Clifford Boyd, Jr.
    1985 *Archaeological Contexts and Assemblages at Martin Farm*. University of Tennessee Department of Anthropology Report of Investigations No. 39, Knoxville, and Tennessee Valley Authority Publications in Anthropology No. 37.

Sellers, George Escol
  1877 Aboriginal Pottery of the Salt Springs, Illinois. *Popular Science Monthly* 11:573–585.
Shetrone, Henry C.
  1928 Some Ohio Caves and Rock Shelters Bearing Evidences of Human Occupancy. *Ohio Archaeological and Historical Publications* 37:1–34.
Shetrone, Henry C., and E. F. Greenman
  1931 Explorations of the Seip Group of Prehistoric Earthworks. *Ohio Archaeological and Historical Quarterly* 40(3):343–509.
Sibley, Lucy R., and Kathryn A. Jakes
  1986 Characterization of Selected Prehistoric Fabrics of Southeastern North America. In *Historic Textile and Paper Materials,* edited by H. L. Needles and S. H. Zermian, pp. 253–275. American Chemical Society, Washington, D.C.
  1989 Etowah Textile Remains and Cultural Context: A Model for Inference. *Clothing and Textiles Research Journal* 72:37–45.
Sibley, Lucy R., Kathryn A. Jakes, and C. Song
  1989 Fiber and Yarn Processing by Prehistoric People of North America: Examples from Etowah. *Ars Textrina* 11:191–209.
Simpson, A. M.
  1936 Archaeological Survey of Peoria County. *Transactions of the Illinois State Academy of Science* 29(2):50–51.
Skinner, A. B.
  1921 *Material Culture of the Menomini.* Museum of the American Indian/Heye Foundation Indian Notes and Monographs Miscellaneous Series No. 20, New York.
Smith, Bruce D.
  1978 Variation in Mississippian Settlement Patterns. In *Mississippian Settlement Patterns,* edited by Bruce D. Smith, pp. 479–503. Academic Press, New York.
Smith, Joyce R.
  1975 *Taaniko: Maori Hand-Weaving.* Charles Scribner's Sons, New York.
Smith, Marvin T.
  1987 *Archaeology of Aboriginal Culture Change in the Interior Southeast: Depopulation during the Early Historic Period.* University Presses of Florida, Gainesville.
Smith, Marvin T., and David J. Hally
  1990 Chiefly Behavior: Evidence from Sixteenth Century Spanish Accounts. Paper presented at the 1990 Southeastern Archaeological Conference, Mobile, Alabama.
Smith, Marvin T., Vernon J. Knight, Jr., and Julie B. Smith
  1989 The Milner Village: A Mid-Seventeenth Century Site near Gadsden, Alabama. Paper presented at the 1989 Southeastern Archaeological Conference, Tampa.
Starna, William A., and John H. Relethford

1986 Deer Densities and Population Dynamics: A Cautionary Note. *American Antiquity* 50(4):825–832.

Stoltman, James B.

1973 The Southeastern United States. In *The Development of North American Archaeology,* edited by James E. Fitting, pp. 117–150. Anchor Press, Garden City, New York.

Strong, John A.

1989 The Mississippian Bird-Man Theme in Cross-Cultural Perspective. In *The Southeastern Ceremonial Complex: Artifacts and Analysis,* edited by Patricia Galloway, pp. 211–238. University of Nebraska Press, Lincoln.

Stuiver, Minze, and B. Becker

1986 High-Precision Decadal Calibration of the Radiocarbon Time Scale, AD 1950–2500 BC. *Radiocarbon* 28:863–910.

Sussenbach, Tom, and R. Barry Lewis

1987 *Archaeological Investigations in Carlisle, Hickman, and Fulton Counties, Kentucky.* University of Illinois at Urbana-Champaign Department of Anthropology Western Kentucky Project Report No. 4.

Swanton, John R.

1918 An Early Account of the Choctaw Indians. *American Anthropological Society Memoirs* 5(2).

1946 *The Indians of the Southeastern United States.* Bureau of American Ethnology Bulletin No. 137, Washington, D.C.

Tankersley, Kenneth B.

1986 Bison Exploitation by Late Fort Ancient Peoples in the Central Ohio River Valley. *North American Archaeologist* 7:289–303.

Tankersley, Kenneth B., and William R. Adams

1989 Holocene Bison Remains *(Bison Bison)* from Greene County, Indiana. Paper presented at the Annual Meeting of the Indiana Academy of Science, New Albany.

Tanner, Helen Hornbeck

1986 *Atlas of Great Lakes Indian History.* University of Oklahoma Press, Norman.

Thomas, Cyrus

1894 Report on the Mound Explorations of the Bureau of Ethnology. *Bureau of Ethnology Annual Report for 1890–91* 12:1–742.

Thruston, Gates P.

1890 *The Antiquities of Tennessee and the Adjacent States.* Robert Clarke, Cincinnati.

Waring, Antonio J., and Preston Holder

1945 A Prehistoric Ceremonial Complex in the Southeastern United States. *American Anthropologist* 47:1–34.

Watson, Patty Jo, and Mary C. Kennedy

1991 The Development of Horticulture in the Eastern Woodlands of North America: Women's Role. In *Engendering Archaeology: Women and Prehistory,* edited by Joan M. Gero and Margaret W. Conkey, pp. 255–275. Basil Blackwell, Oxford.

Webb, Clarence H., and Ralph R. McKinney
1975 Mounds Plantation (16CD12), Caddo Parish, Louisiana. *Louisiana Archaeology* 2:39–127.

Webb, William S.
1938 *An Archaeological Survey of the Norris Basin in Eastern Tennessee.* Bureau of American Ethnology Bulletin No. 118, Washington D.C.
1952 The Jonathan Creek Village, Site 4, Marshall County, Kentucky. *University of Kentucky Reports on Anthropology* 8(1).

Webb, William S., and William D. Funkhouser
1929 The Williams Site in Christian County, Kentucky. *University of Kentucky Reports in Archaeology and Anthropology* 1(1):5–29.
1931 The Tolu Site in Crittenden County, Kentucky. *University of Kentucky Reports in Archaeology and Anthropology* 1(5):307–410.
1936 Rock Shelters in Menifee County, Kentucky. *University of Kentucky Reports in Archaeology and Anthropology* 3(4).

Weiner, Annette, and Jane Schneider (editors)
1989 *Cloth and Human Experience.* Smithsonian Institution Press, Washington, D.C.

Wesler, Kit W.
1985 *Archaeological Excavations at Wickliffe Mounds, 15BA4: Mound A, 1984.* Wickliffe Mounds Research Center Report No. 1, Wickliffe, Kentucky.
1986 Return to Wycliffe Mounds: Excavations in Mound A. *Central States Archaeological Journal* 33(2):83–87.
1988 Ceramics and Mississippian Chronology at Wickliffe Mounds, 15BA4 (Grant No. 21–88–30089). Ms. on file, Kentucky Heritage Council, Frankfort.
1989a *Archaeological Excavations at Wickliffe Mounds, 15Ba4: Mound D, 1987.* Wickliffe Mounds Research Center Report No. 3, Wickliffe, Kentucky.
1989b Ceramics, Chronology, and Horizon Markers at Wickliffe Mounds. Paper presented at the 1989 Midwest Archaeological Conference, Iowa City, Iowa.
1990a Ceramics, Chronology, and Horizon Markers at Wickliffe Mounds. Ms. in possession of author.
1990b An Elite Burial Mound at Wickliffe? Paper presented at the 1990 Mid-South Archaeological Conference, Pinson, Tennessee.
1990c The 1990 Excavations at Wickliffe Mounds: As Many Questions as Answers. Paper presented at the 1990 Midwest Archaeological Conference, Evanston, Illinois.
1991 Ceramics, Chronology, and Horizon Markers at Wickliffe Mounds. *American Antiquity* 56(2):278–290.

Wesler, Kit W., and Sarah W. Neusius
1987 *Archaeological Excavations at Wickliffe Mounds, 15BA4: Mound F, Mound A Addendum, and Mitigation for the Great River Road Project, 1985 and 1986.* Wickliffe Mounds Research Center Report No. 2, Wickliffe, Kentucky.

White, Ellanor Peiser

   1987 *Excavating in the Field Museum, a Survey and Analysis of Textiles from the 1891 Hopewell Mound Group Excavation.* Unpublished Master's thesis, Department of History, Sangamon State University, Springfield, Illinois.

White, John K.

   1969 Twined Bags and Pouches of the Eastern Woodlands. *Handweaver and Craftsman* (Summer):8–10, 36–37.

Whiteford, Andrew Hunter

   1977 Fiber Bags of the Great Lakes Indians. *American Indian Art* 2(3):52–64, 85; 3(1):40–47, 90.

   1978 Tapestry-Twined Bags, Osage Bags, and Others. *American Indian Art* 3(2):32–39, 92.

Whitford, A. C.

   1941 Textile Fibers Used in Eastern Aboriginal North America. *Anthropological Papers of the American Museum of Natural History* 38(1):1–22.

Wild, John-Peter

   1970 *Textile Manufacture in the Northern Roman Provinces.* Cambridge University Press, Cambridge.

Wilder, Charles G.

   1951 Kincaid Textiles. In *Kincaid, a Prehistoric Illinois Metropolis,* by Fay-Cooper Cole et al., pp. 366–376. University of Chicago Press, Chicago.

Wilkinson, Leland

   1987 *SYSTAT: The System for Statistics.* SYSTAT, Inc., Evanston, Illinois.

   1988 *SYGRAPH.* SYSTAT, Inc., Evanston, Illinois.

Willey, Gordon R., and Phillip Phillips

   1944 Negative Painted Pottery from Crystal River, Florida. *American Antiquity* 10:173–186.

Williams, Stephen

   1954 *An Archaeological Study of the Mississippian Culture in Southeast Missouri.* Unpublished Ph.D. dissertation, Department of Anthropology, Yale University, New Haven, Connecticut.

   1971 Round Table on Definition of Mississippian. *Southeastern Archaeological Conference* 10(2):1–19.

   1980 Armorel: A Very Late Phase in the Lower Mississippi Valley. *Southeastern Archaeological Conference Bulletin* 22:105–110.

   1990 The Vacant Quarter and Other Late Events in the Lower Valley. In *Towns and Temples along the Mississippi,* edited by David H. Dye and Cheryl Anne Cox, pp. 170–180. University of Alabama Press, Tuscaloosa.

Williams, Stephen, and Jeffrey P. Brain

   1983 The Yazoo and Cultural Dynamics in the Lower Mississippi Valley. In *Excavations at the Lake George Site, Yazoo County, Mississippi, 1958–1960,* by Stephen Williams and Jeffrey P. Brain, pp. 393–420. Harvard University Peabody Museum of Archaeology and Ethnology Paper No. 74, Cambridge, Massachusetts.

Willoughby, Charles C.

1952 Textile Fabrics from the Spiro Mound. *Missouri Archaeologist* 14:107–118, Plates 140–152.

Wimberly, Steve B.

1960 *Indian Pottery from Clarke County and Mobile County, Southern Alabama.* Geological Survey of Alabama Museum Paper No. 36, University, Alabama.

Wobst, H. Martin

1977 Stylistic Behavior and Information Exchange. *University of Michigan Museum of Anthropology Anthropological Papers* 61:317–341.

Yerkes, Richard W.

1988 The Woodland and Mississippian Traditions in the Prehistory of Midwestern North America. *Journal of World Prehistory* 2(3):307–358.

1989 Mississippian Craft Specialization on the American Bottom. *Southeastern Archaeology* 8(2):93–106.

1991 Current Research: Great Lakes. *American Antiquity* 56(3):538–544.

Young, Jon N.

1962 *Annis Mound: A Late Prehistoric Site on the Green River.* Unpublished Master's thesis, University of Kentucky, Lexington.

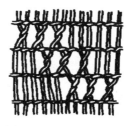

INDEX

Circle-and-cross motif, 7, 77, 79, 172, 173, 200, 202, 236

Clarke County, Alabama: saline sites, 19. *See also* Beckum Village; Salt Creek

Cleburne County, Arkansas: bag from, 64, 66; sites, 59 (Fig. 12)

Cleland, Charles, 92

Cliffty Creek Rock-shelter, Tennessee: awls from, 159; bag from, 62 (Fig. 14), 65–66; garments from, 80, 81 (Fig. 20), 153, 166, 169, 214; hemp fiber from, 159; location, 59 (Fig. 12); mat from, 86, 87 (Fig. 21)

Cloaks. *See* Mantles

Cloth: definition, 244

Cofitachequi, South Carolina: garments at, 75, 235; stockpiling of textiles at, 235

Cole, Missouri, 19, 180 (Table 12); location, 177 (Fig. 49); saltpan production at, 16

Color symbolism, 74, 239

Communication through costume, 83, 172–74, 237–41

Conrad, Anthony, 170

Copper artifacts: depicting garments, 76; fabrics in manufacturing process of, 93–94; as high value exchange items, 7, 236, 237; preserving textiles, 167, 197, 200

Cordage: definition, 244

Cotton: fiber, 162, 201, 232, 234, 239; textile, 202; yarn, 166

Craft specialization, 8, 231, 232

Crosno, Missouri: "saltpans" from, 14 (Fig. 3), 15, 145; textile structures, 28

Crowder, Missouri: textile structures, 28

Dallas focus, 193, 222

Davenport, Iowa, 204

De Batz, A., 75, 154, 204

De Bry, Theodore, 80

Decorated textiles: geographic variation, 214–18, 220; as indicators of social status or affiliation, 44, 172–75, 237–41; temporal variation, 221–22

Decorative motifs: in basketry, 86, 88, 202, 214; colored, 44, 62, 66, 69, 71, 106, 107, 155, 164, 172, 173, 197, 200, 218, 222, 226, 239, 241; figurative, 70, 71 (Fig. 17), 155, 159, 238–39; geometric, 70 (Fig. 16),

78 (Fig. 18), 158, 186 (Fig. 51), 191–92, 214, 218; scale, 172, 173, 240, 241; by stripes or bands, 182 (Fig. 50), 215, 216; structural, 44, 186 (Fig. 51), 191–92, 201, 203, 214–16, 218, 239, 240, 241; symbolism of, 237–41. *See also* Banded twining

De Montigny, Dumont (missionary), 160

De Soto, Hernando, 8, 75, 154, 235

Dickens, Roy, 174

Discoidals: as possible spindles, 159

Distaff, 160

Diversity in material culture: as indicator of intergroup contact, 174

Division of labor by gender, 11–12, 18, 237

Douglas, Frederick, 69

Down fiber, 73, 83, 231, 239

Duffield, Lathel, 77

Du Ru, Paul, 74, 80, 160, 235

Dyeing: as potentially harmful to yarn, 66; time requirements, 231

Early Mississippian, 220, 222, 227. *See also* Mississippian

Eastern Woodlands Indians: spinning, 159

Edge structures, 48; for bags, 60, 63 (Fig. 15), 64–65; functional characteristics of, 58; for garments, 63 (Fig. 15), 82; geographic variation, 218, 219 (Table 16); as indicators of artifact function, 48; as indicators of cultural affiliation, 48, 218; as indicators of fabric construction technique, 48, 229–30; production time of, 58, 168; side, 49, 60, 134 (Fig. 41), 136–38, 179, 202, 218, 219 (Table 16), 224, 229; starting, 48, 60, 61 (Fig. 13), 63 (Fig. 15), 133–34, 135 (Fig. 42), 179, 182 (Fig. 50), 183, 189, 193, 218, 219 (Table 16); temporal variation, 218; terminal, 48–49, 63 (Fig. 15), 64–65, 134–36, 179, 193, 213, 214, 218, 219 (Table 16), 231

Effigy figures, 76–77, 79, 85

Element: definition of, 244–45

Elvas, Gentleman of, 74, 235

Emergent Mississippian, 220, 234. *See also* Mississippian

Emery, Irene, 40, 243, 253

Equality, Illinois, 19; "saltpan" production at, 16

Etowah, Georgia, 6, 7, 29, 194, 197, 200; dates, 200; effigy figures from, 77; location, 6 (Fig. 1), 200; site description, 200; textiles, 9, 65 (Table 3), 84, 90–91, 170, 173, 200–202, 205 (Table 14), 210 (Fig. 55), 213, 217, 218, 221, 226, 231, 232, 233, 239, 241; yarns, 73, 201, 207–08, 209 (Fig. 54), 217, 218

Exchange: of animal fibers, 236–37; of animal skins, 235–36; Mississippian, 7, 234–37; networks, 7, 236–37, 240; at Spiro, 201, 236, 237; of textiles, 74, 171, 235–37; at Wickliffe, 25, 29, 174–75, 240. *See also* Copper artifacts; High value exchange items; Low value exchange items; Shell artifacts

Fabric count, 46, 50, 184, 185, 187, 191, 197, 208, 217, 225; calculation of, 50, 254; definition of, 245; as indicator of fabric scale, 46, 50; as indicator of production time, 50. *See also* Wickliffe impressed textiles, fabric count

Fabric-impressed pottery, 13, 39, 54. *See also* "Saltpans"

Fabric-marked pottery, 13

Fabrics. *See* Textiles

Feather: fiber, 73, 83, 231; mantles, construction of, 73–74, 90, 170, 226, 235; work, 73–74, 80, 95 (Table 4), 205 (Table 14), 218; yarns, 73–74, 83, 200, 201, 226

Fiber: definition of, 245

Fiber processing. *See* processing; Bark, fiber processing; Bast fiber, processing of; Yarns, fiber

Fishing nets, 92–93. *See also* Nets

Flax, 165

Float, definition, 245

Florida, Pensacola Bay site: spindles, 160

Foreman, Mary, 89

Fort Ancient: bag, 68; knotted netting, 93; yarns, 207

Fort Loudon, Tennessee: impressed textiles, 180 (Table 12), 198 (Table 13), 213, 219 (Table 16); location, 177 (Fig. 49)

Fraser, David, 40, 228, 243

French Lick, Tennessee, 19

Fringe, 75, 81 (Fig. 20), 82, 83, 85, 134–35,

136 (Fig. 43), 168; definition of, 245

Fundabark, Emma, 89

Funkhouser, William, 17, 183, 185, 187

Fur: garments, 73, 75, 84; yarn, 200, 227

Garments: archaeological, 65, 73–77, 80, 81 (Fig. 20), 82–83; attributes of, 65 (Table 3), 95 (Table 4); ceremonial, 74, 76–77, 79–80, 83, 153, 226, 231–32, 237–41; colored, 79, 83, 239; as communication devices, 83, 172–74, 237, 241; construction of, 73, 82, 83, 84; decorated, 30 (Fig. 6), 32, 76, 77, 78 (Fig. 18), 82, 83, 84, 238–39; depictions of, 74, 75, 76–77, 78 (Fig. 18), 79; edge structures, 48, 63 (Fig. 15), 82; energy requirements for those made from skins, 233–34; as gifts, 239–40; historical, 73–76, 77, 80, 82; interlaced, 80, 82, 226; leather, 73, 74, 75; Mississippian, 65, 73–83, 85; production time for, 166, 168; ties on, 82; twined, 80 (Fig. 20), 81, 82, 84; types, 73; utilitarian, 81 (Fig. 20), 82–84; worn by females, 73, 75–77, 79, 85; worn by males, 73–75, 78, 79, 83, 85; yarn fibers, 74–76, 83, 84, 85. *See also* Belts; Mantles; Sandals; Sashes; Skirts; Slippers; Tunic-like garments

Geographic variation: in textile attributes, 207–08, 210–20, 224, 233, 240; in yarn attributes, 162, 207, 208, 209 (Fig. 54), 218. *See also* individual attributes

Gramly, R. Michael, 233

Grass fiber, 92, 159

Gray Farm, Tennessee: location, 217 (Fig. 58); impressed textile from, 216

Great Lakes region: bags from, 67–68, 72, 106, 160; mats from, 88, 156; nets from, 92; spinning, 159; yarns from, 160

Great Salt Spring. *See* Salt Spring

Griffin, James, 193

Guajiro textiles, 164

Guntersville Basin, Alabama: impressed textiles, 180 (Table 12), 198 (Table 13), 213 (Fig. 56); location, 177 (Fig. 49)

Haag, William, 16

Hair nets, 76, 154

Hall, Robert, 234

Plains region: bags, 67, 68, 106
Plain weave: definition, 246
Ply. *See* Yarn ply
Positive molds. *See* Casts of textile impressions
Potawatomi: bag, 64, 69, 154
Pottery types: Bell Plain, 35, 142; Hawkins Fabric Marked, 13; Kimmswick Fabric Impressed, 13, 14, 33, 35, 142, 212; Kincaid Net-Impressed, 13; Langston Fabric Marked, 13, 195; Mississippi Plain, 33; Morris Fabric Impressed, 13; Saline Fabric Impressed, 13; Salt Creek Cane Impressed, 13, 195, 196; Tolu Interior Fabric Impressed, 13; Weeden Island, 174; Yates Net Impressed, 13. *See also* "Saltpans"
Pre-Mississippian textiles, 9, 11, 54, 68, 197, 200, 205 (Table 14), 209 (Fig. 54), 210 (Fig. 55). *See also* Hopewell, textiles
Putnam Farm shelter, Arkansas: bag from, 64; location, 59 (Fig. 12); shuttle from, 159; textiles from, 203, 217

Rabbit hair, 83
Rachlin, Carol, 10, 15, 68, 183–84
Ranjel, Rodrigo, 75
Raudot, Antoine, 159
Repaired fabrics, 139, 169
Replication: of bags, 167; of feather mantles, 170; of hammocks, 166; of interlaced fabrics, 93–94, 167; of mat, 167; of slippers, 167; of tapestry, 231; of twined textiles, 166–67; of yarns, 161, 165–66
Robes. *See* Mantles
Rogers, Nora, 229
Royal Tapestry Factory, Madrid, Spain, 231
Rushes: in mats, 88, 156

Ste. Genevieve County, Missouri: impressed textile from, 69
Saline River, Illinois: "saltpans," 19; textile structures, 28
Saline River, Missouri: impressed textiles, 181 (Table 12), 199 (Table 13), 213; location, 177 (Fig. 49)
Salt: exchanged for shawls, 235–36
Salt Creek, Alabama, 196; impressed fabrics, 180 (Table 12), 199 (Table 13), 212,

220, 224; location, 177 (Fig. 49), 195; site description, 195; yarns, 195
"Saltpans," 12–20, 52–54; estimation of diameter, 34, 53, 253, 254; fabric as ornamentation on, 17; fabric-impressed, 13, 14 (Fig. 3), 15, 52–54; fabric orientation on, 150–52; fabric orientation on, as indicator of textile impression function, 53; fabric orientation, measurement of, 253–54; fabric position on, 13, 16, 54, 139–40, 150–52, 179, 182; function, 18–20; geographic distribution, 15–16; not trade items, 16; production, use of fabrics in, 17, 18, 49, 94, 211, 212, 223–25; production location, 15; production time, 18; shapes, 13, 14 (Fig. 3), 15, 35 (Fig. 7); sizes, 13; smooth-surfaced, 15; temper, 13; temporal variation, 15, 145. *See also* Wickliffe "saltpans"
Salts Cave, Kentucky, 59 (Fig. 12)
Salt Spring, Illinois, 19; impressed fabrics, 181 (Table 12), 199 (Table 13), 215; location, 177 (Fig. 49); "saltpan" production at, 16; "saltpans" at, 14
Samuel, Alena, 161
Sandals, 73, 94, 163, 171, 230
San Marco, Florida: mats, 86
Sashes, 30–32, 73, 154, 164, 171, 174, 229
Sassafras Ridge, Kentucky, 28
Schambach, Frank, 236
Schmoo Effect, 234
Scholtz, Sandra, 68, 73, 230
Schreffler, Virginia, 84, 90, 173
Selvage: definition of, 246; as indicator of fabric construction technique, 43. *See also* Edge structures
Shawls. *See* Mantles
Shell artifacts: engraved, depicting garments, 76, 77; as high value exchange items, 7, 201, 236, 237
Shuttles, 159, 161
Sibley, Lucy, 201, 239
"Silk grass" fiber, 75
Sinew: deer, 159
Siouans, Eastern: garments, 75
Skirts, 73, 74, 77, 78, 79, 80, 82, 85, 95 (Table 4), 154–55, 171, 226; fibers, 75; sizes, 75, 77, 85, 95

39); as indicator of social status, 52; measurement of, 51–52, 254. *See also* Modified Textile Production Complexity Indexes; Textile Production Complexity Index

Textile condition: applications, 49; of impressed fabrics, 138–39, 182, 185, 187, 190, 192, 196; as indication of "value," 169; measurement, 49

Textile density: calculation of, 51, 254; of impressed fabrics, 99 (Table 6), 116–19 (Table 8), 120, 125, 127 (Fig. 38), 128, 148, 155–56, 185, 225; relation to textile function, 51, 57; total, 51, 127–28; warp, 51, 127–28; weft, 51, 127–28

Textile design motifs. *See* Decorative motifs

Textile diversity: 57–58, 218, 220; calculation of, 57–58; geographic variation, 218, 220; as indicator of social organization, 58; as indicator of textile functions, 58; temporal variation, 222. *See also* Wickliffe impressed textiles, diversity

Textile edge structures. *See* Edge structures

Textile-impressed pottery. *See* Fabric-impressed pottery

Textile impressions: analysis of, 196–97 (problems), 251–52; casts of, 39, 251–54; functions on "saltpans," 17, 18, 53, 54; on non-"saltpan" pottery, 54, 142

Textile production: artifacts, 158–59; by men, 12; place in subsistence economy, 232–34; specialization, 169–71, 231–32, 236; techniques, 84, 160–61, 163–64, 228–31, 232; technology, 84, 158–61, 163, 228–31; time requirements, 93–94, 166–68, 170, 173, 226, 231, 233; by women, 11–12, 237

Textile Production Complexity Index, 32, 51, 52, 91, 232; calculation of, 51–52. *See also* Modified Textile Production Complexity Indexes

Textiles: decorated, as indicators of social status or affiliation, 44, 90–91, 172–74, 218, 238–41; double-sided, 75; elite, 90–91, 197, 200–202, 205 (Table 14), 208, 218, 226, 235–41; exchange of, 74, 171, 234–37, 239–40; functional standardization, 57, 93–94, 224–25; function in

"saltpan" production, 17, 18, 49, 53, 94; as gifts, 74, 239–40; as indicators of "affluence," 234, 240; as indicators of belief system, 235, 237–41; as items of value, 234–37; as manufacturing tools, 93–94; mortuary, 89–92, 197, 200–204; production time, 165–68; repaired, 139, 169; stockpiling of, 234–35, 241; symbolism of, 237–41. *See also* Mississippian, textiles; individual site names

Textile scale, 46; definition of, 245; geographic and temporal variation, 208, 209 (Fig. 54), 210 (Fig. 55); relationship to function, 57, 224–25

Textile structures, 40, 41 (Fig. 9), 42 (Fig. 10), 43–44, 100–14, 115 (Fig. 32); effect of missing elements, 49; functional characteristics, 54–58; geographic variation, 211–20, 224, 240; temporal variation, 143–44, 220–22, 224. *See also* individual sites; individual structures

Thigh spinning, 47, 159–62, 227–28

Thread: definition, 249

Threddles (heddles), 161

Thruston tablet, 77–79

Tinsley Hill, Kentucky, 29, 177 (Fig. 49); impressed textiles, 181 (Table 12, 199 (Table 13)

Tolu, Kentucky, 13, 28, 159, 183; impressed textiles, 181 (Table 12), 187, 199 (Table 13), 202, 210 (Fig. 55), 212, 215 (Fig. 57), 216, 217 (Fig. 58), 220, 240; location, 177 (Fig. 49), 185; site description, 185; yarns, 187, 209 (Fig. 54), 212

Tonti, Henri de, 74

Toqua, Tennessee: impressed textiles, 181 (Table 12), 199 (Table 13), 213 (Fig. 56); location, 177 (Fig. 49)

Tr/10, Kentucky: impressed textiles, 181 (Table 12), 199 (Table 13); location, 177 (Fig. 49)

Trowels: for pottery production, 16, 25

Trudeau, Louisiana: basketry, 204, 205; textile, 204

Tunic-like garment, 74, 75, 77, 78 (Fig. 18)

Twill interlacing, 43, 44, 194, 195, 196, 198–99 (Table 13), 200, 202, 205 (Table 14), 225; in artifacts, 95 (Table 4); in

Wickliffe impressed textiles (*continued*)
as fishing and hunting nets, 158; flex-ibility, 148; functions, 146–58, 223; interlaced, 101 (Table 7), 113, 115 (Fig. 32), 125, 153, 157, 158, 214, 220; joins, 133–35 (Fig. 42), 139, 142, 152, 155, 219 (Table 16); knotted, 101 (Table 7), 113, 114 (Fig. 31), 117–18 (Table 8), 119, 125, 128, 129, 131, 144 (Table 10, Fig. 47), 153, 157, 158, 169, 171; as mats, 157, 158; orientation on "saltpans," 139–40, 150, 151, 152; overlays, 135, 137, 140, 141 (Fig. 46), 142, 152, 157; overlays, correlation with fabric structure, 142, 152–53; plain twined, 100, 101 (Table 7), 102 (Fig. 22), 104, 106, 109, 110, 111, 116 (Table 8), 119, 120 (Fig. 33), 128, 129, 131, 132 (Fig. 40), 133, 139, 142, 144, 152, 154, 155, 156, 158, 167, 168, 173; production specialization, 169–71; production technology, 163–64; produc-tion time, 131, 165–68 (Table 11); as rags, 169; removability from "saltpan" surface, 148; representativeness with regard to entire Wickliffe textile complex, 170–71; in "saltpan" production, 142, 147–50, 152, 169, 171, 175; in "saltpan" use, 142, 150–52; shape, 153; side edges, 134 (Fig. 41), 136–38, 155, 156, 219 (Table 16); size, 148–49, 152–53; spatial distribution, 143; spinning techniques, 161–63; stan-dardization, 147, 170; starting edges, 133–34, 135 (Fig. 42), 138, 158, 219 (Table 16); strength, 147–48; "stripe" designs from warp yarn variation, 104, 105 (Fig. 24), 216; structure frequencies, 100, 101 (Table 7), 211 (Table 15); structures present, 40, 100–114, 199 (Table 13); temporal variation, 143–44, 175, 220–22, 240; terminal edges, 134–36, 155–58, 163, 219 (Table 16); as textile artifacts, 152–58, 170–74, 185, 223; twined, attributes, 116–39; twined, struc-tures, 100–114; twined, with crossed warps, 101 (Table 7), 106–08, 154–55; twined, with diagonally diverted warps, 101 (Table 7), 104, 106, 107 (Fig. 25); twined, with interlinked warps, 101 (Table 7), 108–11, 118–19 (Table 8), 120 (Fig. 33), 125, 128, 158, 163, 164, 167–68, 169, 172, 187, 211 (Table 15), 215, 216, 217 (Fig. 58); twined, with oblique interlacing, 101 (Table 7), 111, 113; twined, over paired non-alternating warps, 100, 104; twined, with three wefts, 108, 138; twining twist direction, 100, 108, 125, 138, 163, 164; warp count, 101 (Table 7), 116–19 (Table 8), 120 (Fig. 33), 125, 126 (Fig. 37), 128, 132 (Fig. 40), 133, 210 (Fig. 55); weft count, 101 (Table 7), 116–19 (Table 8), 120 (Fig. 33), 125, 126 (Fig. 37), 128, 132 (Fig. 40), 133; weft-faced, 101 (Table 7), 108, 112 (Fig. 30), 113, 117 (Table 8), 119, 120 (Fig. 33), 123, 125, 128, 129, 131, 132 (Fig. 40), 133, 136 (Fig. 43), 142, 144, 152, 153, 154, 156, 157, 158, 167, 168 (Table 11), 169, 175, 212, 221; wrapped twining, 100

Wickliffe impressed yarns, 113, 114–15, 119–25, 132–33, 155, 157, 161, 212; braided, 123, 124 (Fig. 36), 155, 156; diameter, 99, 114–15, 116–18 (Table 8), 119, 120 (Fig. 33), 121 (Fig. 34), 123, 132 (Fig. 40), 208, 209 (Fig. 54); "fluffy," 103, 122, 123, 153–54; ply, 99 (Table 6), 114, 115, 116–18 (Table 8), 119; process-ing of fibers, 119, 122 (Fig. 35), 123; production methods, 162–63; yarn twist angle, 115, 119, 121 (Fig. 34), yarn twist direction, 114, 123–25, 162, 207, 220; wrapped, 123, 124 (Fig. 36); **Z**-twisted, 123, 124 (Fig. 36), 125

Wickliffe Mounds: burial pattern, 25, 28, 174; ceramic seriation, 26; chronology, 26–27, 29; embankment, 26; excavation history, 23–26; exchange, 25, 29, 174–75, 240; location, 6 (Fig. 1), 177 (Fig. 49); Mound A, 23, 26, 27, 28, 97, 98; Mound B, 24, 26, 27, 28, 97, 98; Mound C, 25, 27, 28, 97, 98; Mound D, 25, 27, 28, 32, 33, 34, 97, 98, 106, 123, 151; Mound E, 26, 27, 97; Mound F, 26, 27, 28, 97, 98; North Village, 26, 27, 98; plaza, 26; population, 23; regional affiliations, 28–29; regional chronology, 29; regional settlement pattern, 23, 28; site descrip-

ABOUT THE AUTHOR

Penelope Ballard Drooker is a weaving instructor and practicing fiber artist who has lectured extensively on weaving and textile history. She earned a bachelor's degree in geology from Wellesley College, a master's degree in hydrology from the University of New Hampshire, a master's degree in anthropology from Harvard University, and currently is completing her doctorate in archaeology at the University at Albany, State University of New York. Her other publications include three books on fabric design and production techniques and one on computer watershed modeling, as well as articles on textiles, textile history, and archaeology in publications ranging from *Archaeology* to *The Weaver's Journal*.